William Graham

The creed of science, religious, moral, and social by William Graham

William Graham

The creed of science, religious, moral, and social by William Graham

ISBN/EAN: 9783743382183

Manufactured in Europe, USA, Canada, Australia, Japa

Cover: Foto ©Lupo / pixelio.de

Manufactured and distributed by brebook publishing software (www.brebook.com)

William Graham

The creed of science, religious, moral, and social by William Graham

THE

CREED OF SCIENCE

RELIGIOUS, MORAL, AND SOCIAL

BY

WILLIAM GRAHAM, M.A.

AUTHOR OF "IDEALISM: AN ESSAY METAPHYSICAL AND CRITICAL"

LONDON

C. KEGAN PAUL & CO., 1, PATERNOSTER SQUARE

1881

CONTENTS.

INTRODUCTION xi

BOOK I.

THE CREED OF SCIENCE, RELIGIOUS AND MORAL.

CHAPTER I.

ON THE CREATION AND GOD.

§ 1. Whence came the physical worlds? 3
2. Answer of Science: (1) Of Laplace and Kant; (2), of Sir W. Thomson and Helmholtz 5
3. Origin of life, according to Haeckel: spontaneous generation ... 15
4. Origin of species, according to Darwin: natural selection ... 21
5. Chance the chief characteristic in the process of natural selection 25
6. Natural selection as a scientific hypothesis, how far proved. Its great significance in a theological, philosophical, and ethical reference 32
7. Natural selection dispenses with Design in the process of Evolution 35
8. Gives a new and sinister solution of the problem of evil. Science optimistic in spite of the struggle for existence. Modern pessimism and evolution 38
9. A Creator, postulated by Darwin, set aside by Haeckel ... 44
10. Real issue raised by the doctrine of evolution,—Whether Chance or Purpose made and rules the world 47

CHAPTER II.

ON MAN AND HIS DEVELOPMENT.

§ 1. The place of man in Nature 55
2. The scientific portrait of man 58
3. The development of the human species. Has been by a series of great individuals rather than by natural selection and inheritance 64

		PAGE
§ 4.	The preceding proved of man during historic as well as prehistoric time	68
5.	The initiative and influence of great individuals a force traversing the law of natural selection	72
6.	In what direction the further development of humanity tends ...	74
7.	Concession to the pessimist. Happiness, though possible, mostly missed. Causes of this	77

CHAPTER III.

ON HUMAN NATURE AND ITS CAPACITIES FOR VIRTUE.

§ 1.	Defects in our past ethical systems	83
2.	Chief cause of the failure of the masters of morals—want of scientific knowledge. Man, as shown by psychology, physiology, and natural history	87
3.	Man fundamentally an animal, self-conserving and moved by sense: far-reaching ethical consequences of these facts, and particularly of the former. The struggle for existence within the human species	91
4.	Man also a social animal: ethical consequences of this fact. Love for others the happiest feat of evolution. Influence of religious founders in its development	95
5.	Origin of the feeling in the primitive man. How far it admits of natural explanation	98
6.	The "love of humanity," and "the greatest happiness of the greatest number." How far the former is a possible feeling, or the latter a practicable or proper aim. Testimony of psychology, experience, and the great writers on the former point	102
7.	The love of humanity and the struggle for existence as exemplified in nations, classes, individuals	110
8.	The love of our species real and possible in the sense of a love of certain individuals as representatives of the whole and redeemers of its unlovable units	112
9.	Defect in the ethical system of Kant	115

CHAPTER IV.

ON FREE-WILL, AND MAN'S AUTOMATISM.

§ 1.	Ethical significance of the free-will controversy	119
2.	Theory of the man-machine, with consciousness superadded as spectator	120
3.	Portion of truth in the theory. Futility and irrelevance of the theory	124
4.	Theory of Mill and Bain: our volitions determined by conscious motives referring to pleasure and pain	126
5.	Substantial truth of the theory. Corrections suggested. Conscious motives governed by unconscious causes. Variation in the strength of conscious motive apparently the same ...	129

CONTENTS. vii

§ 6. Our actions: how far from automatic and unconscious, how far from conscious causes. Analysis of the possible kinds of causes allows no room for free-will 130
7. Logical consequence of free-will,—involves the miracle of the creation of force or energy 133
8. The power of improving our character does not imply free-will 136
9. Merit and demerit, how far affected by the motive theory ... 139
10. Is punishment justifiable on this theory? 141
11. Practical freedom—the freedom to pursue desired ends—untouched by the theory 146

CHAPTER V.

ON IMMORTALITY.

§ 1. Verdict of Science: of the physicist, the physiologist, and the naturalist 150
2. Metaphysical theories of the soul. Arguments in favour of its immortality. Theological theories of the soul. Immortality a revelation, not an inference of reason 152
3. Scientific arguments against a future life: (1) From physiology 156
4. (2) From the Darwinian theory of descent. Natural origin and history of the belief in a future life. (3) From evolution in general; because the human species and all species will disappear, and because the earth itself shall perish 159

CHAPTER VI.

ON IMMORTALITY: COUNTERTHESIS.

§ 1. Objections, other than theological, to the scientific arguments: (1) Of the spiritualist; (2) of the mystic. Reply of Positive Science to each 169
2. (3) Of the universal human heart founded on the desire to meet again our loved ones. Reply of Science 180
3. Review of discussion. What Science has proved, what failed to prove. A future existence possible without memory of the past. Belief of greatest philosophers and poets. Why opinion of great poets is important. Belief of Shakespeare and Goethe; belief of Kant. Conclusions of Kant and Goethe specially noteworthy because they were also men of science ... 182
4. Conclusion maintained: that further conscious existence is possible, that existence other than consciousness, and perhaps better, is also possible. Is annihilation possible? 188
5. Is the future one of rewards and punishments? How far virtue and vice have received their wages on earth. Possible objections to conclusion 193
6. Recapitulation: how far a scientific philosophy can believe in a future life 197

BOOK II.

THE GOSPEL, AND THE SOCIAL CREED OF SCIENCE.

CHAPTER I.

PESSIMISM AND POSITIVE SCIENCE.

	PAGE
§ 1. Modern pessimism—"The Occidental Buddhism." Explanation and meaning of the phenomenon	203
2. Answer to the pessimist: from the experience of the majority; from the interpretation of consciousness. Consciousness not essentially a want and a pain. Pessimism not the word of life to-day in Western Europe. The "denial of the will to live" and the struggle for existence	210
3. Positive science and positivism. Common principle and point of view. Science and Metaphysics	214
4. Causes of the rise and spread of the positive spirit. Whether the old metaphysical questions, stripped of their unreal elements, may not be answered from the positive point of view	219
5. The positive standpoint suffices at least for all questions relating to practice	224

CHAPTER II.

THE MESSAGE AND THE PROMISES TO MANKIND.

§ 1. The revelation of science	227
2. The truths of science calculated to beget a resigned and religious frame of mind	229
3. Knowledge the emancipator and deliverer. The pursuit of knowledge the worship and sacrifice accepted by Nature. Grace and favours which physical science has gained for us from Nature	232
4. What medical science and physiology have done for us ...	237
5. The new philosophy and the general probation of life. How far the latter may be mitigated by knowledge. Need of stoicism and resignation for which a knowledge of the universal order prepares us	240
6. Good side of the struggle for existence. Competition, its uses and necessity. The Race in the future	246

CHAPTER III.

TO THE POOR. SCIENCE AND SOCIALISM.

§ 1. The socialist's indictment against modern society. Causes of poverty and all social evils, according to the socialist. The only cure	252
2. Reply of the sociologist and political economist. Social evils spring from imperfect human nature, not from unjust laws, or imperfect constitution of society. Further development of this view. Consequences. Advice of the sociologist and economist to the poor	265

3. Truth and error in both preceding views. The socialist's programme impracticable, human nature stopping the way. Mistake of the sociologist. Human nature modifiable for a time during which important social changes are possible. Examples 278
4. Co-operative labour. Limits to the application of the principle. Why it must fail for a long time to solve the problem of capital and labour 286
5. Under one contingency, the normal slow rate of social evolution might be greatly accelerated. The aristocracy of thought and letters on the side of labour. Best present advice to the toiling many. The social agitation in all civilized states a practical admonition to statesmen and rulers 291

BOOK III.

THE FUTURE OF RELIGION AND MORALS.

CHAPTER I.

ON THE MATERIALISM OF ATOMS AND FORCES.

§ 1. Is science atheistic? Distinction between science and the philosophies professing to be based on science: positivism, materialism, and evolution. Positivism and theism ... 297
2. Two kinds of materialism, one constructing the universe from atoms, and one from force or energy. How far these are severally atheistic. The theory of man's automatism a logical consequence of the reduction of all to physical energy. Refutation. The two species of energy, physical and spiritual. The latter ever on the increase 299
3. A third Something behind all phenomena material or mental. Admitted by materialists like Haeckel and Huxley. Effect of admission on their philosophy 309

CHAPTER II.

ON THE EVOLUTION-MATERIALISM AND THEOLOGY.

§ 1. What is necessary to establish a complete materialism. The Design argument and the Darwinian theory 317
2. The argument for God's existence as the Author of the moral law attacked by evolution. Evolution account of the origin and development of morality and religion. Explanation by the evolutionists of the admitted fact of conscience 324
3. Continuation and conclusion of the evolution-materialist's argument. A Creator need not be postulated at the introduction of life, or at the first appearance of consciousness 332
4. Reply to this materialism. How far the controversy with the materialist may now be narrowed. Futility of all materialism to-day 337

CONTENTS.

§ 5. Real danger of Darwinism and the evolution philosophy in another direction; tends to make not Matter but Chance the author of all. Proof of this. Why and in what sense we must believe in Purpose 344

CHAPTER III.
ON THE DEVELOPED CONCEPTION OF GOD.

§ 1. The modern conception of God. Its origin and development ... 351
2. The conception illustrated in detail. How far it coincides with the Ultimate Reality of Herbert Spencer, with the Infinite Substance of Spinoza 353
3. The conception of Kant and Schliermacher 358
4. Will the new conception offer a barrier to the new materialism in alliance with evolution? 360
5. Can theology accept it? 362
6. Theory considered that God can be known in other and human relations by a special religious sense 365
7. True source of the supposed intuitions of the religious sense ... 369
8. Source of the complete conception of God so far as possible by our minds. Elements of the conception furnished by religion, philosophy, art, and science 373

CHAPTER IV.
OBJECTIONS TO THE EVOLUTION ETHICS.

§ 1. (1) That the new teaching destroys virtue by making it a matter of human invention. (2) That it makes the authority of conscience questionable and of no effect 376
2. (3) That the relaxed sense of moral obligation will destroy society and civilization. Parallels of history. Stages of moral decay specified. This result more to be dreaded if the theory of the mechanical or materialistic derivation of all actions is accepted 385

CHAPTER V.
CONFLICT AND PARTIAL CONCILIATION BETWEEN THE NEW AND OLD ETHICS.

§ 1. Only mode of partial conciliation. Concession by evolutionist to the spiritualist and moral idealist. Nature of our moral impulses to be learned from the impulses themselves, not from their origin. Our obligation to truth and justice. Limitation to the possible 391
2. Evolutionists may concede that men follow ideals more than ever. Morality will not be touched in essence; but a new valuation of the virtues may be required. Doctrine of heredity ... 399
3. Irreducible contradictions between real and ideal morality. The contradictions in our nature and in the conditions of life. Tendency to further conciliation, ever short of full harmony 406

INTRODUCTION.

§ 1. I PROPOSE in the following pages to give the chief conclusions reached by Modern Science on the central questions of religion, morals, and society,—to state, in a word, the general creed of Science; and, as the scientific faith may still be fallible, or of unequal degrees of credit, I propose, in the second place, to offer some comments and criticisms on some of its more doubtful articles, with a view to their reconsideration or revision.

Already many have taken in hand to set forth the scientific faith, together with the grounds on which it rests. In particular, eminent physicists and naturalists both in this country and in Germany—Huxley, Clifford, Tyndall, Haeckel, Helmholtz, Tait, and Balfour Stewart have all attempted it in essays, addresses, or books, with more or less pretence at fulness. But the physicists and naturalists, though they may be depended upon to reflect accurately the tendency of scientific thought on the questions within their respective provinces which touch on the sphere of religion, do not speak with the same authority on questions moral, social, or philosophical.

The scientific thinkers, to whom the work more properly belongs, have also attempted to give expositions of scientific faith and doctrine. Within the past forty years Comte, Mill, Strauss, and Herbert Spencer have all essayed it. But as the two former wrote before the discovery of the two most comprehensive generalizations in physics and biology—the law of the Conservation of Energy and the law of Natural Selection—they failed to reach the new and more commanding point of view which these two laws place henceforth at the disposal of thinkers. Their systems are accordingly to a considerable extent superseded as incomplete scientific explanations of the universe, while the moral and social doctrines of both are pronounced by Herbert Spencer inconsistent with the deepest and widest generalizations of the laws of life and society.

Herbert Spencer has himself, in the various volumes of his new system of evolution-philosophy, given the most complete and philosophic statement of the scientific faith, and he has given it with special references to the above-named highest laws. But waiving the fact that physicists object to some of his physics, and philosophers to some of his philosophy, the system is itself so voluminous and vast—in fact, so severe a course of reading, which postulates a special facility in the art of quickly apprehending the meaning of a train of abstract symbols, scientific and philosophic—that a more compendious if not an easier exposition would seem a matter to be desired. To supply some such condensed exposition to the large and increasing class who have an intelligent human interest in the new scientific theories, and in the great collision and controversy now going on between the new and old beliefs is one object of this book; to supplement the exposition with a criticism which may assist them to separate the false from the true elements in the new creed, is the second and possibly more important object.

§ 2. In the absence of any single and universally acknowledged authority on all articles of faith and doctrine I have taken the consensus of scientific opinion amongst the few highest authorities on each particular article, and I have treated this as the orthodox teaching of Science—as what would have been the decision had all such authorities met together in Council to fix the faith. Thus, on the question of the origin and future dissolution of our earth and solar system, the most eminent physicists are in the main agreed, however much they may differ on such philosophical questions as the immortality of the Soul or the existence of God. Professors Tait and Helmholtz, for example, differing on the latter, are still agreed that a widely dispersed nebulous matter, closing together under gravitation, awoke the sun's fires, and produced the earth and planets originally at molten heat. They are further agreed, and so also are Professors Balfour Stewart and Clifford, in accepting Sir W. Thomson's doctrine of the Dissipation of Energy with the consequent future dissolution of all the systems of the universe. There is a consensus of opinion, that is to say, amongst the foremost physicists as to the remote physical beginning and far-off end of the material universe, though they differ widely as to the nature and destiny of the human soul. Accordingly, this consensus of opinion may be accounted an article of scientific faith, even though some physicists seem disposed to doubt it.

In like manner, I have treated as the orthodox belief the Darwinian doctrine of the origin of Species, and in particular of the animal origin of Man, even though there still exists with respect to both an eminent body of scientific dissent. It is to be so held because the balance of biological authority, estimated not less in quality than in quantity, has clearly pronounced in its favour; and because on these two points the biologists form the final court of appeal.

But when we come to mental, moral, and social questions, neither physicists nor naturalists are any longer authorities, however little some of them seem disposed to concede the point. In particular, when the question relates to man and his behaviour under the complex motive forces, conscious or unconscious, which determine it (supposing the question to come at all within the range of scientific methods or treatment), we shall no longer refer to the physicist or the naturalist for the scientific doctrine. Not to the physicist certainly, whose special studies of the invariable behaviour of matter or the settled sequences of physical phenomena prepare him very imperfectly for the investigation of the widely different phenomena presented by human conduct; nor yet to the naturalist, whose infinitely wider subject of plant and animal life forbids the due concentration of regard upon the special human subject, particularly on its inner conscious side. Nor need we greatly care as yet to consult that new man of science, the anthropologist,—not at least until he has a little more systematized the miscellaneous mass of facts referring to man in all times and climes which at present forms the subject-matter of his study.

On all questions concerning man himself, his virtues and vices, and the uniformity, such as it is, which his life in society presents, we are properly referred, on the part of science, to a different order of specialists—to the psychologist, the moralist, the sociologist, to such authorities as Mill, or

Bain, or Herbert Spencer, who, in addition to their writings on the philosophy or the logic of the sciences, have dealt expressly, and from the scientific point of view, with ethical and social questions. It is true, indeed, that both physical and vital phenomena are manifested in the human subject, that man is both a machine and an organism in which the law of the transmutation of energy is fulfilled; true, therefore, that he is so far a proper subject for physical and biological investigation; still, neither the most important nor the most interesting problems presented by man relate to the mechanism, however express and admirable, of his physical structure, nor to the transmutations of physical into vital and mental energy which really has place within the human machine. Nor do they relate to those other facts of organic functions and their various relations, with which the science of physiology deals. The most important problems presented by man from the point of view of science are psychological, moral, and social, and our scientific authorities may be credited with having taken into consideration such physical and physiological conclusions as have special and important bearing on these questions.

§ 3. Thus far on the subject of authorities. But it may be said, If your exposition be unexceptionable, and your finding of faith and doctrine accurately gathered from the first and surest sources as respects each particular article, is it not a little presumptuous to affect thereafter to criticise such acknowledged authorities?

I think not, and for the following reasons:—In the first place, we must distinguish between scientific faith and scientific fact, between a fully verified law and a supposed inference hazarded from it without being contained under it, between a well-established theory and a hypothesis only probable, perhaps only possible. The facts, the laws of science are true and certain: nothing can be more so. But the same cannot always be said of the interpretations of the facts, of the inferences from the laws, of the temporary tentative hypotheses framed to give some sort of systematic unity or supposed causal connection to a collection of facts or of laws. And some, though by no means all, of the articles of belief fall under this description. They are only hypotheses of different degrees of probability, and consequently of fallibility; whilst one or two, confidently accepted by Herbert Spencer and Strauss at the hands of the physical speculators, do not merit even the name of good hypotheses, being predictions which have yet to be fulfilled from hypotheses which are acknowledged to be uncertain. The articles, in particular, which touch on the religious sphere are mostly inferences without scientific justification, because from the nature of the case they can never receive that verification by comparison with facts, which Mill, Bain, and Lewes, our authorities on the logic of science, insist on as essential to legitimate inference or confident prevision.

Thus, any one with a moderate acquaintance with physics, who has mastered the principles of inductive and deductive logic as taught by Mill or Bain, may without presumption point out, what some physicists are ready enough to tell us, that the nebular hypothesis of Nature's mode of manufacture of the earth and worlds of space, now somewhat confidently offered as an article of belief, is still only a hypothesis, subject in all its forms, and after all its revisions, to very serious doubts; while at the best it does not admit of that decisive proof which other hypotheses, at first doubtful, in process of time received.

And happily, it is still more permissible to doubt the recent apocalyptic vision and gigantic prediction of the greater prophets of physics so circumstantially recorded by Professors Tait and Balfour Stewart, in *The Unseen Universe;*—the prediction that the sun will one day, Saturn-like, devour his own offspring, the earth and planets, with their satellites; that thereafter the nearer suns—our own and Sirius, for example—"having each long since devoured his attendants," will rush together to absorb each other or reduce themselves to a nebulous vapour in the attempt; that after an infinite series of such collisions, after each of which there is a sun or perhaps two suns the less in space, after innumerable deaths (as well too as occasional births) of suns and systems, the final consummation, however long delayed by the latter disturbing element in the calculation, will be the coalescence of all the matter of all previous suns and systems into one widely diffused matter of uniform temperature, which, as such, can make no fresh attempt at world-generation.*

I say we may be fairly permitted to doubt this very "big" physical speculation, even without being extreme sceptics with regard to the general scientific creed; more especially as the first though worst calamity, the fall of our earth upon the sun, is confessedly such a very long way off that the unbeliever can never be convinced in the only effectual way—by fulfilment or unmistakable tendency to fulfilment of the prophecy. Besides, the supposed finer matter dispersed through space, the universal ether or "resisting medium," whose imperceptible but ceaseless friction in opposition to the earth's motion is the small

---

* *The Unseen Universe*, pp. 165, 166; see also H. Spencer's *First Principles*, p. 528.

cause which is to bring about the great catastrophe of the fall of the earth on the sun,—this ether may still further attenuate itself, or it may grow denser in some regions and rarer in others, thus possibly allowing a freer or a void space for the earth's unimpeded movement. Or better still, and more likely, the resisting medium, as eminent astronomers now begin to think, may have no existence, or, if any, only within a safe and limited region which does not concern the earth. The whole disturbing prediction may be only a false alarm, founded on the eccentric behaviour of Encke's comet, whose slight anticipation of its calculated time of return led, as is well known, the perplexed astronomers to this hypothesis of a resisting medium. But even if the ether does exist, as Herbert Spencer and Professors Tait and Balfour Stewart believe, we might still escape the apprehended disastrous consequences. Something might always turn up in the long chapter of chances to save the earth. Our present laws of Nature, as Mill suggests, may not keep quite steady and invariable so long. Or, on the other hand, they may; and the earth, which has got on so many millions of years in spite of the efforts of the ether, may still contrive to keep off from the sun. But the best encouragement of our scepticism comes from the fact that a shade of it, at moments, appears to cross the mind, at other times so confident, of our physical speculators themselves. Thus, Professor Balfour Stewart, after describing the chaotic beginning of the visible universe to which "our modern knowledge enables us to look back with almost certitude," and after predicting the inevitable end with equal certainty, lets fall the significant sentence, not unsuggestive of scepticism in its author, "It ought, however, to be borne in mind that our knowledge of the laws of matter is in reality very limited."

In like manner, though to a less degree, we may entertain doubts respecting the far more important and significant Darwinian hypothesis. We may doubt that the hypothesis of Natural Selection is as well-founded as the Newtonian theory of Gravitation; or, admitting Natural Selection as an undoubted *vera causa*, we may still doubt that it was the sole agency employed by Nature in the derivation and fashioning of her innumerable types and varieties of life. We may doubt the universal applicability of the hypothesis, even though we must acknowledge that our biologists have produced much evidence in its favour. And those who prefer to doubt may still doubt the descent of man from an extinct variety of the ape species, though it is really easier to believe, and is more likely to be true, than the infinitely wider Theory of Development, from which, if established, it would of course follow as an evident corollary. In the present case, the corollary, if the least satisfactory, is the most significant part of the theory; and already, independent of the theory, in our undoubted ancestor, the Cave-man, we have more than half-way bridged the gulf between us and our still more questionable "country cousin," the gorilla.

But, as said, we may still doubt a little longer our alleged animal origin, as we may doubt Haeckel's hypothesis of the Spontaneous Generation of life, which, though it can hardly as yet be pronounced an article of scientific faith, is probably destined at no distant date to become one. And we may entertain degrees of doubts about all these hypotheses, even though we concede that each one of them is on the right lines of truth, and is gradually feeling its way nearer and nearer to it. For that some doubt is inseparable from every hypothesis is implied in the very notion of a hypothesis; and all who know the logical and psychological conditions which govern our assent when rightly yielded, know also that all degrees of doubt may and do attach to hypotheses, even in the minds of their originators themselves.

So stands it with the Darwinian hypothesis when looked at from the scientific point of view. A degree of doubt still hangs over it, as to the amount of which and the co-relative amount of evidence in its favour we must defer to the opinion of the best biologists, supposing them logical and free from mental bias. But it is otherwise when the *scientific hypothesis* is converted by biologists like Haeckel into a universal *philosophical theory*—a change which, though great and significant in its consequences, is easily and often made without notice being taken of it. When the scientific hypothesis of Darwin is turned into a philosophical system, called Darwinism, or is made the leading principle in the allied though more complete system of Herbert Spencer, called the Evolution Philosophy; when it is regarded not merely as a probable scientific hypothesis, but as a full philosophical interpretation of the universe and of the whole course of organic evolution, to say nothing of mental, moral, and social evolution in man;—then it is quite another matter, and we have a right to object to the all-embracing pretensions of the hypothesis, even though we are neither specialists nor advanced students in biology.

In fact, when Natural Selection—a name barely serving to mask the infinite play of Chance, which is its essential feature—is offered us as the chief or sole creative agency; when the only principle employed by Nature in the elaboration of the marvels of organic and of all other evolution is said to have been the principle of utility; when the unfolding of the purpose of the universe is resolved into movement in "the line of least resistance;"—in a word, when Chance and physical necessity, to the exclusion of Reason, Morality, and Purpose, are announced by Haeckel and Huxley, if not by Darwin himself, as the fundamental principles of the universe and of its process of development, we have the strongest philosophical grounds for objecting to the Darwinian doctrine so understood.

It is our right and our duty to challenge the conclusions of Science, or rather of the current philosophies which profess to speak in her name and with her credit, when they affect to be authoritative and final deliverances on philosophic or religious questions of supreme import. On the question of a future life, and of the existence and nature of God, we cannot allow the decisions of scientific specialists or even of scientific philosophers to contain the whole truth and the final word. On these two questions, that have been discussed since the days of Plato by the supremest intellects of our species, it cannot be allowed that the greatest of these were wholly away from the truth which has been only revealed at last in our own day by the latest great scientific hypothesis in conjunction with the law of the Conservation of Energy. Our new scientific philosophies must be content to have their pretensions tried by the same tests as all previous philosophies, namely, by criticism. They must be content to be valued by their powers of recommending themselves to the most developed human reason, including the universal human instincts; and when they have been thus tried and valued, I venture to predict that none of our new interpretations of the universe, neither the revised Materialism of Democritus resting on the doctrine of atoms and energy, nor the Evolution-Materialism of Haeckel which mingles the germs of life with the atoms, nor the still higher Evolution Philosophy of Herbert Spencer, will give full and final satisfaction. The last is the greatest, but as it takes away the attribute of Purpose from the Ultimate Reality and Power which it acknowledges in the universe, it will fail so far to find general acceptance with men.

§ 4. The question of a future life does partly belong to Science; and physics, physiology, and natural history under the light of the Darwinian theory, have all apparently decided against the possibility of it. When the cunningly constructed human machine breaks up; when the bodily organism, with all its functions, including thought, collapses; when man, the merely developed animal, dies like the rest;—there is a common scientific verdict that the end has veritably come, that the career of man as a conscious individual being has for ever closed. And it is not to be denied that the apprehension that it is really so has been deepened in our generation by the discoveries of Science. Nor has the apprehension been lessened by the application of the new Historical Method which tries to show the natural origin and genesis of the doctrine itself, and which, moreover, points to a period in the infancy of the species when the notion of immortality did not even exist. Nevertheless, the question of a future life is only in part a scientific one; nor is the doctrine disproved by showing that in the infancy of the species it was no more thought of than it now is in the infancy of the individual. The question is also philosophical, or, if the reader is not afraid of the word, metaphysical. It is metaphysical; for on the two questions of God and immortality, if one raises them at all, there is no escape from metaphysics, which, in fact, since the days of Kant, has been concentrating itself mainly round these two questions. Happily, from the side of philosophy, the question of a future life shows itself in an aspect quite other than it does from that of Science. In the two concluding chapters of the First Part of this book the whole question is discussed anew, and with special reference to the new scientific theories which bear upon it. I have fronted the arguments of science with the counter-theses of philosophy and religion, supplemented by the instincts of the human heart, and I have endeavoured, finally, after assigning to the several arguments the degree of weight that seemed in each case due, to take the fair measure of our fears as well as of our hopes.

§ 5. As regards the scientific ethics, in addition to exposition, some criticism is called for; because, though a certain agreement is apparent, one is also soon forced to recognize very serious differences amongst the scientific authorities; and also because the doctrine the most apparently well grounded does not appear wholly unexceptionable. Thus, scientific moralists agree that the will is not free, and here I agree with them; they agree further that the ultimate end of action is happiness or the lessening of pain; that the proper standard of virtue or right action is the amount of resulting good or happiness or utility; and with neither of these principles am I disposed to quarrel much. But though utilitarianism is thus the common ethical creed of scientific moralists like Mill and Bain and Herbert Spencer, it is by no means conceived alike by all of them. The utilitarianism of Mill, which places the happiness of others first, that of self only second, is very different in itself and in its consequences from the utilitarianism of Spencer, which reverses this order; and if the latter doctrine, backed as it is by evolution, and reposing on wider and deeper generalizations of the necessary laws of life, is to be held the more scientific and defensible presentment of utilitarianism, then the reflection is forced upon us that certain celebrated formulas, such as "the greatest happiness of the greatest number," and the "love and service of humanity," which have made much noise in these latter years, must be either henceforth dropped, as moral mottoes referring to delusive because impracticable goals, or else must be narrowed to more modest and possible aims, with a corresponding abatement as well in their dignity as in our obligation to follow them. For if the claims, the happiness, the well-being of self, must come first, both in the order of time and of reason; if the struggle for existence in some form, however disguised, is, as implied by Spencer, inseparable from all life,—it clearly follows that the happiness of others, even of those nearest us, must give place, and can only come second; while the happiness of the greatest number should be no aim of ordinary people at all, and can only be an aim to the statesman or even the most autocratic ruler within the limits of his own nation or race, and even within further limits determined for him by social facts and forces which he must take into account.

There is, in reality, opposition wide as the poles between the new and the old utilitarianism, between the humanitarian ethics of Mill, which makes the happiness of the species its aim, and the evolution ethics of Spencer, which, although it assigns a place to the facts of sympathy and sacrifice, nevertheless recognizes "the struggle for existence" as the most universal and necessary, the most controlling and comprehensive generalization; and if we elect to stand by the utilitarian creed at all, we must further make choice between these its divergent forms, or else we must make some compromise between them.

It is with the utilitarianism of Spencer that we shall be chiefly concerned; for it must be allowed that it is not only more practicable, but also more scientifically grounded than any previous presentment of the utilitarian creed. It is more truly rational than the famous rationally deduced system of Kant, because, unlike the latter, it is founded on human nature and can be followed by human beings. It is better based on human nature than the ethics of Butler; more consistent than the orthodox popular system, a compound of Butler and Kant, which goes by the name of the *a priori* or intuitional morality. But when all this has been said in its favour, we have to add that there are grave objections to some of its tenets, and still graver ones to its inmost spirit and practical tendency. There are the most serious questions raised by it; nay, that most serious and sinister of all questions,—whether Virtue has any reality beyond convention,—is once more irresistibly raised by it; and the answer to the question from the evolution point of view is not quite satisfactory. In fact, if virtue is not to be attacked at a vital point by being resolved in the last analysis into selfishness; if morality is to be regarded as other than a useful invention, to abate social jar and friction; if moral rules are not to be brought to the level of police regulations;—then there are some qualifications or concessions that must be made by the evolution moralist over and above those made by Mr. Spencer, in his recent remarkable work, *The Data of Ethics*.

Whatever becomes of moral systems, the practical morality, the ethics to be preached and enforced on men in future, must be the result of a compromise between the new and old teaching; and an attempt is made in the last two chapters of the book at a partial conciliation between the evolution ethics on the one side, and the transcendental, intuitional, and humanitarian ethics on the other. It is there maintained that the evolutionist must concede to the moral idealist that sacrifice is an actual ultimate fact, as well as an eternally necessary thing in life; further, that he must acknowledge the reality and binding obligation of the ideals of Truth, Justice, Charity, as true and not illusory lights, whose meaning, as given in the impulses to them, is that they should be followed, within rational bounds indeed, but sometimes at all hazards. He must also concede to the Kantian that there does exist *somewhere* a moral "ought," absolutely imperative, and a duty that must be done at whatever cost. But the latter, on his side, will have to give up the notion that the whole complex and sometimes contradictory field of conduct can be reduced under the all-embracing category of duty, equally obligatory and equally inexorable, even when the duties are in evident conflict. It will have to be given up, under penalty of the whole Kantian scheme of moral legislation being pushed impatiently aside, as not properly addressed to men, but to a wholly different order of beings—to beings possessed of free-will, which assuredly cannot be men; to noumenal egos, who are not swayed by our phenomenal passions and motives; in short, to hypothetical beings, existing nowhere on earth or in space, but only in the strange sphere of Things-in-themselves, or in the philosopher's imagination.

In order to get a suitable practical ethics for men, there

must either be a further element of sacrifice, of devotion, of absolute allegiance to duty, borrowed and added on to the evolution ethics, that it may contain the proper moral prescriptions for men in an imperfect moral world, which is improved less by moral systems than by individuals who manifest these qualities; or else the absolute systems must soften a little their rigid and unconditional moral code. They must stoop to consider the actual circumstances of men subject to facts and conditions of nature and environment under which action must be taken, and subject sometimes to perplexities and moral antinomies, where no right course is visible, no moral rule applicable. And if they cannot do this,—if the absolute moralist, like Kant, must plead a *non possumus*, then we must be content to improve our evolution and utilitarian ethics, and do the best we can with them.

Where our scientific authorities are all agreed, as on the question of the ultimate moving principle of action, and again on the question of the freedom of the will, I am in the main agreed with them. But on the last-named famous controversy a new statement of the necessitarian theory seems necessary, as well to supply certain points omitted by Mill and Bain, as on the other hand to show the futility of the merely mechanical theories of certain physicists and biologists, who, by reducing all action in man to the play of physical forces in the man-machine, would destroy the moral man altogether, as well as drag this old controversy back once more to the dark regions from which, after infinite vain wrangling, it had just emerged.

§ 6. There remains an important aspect of Science to be

considered; an aspect in which she is distinguished equally from the metaphysical as from the hypothetical speculations which so often pass current under her name and assume her credit; an aspect under which she shows herself, her character, and pretensions in their fullest and clearest light.

There is the Baconian view of Science, according to which she challenges our attention, not upon the strength of uncertain theories or provisional hypotheses, which for the most part she sets lightly by, but upon the evidence of her established laws, their worth and certainty; an aspect in which, far from being subject to the doubt that hangs over her hypotheses, she offers herself to us as the only assured truth, and the highest conceivable type of certainty and reliability.

There is positive science regarded as a vast and ever-increasing body of verified natural laws, of ascertained natural sequences, which, arranged in their proper groups and sub-groups, constitute the several sciences; positive science, which, having divided the phenomena of the outer world into their proper provinces—physical, chemical, natural—and having successfully reduced these to law and order for the intelligence, is now engaged in reducing physiological, psychological, and social phenomena to law also; positive science, which, before evolution had even been heard of, had already, in large measure, revolutionized man's previous conception of the universe, and which is further destined, if not to revolutionize wholly, at least to greatly modify, the current theories of religion, morals, politics, and the conduct of life.

There is positive science (not Positivism), which in itself is truth, which in its searching methods furnishes the surest test of truth, and the potent instruments in its further discovery; positive science, which, in its application, has given man the mastery over Nature, and tamed and turned her once formidable and destroying forces into his potent and submissive slaves; positive science, which, besides ministering to the higher wants of his intelligence, has multiplied manifold man's comfort and the material factors of his happiness, while confidently promising indefinite further gifts and services.

This aspect of Science, in which she is properly herself and truly great; in which she brings not merely the fruit which Bacon chiefly sought, but also truth, not merely material but spiritual bread, not merely the power which knowledge gives but the satisfying knowledge itself, and the pleasure from its discovery or rediscovery,—I have dwelt upon in the Second Book, on account of its intrinsic importance and the constant extension of this positive spirit over all departments of inquiry. Further, it is from this positive point of view that the Socialism and Pessimism of our time can be most profitably considered and best answered.

It must, however, be allowed that hitherto it has been chiefly in the physical and biological sciences, and in the practical sciences and arts to which these supply the necessary knowledge, that the conclusions and results of the positive methods have been of great and evident value. It is the positive conclusions of astronomy, chemistry, physics, physiology, and their applications in engineering, medicine, surgery, navigation, and the numerous other useful arts, that have multiplied man's power and increased the material conditions of his happiness. It is these same positive conclusions that have slowly altered and aggrandized his conception of the universe. But when we come to the mental, moral, and social sciences, there is less unanimity in their cultivators. Neither the laws of mind nor those of society are beyond dispute, like physical laws. There is less universality, and less permanence in the laws, because mental and social phenomena vary with the individual and the society. Nevertheless, of psychology at least it may be said, that, however its scientific claims be rated, it will at no distant day be regarded as an important department of study in connection with physiology, having its uses and applications in an order of things higher than material interests —in philosophy, criticism, ethics, politics, education, and even, in union with physiology, in the preservation of health and the conduct of life.

It is chiefly in the sphere of society that the discovery of settled laws becomes difficult, and the worth of those discovered questionable. For how, it is asked, can we reduce social phenomena to any permanent laws, when, as history clearly teaches, the appearance of a single great spirit, of a religious founder like Buddha, or even of a conqueror like Cæsar, might greatly modify them; and when the rise and spread of a new religious faith, or the growth of a new social system, might almost wholly dissolve them? The objection has weight; and we shall see reasons of a different sort for objecting to any science of society which would appear to bind man's power of social or political initiative in the fetters of necessity in the shape of scientific laws, social or economic, few or none of which are true for all ages and all societies. Sociological and even economic laws, it may be said, unlike physical laws, are revocable. They are made by the will of men, and the will of men can unmake them. They are made possible only by the consent of men, which can be revoked if it suits the general interest and convenience to do so. In short, the struggle of classes to enfranchise or to better themselves, the general movement of modern society to greater social equality and justice, the whole of what we call social progress, tend to make many sociological and economic laws merely temporary expressions of social facts, and the quicker the progress, the less durable all such laws. The notion of social evolution, and still more of revolution, is incompatible with permanent laws of social equilibrium, though it allows of laws of change or growth; and therefore the application of the term "science" to the ascertained order, such as it is, of social phenomena, is a matter of doubtful propriety. In this region of interesting speculation, scientific *methods* are unquestionably applicable; methods which have borne fruit in the explanation both of the facts of existing and of past societies; but whether the utmost possible systematization of which the infinite body of facts of a complex modern society admits, is to be called by the name of science or by some more fitting term, is still a disputed question.

I must add, too, that it is to a considerable extent a verbal one, since the applicability of scientific methods is universally admitted; while, further, that there is some order amongst social phenomena which lasts for a considerable time, is also allowed by all, and an accurate statement of this, together with the prediction of the next term in social progress, might fairly be regarded as scientific. But whether a science of society in a stricter sense be or be not possible, what is certain is that as yet the science has not been fully developed in any sense. The entire scope and boundary of the science are, in fact, not conceived alike by the only two thinkers who have laid claims to the creation of it—Comte and Herbert Spencer. And it still remains to be seen how far the latter eminent thinker, when he has finished his task, will have succeeded in at last creating the grand Science of Society, embracing, amongst other things, the subjects already more or less systematised, of political economy, politics, and jurisprudence.

In what precedes, I have given a general indication of what is to follow; of the chief questions that will be raised, of the methods of exposition and criticism that will be employed, of the general spirit in which they will be treated, and, in some cases, of the conclusions that will be contended for. We shall now proceed to the development in detail of the outline indicated.

BOOK I.
THE CREED OF SCIENCE
RELIGIOUS AND MORAL.

CHAPTER I.

ON THE CREATION AND GOD.

§ 1. THE earth, the sun, and the worlds of space stand before us as existing facts, poised in space and governed by law; and unless on the hypothesis of their eternal existence, as we now behold them, they must have had an origin of some kind. What was the origin? the mind of man naturally and persistently asks. To this question only three answers seem possible. They were created, or suddenly summoned into existence from nothing, by fiat of the Creator. They were slowly evolved by natural processes such as are still in operation, from elementary matter. Lastly, the question is too transcendent for human capacity: we do not know; and we can never know from the necessary and eternal limitation of our faculties and means of knowledge.

The hypothesis of the eternal existence of the earth, the sun, and the other heavenly bodies would seem at first the most natural one to hold; but it is negatived, as regards the earth and the solar system generally, by the consideration that the sun itself, on which the earth and planets depend, is, according to scientific showing, a consuming energy, a lit lamp and fire that could not have been burning for ever unless recruited by agencies of which Science has no knowledge and can form no guess.

The hypothesis of creation in time need not be long considered, because the thing itself is in fact unthinkable. Creation *ex nihilo*, the creation of matter from pure nothing, is entirely unthinkable;* while creation in the less proper sense of architectonic world-building from pre-existing materials, though not beyond the reach of a certain rude anthropomorphic imagination, is an unsatisfactory and inadequate explanation, for besides that the highest philosophic thought lends no countenance to such a conception, it is also opposed to the view which geology has accustomed us to take of the extremely slow transition of our earth through an indefinite series of changes, due to the action of natural causes, which still continue their work. It is opposed to the whole modern conception of evolution, which, however satisfactory or otherwise it may itself turn out as a complete hypothesis (a point to be considered in its turn), has at least so far established its claims on our credit as to set aside in comparison the notion of the sudden construction of the earth and worlds by a world-builder. We are still at liberty, indeed, to believe in a Power, one and eternal, immanent in matter, and moving it when it is supposed to move by its own laws; but, though we may even continue in imagination to represent this Power as still at work like the architect or the engineer, we can no longer believe in it as really working in such fashion, or concede to the conception of the Great Architect who fashioned worlds and launched

---

* See *Critique of Pure Reason*, p. 139, Meiklejohn's translation, where Kant, treating of "The Permanence of Substance," tells us that annihilation and creation are alike inconceivable in the field of possible experience, and that the two maxims, "*Gigni de nihilo nihil,*" "*in nihilum nil posse reverti,*" should never be separated.

See also Herbert Spencer's *First Principles*, ch. iv., "On the Indestructibility of Matter."

them fully finished on their paths in space, other than a poetic significance of no scientific or philosophical value.

The negative doctrine of Nescience, or the necessary insolubility of the problem from the limitation of our faculties, is one only to be fallen back upon finally, after the complete and demonstrated failure of Science to solve the mystery of the origin of things by a positive and probable hypothesis. At least, Nescience will only be listened to without impatience after Science has made her utmost attempt at explanation and signally failed. But Science is now in possession of the ear of the court; she professes to have a satisfactory hypothesis to offer explanatory of the origin of the material universe, as well as of the world of life. It remains, therefore, to let her unfold her hypothesis, and apply it to the explanation of the facts, that we may see how far we can accept it.

§ 2. According to Science, the earth, the sun, the moon, the planets, and all the host of heaven are the results of the condensation, millions of years ago, of a nebulous vapour or extremely attenuated matter diffused throughout the expanse of space.

This dispersed matter, with a stock of potential energy, existed from eternity, but into their previous possible states or transformations, Science does not inquire. She commences her story at the beginning of the evolution of the present existing universe, without raising the question whether the necessary materials might not have entered into the composition of a previously existing one which had become dissolved; and for purposes of explanation she postulates at this beginning our present quantity of matter and energy, subject to the law of gravitation, and the law of the transformation of energy.

The primitive matter, at first in a chaotic state, we are to suppose slowly reduced to order under the continued agency of these two laws. Its isolated atoms, under gravitation, congregated into groups more or less close, and these again into larger and larger groups, until at length the original diffused matter became resolved into a number of rotating nebular masses of spherical form, of immense volume, and in a state of high heat from the previous shock of their atoms and constituent parts.

According to the nebular hypothesis, these vaporous and rotating spheres slowly cooled by radiation, in cooling contracted, in contracting acquired a more rapid rotatory motion, in consequence of which, through the increased centrifugal force, huge rings of vapour were at length flung off from the equatorial regions. These Saturnian rings successively projected from the spinning spheres as the cooling of the central nebulous mass still continued, in their turn condensed, broke from their annular shape at their points of feeblest cohesion as rings of smoke, united again by the law of gravitation, and settled into the spherical form like their parent masses, with which, however, they continued still connected, as planets, by the powerful invisible chain of gravitation. But the planets, in cooling, had early imitated the process of the parent nebulæ by also expelling rings of vapour which, having gone through the same steps as their generating primaries, appeared as younger families of planets, or planetoids—a third generation, so to speak, and faithful copies, both in form and movements, of their progenitors. Such was the origin of our earth and planets, as well as of their moons—their lawfully-born offspring, and still the followers of their fortunes; while in the rings of Saturn we have an instance of a former potential moon, whose course of development was checked, the broken fragments not having united—a mishap which, however, had the good result for Science of suggesting the whole hypothesis to its originators.

Such is, in substance, the celebrated speculation of Laplace and Kant, concerning the origin of the earth and the solar system; the first of that startling series of tales issued by Science during the past century, and which has now been seemingly completed in the Darwinian story of the origin of plants and animals, and above all in the crowning one—the metamorphosis of the ape into the man.

The hypothesis is generally allowed to be of a legitimate and scientific character. It postulates only a *vera causa*, and such laws as we still see in operation. It postulates only a nebulous mass subject to present physical laws; and such nebulæ now exist, while such laws, we may fairly be asked to believe, did govern from eternity the behaviour of matter and energy. Moreover, the hypothesis explains many of the facts requiring explanation, as the fact that the motions of the planets are all nearly in the same plane; that the central mass of our system remains a blazing sun, while the surface of our earth has long since cooled; the fact of the rings of Saturn, the satellites and the various temperatures of the planets, and many other things. Nevertheless, as will presently appear, the hypothesis is not without great and as yet unexplained difficulties.

"The greatest of them," as Professor Newcomb urges, "perhaps, is to show how a ring of vapour surrounding the sun could condense into a single planet encircled by satellites." * For the ring of vapour that by supposition

* Newcomb's *Astronomy*, Part IV. ch. iii., which contains a full consideration of the subject.

condensed into our earth, for instance, must have been at least the diameter of the earth's orbit, that is, some two hundred millions of miles, in breadth. But now, even if we suppose this enormous ring to have been successfully expelled after the manner described by Laplace—a supposition not without its difficulties; if we suppose it to have subsequently condensed as it certainly would, and to have broken up as it probably would;—the further suppositions that we must make constitute a demand on our scientific faith that is scarcely justified by either physical science or analogy. For we are asked to believe that all the sundered parts, probably extremely numerous, some of them separated by the interval of the earth's orbit, and all of them necessarily moving with great velocity in the same direction, at length, after paroxysmal efforts due to the action of gravity, found themselves together again in one symmetrical sphere of vapour, moving orderly round the sun. The exercise of faith required is great; for physical science would rather predict that the broken parts of such a ring, instead of coalescing into a single sphere, would, as the authority just quoted affirms, "condense into a swarm of smaller bodies like the asteroids," or like those still smaller, which compose, according to conjecture, the rings of Saturn. And then we must believe that this precarious process of generating worlds repeated itself without accident again and again; the rings of Saturn showing the only abortive attempt. The earth was also a sphere of vapour which, in shrinking, left behind a ring, which in its turn condensed, broke up, joined again, and finally formed our moon. And Jupiter must have been thus successfully delivered of his numerous progeny of eight. But a much more serious difficulty presents itself in the case of Uranus, whose moons move in a direction nearly the reverse of that required by the hypothesis. It would seem that either Uranus received a temporary tilt over in his orbit at the moment when each of his rings was disengaged, or else some great perturbation or other exceptional experience occurred to each of his progeny after they were born. And the same must be said of Neptune, whose single moon moves in a more decidedly retrograde order.

Moreover the conditions, if any, under which such a ring could be thrown off from a rotating sphere of cooling vapour have not been investigated mathematically, nor is there any experiment in point,* while under the conditions supposed by Laplace, it has been objected that in the absence of all cohesion between the particles of vapour, the throwing off the ring in the manner alleged was in fact impossible. Finally, the existing nebulæ do not manifest that symmetry of outline which is requisite if they are destined to condense into suns and planets. All which objections, together with others that might be urged, tend to discredit the hypothesis very considerably in the forms propounded by its originators.

The authors of *The Unseen Universe* have given an improved statement of the nebular hypothesis. They begin with a chaos of atoms compelled to order by the law of gravitation, instead of reaching it slowly by chance after many false starts and failures as in the system of Democritus. We are told that "the original state of the visible universe was a diffused or chaotic state, in which the various particles were widely separated from one another, but

* That of Plateau, sometimes adduced, of a sphere of oil rotating in water, is no confirmation, as it relates to a different thing under different conditions, and on an infinitely smaller scale. See Jevons's *Principles of Science*.

exerting on one another gravitating force, and therefore possessed of potential energy. As these particles came together, impinged on one another, or gathered into groups, this potential energy was gradually transformed into the energy of heat, and into that of visible motion. We may thus imagine the cooling and (except under very strict conditions of original distribution) *necessarily* revolving matter, in course of time to have thrown off certain parts of itself, which would thereafter form satellites or planetary attendants, while the central mass would form the sun." *

Now, if this be the development hypothesis of Kant and Laplace, as we are expressly told it is, it must be allowed that most of the difficulties which beset the more audacious presentments of it are avoided. But also, it must be said, with this more guarded and general statement of it, nearly all the grandeur of the hypothesis vanishes. With the contracting spheres and the mighty rings of vapour suppressed, which closed together and became worlds, all the charm and attractiveness is gone. That, however, should not signify in a matter that respects only scientific accuracy. True; but also with the removal of the rings and the sphere of vapour, the hypothesis itself is gone. There is nothing remaining but a mass of matter which threw off parts of itself in its revolution—a different, if a safer, theory. Nor is it wholly satisfactory either. For unless the parts were propelled in a skilful manner that has not been described, they must have either fallen back again or travelled into space, to return no more; and why neither of these accidents, antecedently possible, did actually happen, we are left to surmise.

This last theory has, however, been presented by Sir W. Thomson, its real originator, from a much more striking and

* *The Unseen Universe*, p. 164, Fifth Edit.

suggestive point of view, from which it claims a further and a special consideration.

According to this distinguished physicist, the sun and the heat of the sun were produced some millions of years ago by the fall together of its materials from a state of wide diffusion, as a cloud of stones and dust and gaseous matter. The shock of its atoms, and the mutual collision of its smaller constituent bodies and masses under the action of gravitation, gradually warmed and lit up the nebulous mass, while the final rush together of the whole immense materials with prodigious velocities resulted, by the law of the convertibility of energy, in a vast development of heat in a single condensed mass, which formed the sun.

In like manner, the fall together of the earth's materials millions of years ago, produced the earth at first at white heat, like the sun; but as the earth's constituents fell in smaller quantity, from less distances, and with consequent less velocities, the amount of heat, though great, was far less than in the case of the sun. Accordingly, the earth cooled down long since, while the sun, though lavishly spending heat from the beginning, will not be reduced to the earth's temperature for millions of years to come.

In the same way, our moon and all the other planets, with their moons, were produced—the meteoric showers and the comets, probably of meteoric composition, still existing to remind us of the like former condition of all the other bodies of the solar system.

Such is the theory of Thomson respecting the origin of the sun and planets. But there is no mention here of rings of vapour, and in other respects we are a good way from the theory of Laplace. It is, in fact, so far, a different and a better hypothesis. It explains the sun's heat, which was assumed by Laplace; and it explains it by a true scientific cause—the impact of masses in motion. Moreover, by a still bolder application of the same conception, and for the first time, we might almost say, since men began to speculate on the matter, it explains in a real way, the actual presence of our old solid earth here in space to-day. It is true that the explanation given—the sudden convergence from the four winds of the materials of our globe—is at first a little startling, and almost as trying to the imagination as the old theory of creation *ex nihilo*. But on reflection we see that the thing is possible, the conception scientific. If we believe our earth to be a globe in space, we must allow that its materials, as well as those of every other heavenly body, *may* have come thus together from a state of nebular or meteoric dispersion, under the strong compulsion of gravitation; and it may have even been, as Professor Tait suggests, "that they fell together in such a way that the whole mass of the earth was agglomerated together almost at once."

We might, I say, even believe in this instantaneous fusion and chemical union following on the mechanical forcing together of the materials, since the chemical change, on the vast scale of a given mass of loose materials into a molten planet, may be quite as easy for Nature to effect as the chemical changes on the small scale in her ordinary operations. It is only when we ask the inevitable further question—Whence came the materials that thus suddenly met together one day for the composition of our globe?—that the theory begins to prove unsatisfactory. For it appears from Sir W. Thomson's expositor, Professor Tait, that the precipitated substances came from, or rather formerly composed, a smaller nebulous cloud that had become severed from the primitive mass before its main body had finally condensed into the sun. But how severed? is still the question, and that which raises the old difficulty. The fall together of the parts of a scattered nebulous cloud we understand, and admit as a possible explanation of the sun and planets; but, precisely for that reason, the fall asunder of the primitive nebulous mass is difficult to understand, and cannot be allowed as an explanation of the separate masses required to compose the earth and planets, with their numerous moons. It cannot be allowed, at least, until some natural force is pointed out sufficiently powerful to produce the separation in opposition to the strong force of gravity drawing the mass ever closer together by hypothesis. No matter how loosely associated the constituents of the original nebulous cloud, in order to break off parts from it (since no original repulsive force is postulated) it must be shown that some such force, centrifugal or other, would be generated within the mass. Nor would this be sufficient. It must be further shown how such a force disintegrated the nebula so skilfully, and gave the transported parts at the moment of projection such precise velocities and in such directions, that, avoiding the other contingencies of the case—of passing off finally into infinite space or describing paths returning on the mass—they have been ever since moving in nearly circular orbits around it.

It must be shown, in short, that all was provided for by law, and that nothing was left to chance, especially at the supreme moment when our earth was cast off. Until this has been shown more satisfactorily than has yet been done, though we may entertain ourselves with the speculation that the earth and planets were formerly nebulous islands floating in space, we shall yet hesitate to believe in their alleged former connection with the mainland of the sun's nebular continent, and all the more when we reflect that the former existence of the islands themselves is not beyond the reach of doubt.

To conclude: we know nothing for certain respecting the mode of origination of the earth, the sun, the planets, the stars. We believe, on the showing of Science, that the sun could not have existed from eternity, because his heat is a limited quantity that could not have lasted perpetually unless recruited from sources of which Science has no knowledge. But still, there may now be, and there may have been, such sources. Nor could we be certain to the contrary, unless we were assured that we know all the physical forces in nature, and that none of these, either separately or by their conjoint action, could have kept up an eternal supply of solar heat. Assuming, however, as more probable, that the sun has not existed from eternity, we are sure that he gathered his fires by natural causes. But we are not sure that the only cause was the impact of falling masses of matter, or the condensation of his diffused matter into closer compass, as Helmholtz has it. And assuming that the sun had a beginning in time, we are equally sure that the earth had also a beginning, since it could not well have existed in the sun's absence. But we are not sure that the earth (any more than the sun) was formed at white heat by the rushing together of its materials, much less that it is the solidified result of a prodigious ring of vapour, thrown off ages ago from a revolving vaporous sphere in the course of its contracting and cooling down to the sun.

Both these hypotheses should, indeed, be treated with the respect that is due to the guesses of men of genius. Still, however scientifically prompted, however skilfully shaped, however superior to the rude cosmogonies of non-scientific ages that we now dismiss as only fit for children, they are only guesses. They are only attempts at the solution of the problem—being given a world or a system of worlds, to determine how they were made; a problem so transcendent that the highest human solutions may be no more than rude approximations. And all real verification is out of the question; since, however true our theory of the past process of construction, a competing and more plausible theory is, we see, always possible; while, if worlds are now anywhere made in stellar space according to our formula, it is still impossible to prove the fact, owing to the remoteness of the phenomenon. We must not, then, with some, treat the nebular hypothesis in either of its forms as if it contained the whole truth which explained fully and finally the process of world-making. We must not erect it into an article of scientific faith with the physicists and geologists, or make it an integral part of our philosophic systems with the evolution philosophers like Strauss and Herbert Spencer. We are simply to consider the two forms of the hypothesis as conjectures—equal in poetic grandeur, but unequal in scientific credit—of the phenomena, possibly portentous, abnormal, and wholly beyond the reach of the scientific imagination to shape, which preceded or accompanied the first appearance of the earth, the sun, and the planets as globes in space. They may both contain a certain proportion of truth; they may both be erroneous and misleading, even though one might be less wide of the facts than the other.

§ 3. Let us now pursue the scientific narrative of the creation, which starts from the nebular hypothesis as accepted truth; and for the moment let us also concede its truth. According to both forms of the hypothesis, though there is independent geologic evidence to the same effect, our globe existed as a molten sphere before it cooled down to a solid one. With this fiery-fluid condition of things, the existence of all life such as we know it was wholly incompatible.* Life was impossible on the earth till, after the lapse of ages, its surface had become sufficiently cooled. And then we are presented with the same question with respect to the origin of life that was before raised with respect to the origin of the earth itself. If life has not been from eternity—and it evidently has not been—whence came its first forms? Now, if we dismiss the strange fancy of Sir W. Thomson, that the first forms of life were transported from some other planet to the earth upon an aerolite—a theory moreover, which would only push back the mystery one step, without solving it—there are only two other possible answers to the question of the origin of life. Either life was created supernaturally from nothing, or from nothing by us conceivable, by the fiat of the Creator, as we read in the Mosaic and Miltonic account; or life was spontaneously evolved by Nature herself from the primitive physical atoms, according to natural process, by chemical and physical laws. The first, it is contended by scientific thinkers, is no answer, since the word "creation" conveys, when closely pressed, no meaning, and the creative fiat is a wholly inconceivable cause—a notion which Science and Philosophy agree in declaring to be unthinkable, and the

---

* There are, indeed, those who think that life may have existed in some form "as an eternal constituent of the universe." And Haeckel has hazarded the notion that "all matter is, in a certain sense, alive." But no life such as we know it could have existed in the first fiery-fluid condition of our globe as Science represents it; and if matter be alive, it must be in a sense wholly inconceivable to us.

attempt to realize which puts all thought to confusion. The second is both the secret conviction of Science and her sometimes openly hazarded opinion through the mouths of her more outspoken and sanguine representatives, who hope, at no distant date, to put the matter beyond the reach of further doubt. They have already endeavoured to make manifest by experiments the fact, if not the process, of spontaneous production, by which, they contend, Nature, in the secret recesses of her vast laboratory, formerly introduced the first germs of organic life—a process which, in the case of certain simpler organisms, she still occasionally repeats. It is true the experimentalists have not yet succeeded in surprising Nature in the very act of creation. But they feel certain they are on the right road. They by no means abandon the hope of tracking the last and greatest of Nature's secrets to its final hiding-place, masked, as they believe it to be, under simple natural processes and physico-chemical laws. This secret, which has hitherto baffled scientific scrutiny, but which, since the dawn of science, has attracted all who had a thirst for real knowledge, the secret that filled Faust with the consuming desire for the power

> To see below earth's dark foundations
> Life's embryo seeds before their birth,
> And Nature's silent operations;

this secret of the first beginnings of life, so long and seemingly so carefully guarded in the deepest recesses of Nature's breast, will, our physicists and biologists are confident, before long, be finally laid bare. The thing which Kant thought impossible—the attempt to explain the facts of life by physical and chemical laws, and which, he affirmed, must be shattered to pieces on a "caterpillar"—

will be successful, and will explain the man as well as the caterpillar. The missing link in the grand chain of evolutionary process from the nebular haze to the sublimed spirit of man, as manifested in Plato, Raphael, Newton, and Shakespeare, will soon be supplied, and the last enigma of existence at length be solved.

Indeed, Professor Haeckel will have it that the problem is as good as solved at present, spite of the want of confirmation by recent scientific experiment, of the asserted fact of spontaneous generation. According to this eminent biologist, the first step from non-living to living matter was made spontaneously by Nature millions of centuries ago at the bottom of the sea, "where the primitive life organisms were formed like saline crystals in water." * Moreover, this process of spontaneous generation, though now less necessary, still goes on at intervals, perhaps even constantly, had we only sufficiently keen and commanding range of vision to see it. Some species of the *monera* are probably produced in this way. But at least it is certain that, in the past, the fact of spontaneous production of life must have occurred. There is no other conceivable or possible hypothesis. Only grant sufficient time—and it is argued, with a whole infinite past to draw upon, there need be no stint in this respect—only grant the necessary time to exhaust possible errors, wrong tentatives, erroneous combinations of chemical atoms, and at last the happy fortuitous meeting and permanent alliance of the proper atoms must take place; the living molecule containing the due though complicated combination of chemical atoms will at length be born; from which, under favour of natural selection, to

---

* Address of Professor Haeckel (see *Times*, August 30, 1878; also *History of Creation*).

protoplasm—the elementary building material of all life, and in particular of the monera—things will, in further course of time and evolution, in duly sequent steps proceed. True, we cannot get down to the dim ocean-beds to witness the actual process of the production of life from matter by chemical combination; but though we cannot descend save only in imagination, we can do the next best thing,—we can summon up from the vasty deep these elementary forms of life in great variety, as witnesses of the truth of our deductions. And they have been brought up in great variety, in particular in the course of the recent expedition of the *Challenger* in the South Seas. Professor Haeckel himself, in his *History of Creation*, gives minute and careful descriptions of several of these remarkable types of life, if such they can be called, which have been thus obtained from an immense depth in the sea. These since celebrated monera are the simplest of all organisms,—if that can be properly described as an organism which possesses in fact no organs, and which consists only of a homogeneous, structureless clot of albuminous matter, or protoplasm. Strictly speaking, the moneron is not an organism,—it is neither plant nor animal, though all the more interesting on that account; for this phenomenon propagates its kind by self-division, and absorbs neighbouring appropriate matter, which displaces some of its own albuminous particles:* that is to say, these ambiguous creatures between mere matter and life possess, in elementary form, the capacities of propagation, of nutrition, and of growth, which are characteristics of all living beings, while they themselves are certainly not organized beings, according to Haeckel. They form, in fact, the bridge between the two worlds, the organic

---

* *History of Creation*, vol. i. p. 186.

and the inorganic; and though not living, they are the original progenitors of all life, including the human. Moreover, to add to the interest which already surrounds this singular class of beings, there is, says Professor Haeckel, amongst its species one " which probably even now always comes into existence by spontaneous generation." *

If it be objected to these views that scientific experiments of an ingeniously searching and seemingly exhaustive character appear to negative the hypothesis of spontaneous generation, it is replied that such are not and could not be exhaustive. What, asks Professor Clifford, do such experiments really prove? Merely that " the coincidence which would form a *Bacterium*—already a definite structure, reproducing its like—does not occur in a test-tube during the periods yet observed. The experiments have nothing whatever to say to the production of enormously simpler forms in the vast range of the ocean during the ages of the earth's existence." And this is clearly true. The experiments do not exclude the possibility that Nature, in her vast laboratory, can and does at present evolve living from non-living matter; far less do they destroy the grounds of the scientific conviction that Nature, working under wholly different and more favourable conditions in the past when the earth, slowly cooling from her originally incandescent state, was warmer, and when her own plastic powers were greater, could evolve life spontaneously from her own breast. But the strongest of all arguments for the theory of spontaneous generation is the inadmissibility of the only rival hypothesis. In no other way can the origin of life be conceived, argues Haeckel. If Nature did not evolve spontaneously the few primordial forms of

* *History of Creation*, vol. i. p. 344.

life which the Darwinian theory postulates, then they must have been supernaturally created. We return to the miracle—the sudden production of things by a Supernatural Personal Creator from blank nonentity—the production of effects without prior natural causes or conditions, and by a process respecting which neither science nor human thought can form any conception. The miracle, from which spontaneous generation would deliver us, and which puts reason to confusion, once again returns, after being everywhere expelled from the wide territory of Science.

§ 4. Without further comment for the present on the hypothesis of spontaneous generation, let us resume the story of creation, which, it should be observed, from the production of the first planet from the nebular vapour, to the production of the first human being from a lower form of life, covers much more than the six days' paroxysmal creative labour as recorded in Genesis, necessitating, as it did, many hundreds, perhaps thousands of millions of years for its slow evolutionary achievement.

We have learned the origin of the worlds of space, according to Kant, Laplace, and the physicists; of the world of life in the dim ocean-deeps, according to Oken, Haeckel, and the naturalists; there remains to be told by Science the origin of the multitudinous and varied species of animals and plants, even should we admit that Nature, the all-bountiful mother, herself unwittingly accomplished the first grand preliminary feat in the spontaneous production of the rudest and simplest forms of life. From the rude and simple to the refined and complex; from the homogeneous moneron to the heterogeneous mammal; from the "few primordial forms" of life which Darwin begins with, and which, let us suppose, have resulted from the due collocation of the chemical atoms after many abortive tentatives, up to the endlessly varied and highly elaborated forms of life which science to-day contemplates,—there is still a vast distance. And the question now rises, How have all these various species in the organic world arisen? How has the elementary life run into such endlessly varied forms, each distinguished by its special kind and degree of adaptations and beauty? Above all, how has life, starting from such low beginnings, soared to such lofty heights in man himself, severed, seemingly, on all sides from the other species by a great gulf apparently not to be bridged, as shown in his outward form, and yet more in his inward nature and in its still growing capacities of invention, of art, of thought, of disinterested virtuous endeavour?

For answer to this most important question we must consult the books of Darwin and of those who have worked in the lines indicated in his world-famed theory. As we there learn, the higher species of plants and animals, including man, were derived from the lower, and all ultimately from "one or a few primordial forms," through the agency of Natural Selection combined with the fact of Inheritance; the first representing the changing and progressive, the second, the conservative factor in the great process of organic evolution. Nature, or to speak more precisely, a complicated but yet connected and continuous process called Natural Selection, whose action has extended over unimaginable ages, and is still at work, was the unconscious sculptor and mechanician that slowly—extremely slowly—elaborated all the various forms of life that we now behold, as well as many long since extinct species. Natural selection it was that separated the different species from each other; that carved their organs gradually, and ever more carefully, from rough rudimentary attempts, and that fitted them each to the other and all to their environment —an unconscious artist, that worked by seemingly disconnected efforts and without any plan or preconception of the result to be finally achieved, but who nevertheless, by the simplest means, reached at length the most surprising and splendid results. For, by acting on the simple rule of selecting those individuals the best fitted to their surrounding conditions to continue their kind, and soon or late letting drop the ill-fitted, and by an undeviating repetition of the process and adherence to the rule, Nature has attained to all the wonderful and varied life that we behold. Moreover, by acting in this manner, she evolved ever higher as well as ever different types. By this means she slowly evolved the wing of the bird, the fin of the fish, the foot of the mammal,—all the different propellers from common germinal beginnings; by this means, by natural selection only, from an optic nerve, coated with pigment and tingling in the sunlight, she elaborated and perfected the living miracle of the human eye, and adapted its lens to the properties of light; finally, by this means she evolved the civilized man from the savage, the savage from the brute, and the brute, through ever lower lines, from the mollusc and the moneron;—results so marvellous without the Darwinian clue, that men were compelled to refer them to the action of a Supernatural and Omnipotent Creator, who, according to our anthropomorphic habits of thought, still worked after our human fashion in fulfilment of a plan and purpose.

Thus Natural Selection, by seizing on favourable variations accidentally offered, by accumulating and intensifying these, and by thereafter handing them on as a constantly increasing capital, from generation to generation, in the fact of inheritance, succeeded in producing all the variety of plant and animal life that now exists. But for the most part, she finished her species myriads of years ago, and has made little alteration since in the type. And having elaborated all her forms, she did her best to efface all traces of her methods of work, and of the slow and laborious steps by which she reached her ends, which, now that we have discovered them, seem at a first view as startling, when morally regarded, as they are simple from the point of view of mechanical contrivance; consisting simply in invariably favouring the strong and the successful, and in leaving the weak to perish in the eternal and necessary "struggle for existence." Nature had only shown to us the finished article of her manufacture, and we all in our ignorance admired greatly; she had carefully reserved the secret of her processes, which would have much diminished our admiration. It is to Darwin that we owe the drawing aside of the mysterious curtain behind which Nature had carried on her secret operations in the elaboration of her species and varieties. He has explained it to us, and the marvel ceases. He it is who has taken us into her inmost laboratory, and shown her at her labour and in her working dress. He it is first and chiefly who has surprised Nature in the act, who has discovered her secret, and disclosed the processes by which, after long-continued practice, she has reached in some cases so great and splendid results.

But if Darwin has diminished our wonder, by showing us the secret of Nature's mechanical skill, he has aroused other, and some of them disquieting, sentiments. For what a process, according to his showing, Evolution has been!

One long-continued battle without quarter, raging fiercely over the whole animal kingdom, and carried on even into the vegetable kingdom, though there less cruelly, because there is no attendant consciousness; a struggle between species and species, where the weak is ever the prey of the strong; and a still more deadly and concentrated struggle carried on within the limits of each species, amongst the component individuals, compelled to compete with each other for the same precarious supply of food which, however cruelly procured, is always less than the demand for it; a conflict where, unless in the few social species, it is to "the near in blood the nearer bloody." Indeed, the revelations of the Darwinian story are in many cases by no means agreeable to dwell upon, although as our own species—the crown and finished masterpiece of Nature's workmanship— has emerged supreme victor from the universal trial by combat, and upon the whole has come well out of the long chapter of most disastrous chances for other species living and extinct, it seems, according to Darwin and Spencer, that, all things considered, we ought to congratulate ourselves on our good fortune. At least, there has been no fall of man; on the contrary, there has been a wonderful rise, that could scarce in reason have been expected at first. There has been no degradation, but a constant and still-continuing development, which opens out great vistas of promise for our future and still more selected successors.

§ 5. Nevertheless, what strikes us most in reading this marvellous story of the origin and process of manufacture of Nature's living forms, is the seemingly chance affair it all was. We are not permitted, on Darwinian principles, to suppose that there was any prevision or forecast of what was to come resident in Nature's blind bosom. There was no conception, not even the vaguest dream, on the part of Nature, at the commencement of the cosmic process, of the forms of life that should emerge in the sequel. Nature did not know what she did, for there was no principle of knowledge within her. Still worse, there was no constant purpose in view, and no controlling Power governing the process of evolution. Nature had no special aims in view; anything, in fact, might have happened. She did not aim particularly at life or the human consciousness. When life first resulted, it was an accident, lucky or unlucky, as we choose to regard it. When the first rudiments of that wonderful revealer of nature, the eye, were laid, they came by chance, and by further repeated chances the eye was improved. It was improved as a telescope is improved, by slow degrees, only, unlike the telescope, it was improved not by an inventor or maker, but by Natural Selection, which preferred the animals with good eyes, and elected them to continue the advantage to the species.

What has resulted need not have resulted, for Nature neither knew, nor cared, nor directed. Things might have taken a wholly different course, on the earth at least, with a slight accidental alteration of conditions at a critical moment in the history of any one of the species. In particular, man himself, the crown of creation, might not have appeared at all. And after his appearance it was only owing to the chapter of accidents unusually favourable that he emerged victor from the general battle-field of existence. Man is here to-day the master and the "interpreter of Nature," because he has escaped a thousand perils and chances of failure, any of which, taking a more adverse turn, might in the infant stages have early closed his since distinguished career. He is here, too, because the particular line of his brute progenitors, itself since extinct, survived sufficiently long to launch him on a precarious world, not too well provided. Had the latter circumstance been other, or had the special branch of the tree of life from which man is descended withered earlier, as other branches have done; had even any of the antecedent branches, which bore other diverging types as well as the human, perished earlier, assuredly man would not have appeared. The splendid series of accidents which prepared the way for him and made his advent possible, could not have happened twice; in which case Nature would have had another master—the dog, the horse, the elephant, or some other promising species now kept in the background, and whose "genius is rebuked" by man's overshadowing superiority.

On the Darwinian hypothesis, man is the child of Chance, as from the Evolution Hypothesis, in its full generality, all life is the result of chance. An eminent expositor of the truths of physical science, and an eloquent expounder and advocate of the evolution hypothesis, Professor Tyndall, by implication denies this. He affirms that in the primitive nebular vapour all the future developments of the universe were potentially contained: life, man; his philosophy, poetry, art, science; Plato, Shakespeare, Newton, Raphael. Speaking of the evolution hypothesis, he says, "For what are the core and essence of this hypothesis? Strip it naked, and you stand face to face with the notion that not alone the more ignoble forms of animalcular or animal life, not alone the nobler forms of the horse and lion, not alone the exquisite and wonderful mechanism of the human body, but that the human mind itself—emotion, intellect, will, and all their phenomena—were once latent in a fiery cloud. . . . But the hypothesis would probably go even further than this. Many who hold it would probably assent to the position that at the present moment all our philosophy, all our poetry, all our science, and all our art—Plato, Shakespeare, Newton, and Raphael—are potential in the fires of the sun. We long to learn something of our origin. If the evolution hypothesis be correct, even this unsatisfied yearning must have come to us across the ages which separate the unconscious primeval mist from the consciousness of to-day." *

And to this we can only say that a serious attempt to substantiate the proposition, and to show how even the human species, to say nothing of its philosophy and art, or of its Platos and Shakespeares, was potential in the cosmic vapour, would involve the construction of a new system of metaphysics—a feat which would present very exceptional difficulties to any one who, like Professor Tyndall, accepts the law of natural selection, with its admitted play of boundless contingency, as the most fundamental shaping agency in the evolution of organized beings.

But it is just possible that we misunderstand Professor Tyndall when we suppose him to imply that Plato, Shakespeare, and Raphael were potential in the original "fiery cloud." What he says is that they "are potential in the fires of the sun." Does he here mean that when the sun is cooled sufficiently, life as on earth will result? It would be a bold prophecy. Or only that if the sun cooled, and if all other conditions be supposed alike, there would be a like result? It might be; but if any difference be allowed, it is safer not to affirm details; since, even on

* *Fragments of Physical Science:* "On the Scientific Use of the Imagination," p. 163.

the earth, the Shakespeares and Platos have not yet appeared in whole continents. But perhaps he only means that thought is potential in the sun's fires because, through a series of transformations, it can be referred back to the sun's energy as source.* And if so, we have only Plato and Shakespeare traced sideways to the sun as their first cause, instead of backwards to the cosmic vapour as their source. We have only the cruder materialism, which appeals for support to the conservation of energy, instead of the more refined materialism of the evolution hypothesis, both of which will be considered at the proper place. But the final sentence in the quotation from Professor Tyndall I confess I find it difficult to refer to any system of philosophy, or even to give to it any definite meaning. He says, if the evolution hypothesis be correct, that the unsatisfied yearning to know our origin "must have come to us across the ages which separate the unconscious primeval mist from the consciousness of to-day." The only meaning that can be given to this, and what probably is intended, is that this yearning, like all very general feelings, is derived by inheritance from the generations behind us, who in like manner inherited it, till we come back finally to our first animal ancestors not far removed from "the unconscious primeval mist." But such a sentiment fades away long before we reach the moneron, and even long before we go back to the monkey, which, as far as we can judge, manifests no desire to know its origin. The sentiment in man is, in fact, a product of philosophical reflection, and of comparatively cultured ages, which scarcely exists in the savage. How, therefore, such a "yearning," born long

* The latter is certainly one of Professor Tyndall's meanings; see *Fragments of Physical Science:* "On Vitality," pp. 437, 441.

after life appeared, could "have come to us across the ages" from the primeval mist, in many of which ages it did not exist, is very perplexing to understand, even when assisted by the extremest use of the scientific imagination.

Doubtless, every material thing, including our own bodies and brains, all that has ever assumed any form of matter, has come out of the original stock of matter, which has only been worked into new forms without any increase or diminution; and therefore we may grant that all these have proceeded from the original cosmic vapour. But this admission does not require us further to say that the highest immaterial things proceeded from the vapour or that they were "potential" in it. Indeed, in what sense could our philosophy or art be said to be potential in the cosmic vapour? That they were bound to come out eventually in course of development. But they did not come out in Mars or Jupiter presumably, certainly not in the moon, all of whom are derived from the cosmic vapour as well as the earth. And they would not have come out on the earth if there had not existed other powers and properties than the physical ones postulated in the cosmic vapour, other agency at work than the play of contingency in natural selection; if there had not been an inner force and necessity that was bent on realizing life and consciousness and the ever higher content of these—Philosophy, Art, Science; an inner Power at work behind natural selection, that manifested both unwearied purpose and all-comprehending executive skill, but of which there is no notice taken in either the Materialist or the Evolution philosophy.

At least, we are certain on Darwinian principles that after life appeared on earth, and when the universal struggle for existence began, the uncertainty repeated again and again that hangs ever over the ordeal of battle must have made the possible future existence of the human species a matter of contingency; as we are certain that after our species appeared, especially in its infancy, there must have occurred crises, when, as in childhood generally, the further existence of the species trembled in the scales of uncertainty. At the first appearance of man the chances were all against his having that long and successful career, which nevertheless a series of fortunate events have since determined for him. His immediate progenitors, half-human and non-human, perished after launching him, not too well provided or appointed, into a precarious life and a world of battle. Moreover, we know that if from any of the other human-resembling and still existing apes a variety at all approaching the human had diverged, such did not survive; so that we must conclude on Darwinian principles that, as the advent of man was not specially contemplated by Nature more than of any other species, and as there was no special fostering or favouring care shown him when he did arrive, his actual survival through so many imminent perils was due, partly at least, to the favour of fortune, as well as the chances of battle.

In one sense it is true indeed that nothing which has ever actually resulted could have been otherwise; when the thing has occurred as a fact, we see that there must have been causes all throughout to determine the fact; and the human species, including its art, science, philosophy, poetry, has resulted as a fact. After the fact has happened, we see that it could not have been different, owing to the antecedent forces at work, just as we see that an infinite intelligence might have predicted the fact before it occurred; but this admission takes nothing from the logical conclusion that, on Darwinian principles, where neither an infinite intelligence nor a controlling purpose is postulated, the appearance of life, of man, and of consciousness must be recognized as a series of fortunate accidents.

§ 6. In maintaining that Chance is the chief characteristic of the Darwinian process of natural selection, when viewed in its philosophical reference, we do not imply any objection to it as a scientific hypothesis. For what appears to be chance, may be, so far as Science is concerned to regard it, a real scientific cause. And natural selection, with all its seeming chances, is undoubtedly a legitimate scientific hypothesis. Natural selection is a *vera causa*, which we can now see actually at work in the organic world, as well as in human societies and nations. The best nations survive, and of these in general the individuals best suited to their environment continue the race. In such ways as natural selection indicates, Nature *must* have travelled. By such a law as natural selection she undoubtedly did do some, at least, of her work in the differentiation and elaboration of her species and varieties; the only question of importance is—Did natural selection, which did some or even much of the work, really accomplish all? Is it the sole scientific cause sufficient to explain all the facts; and if it be so, is the scientific explanation also a full and satisfactory philosophical explanation?

Even as a scientific hypothesis, natural selection is far from being free from defects, which have been pointed out by both friends and adversaries, and some of which have even been admitted by its distinguished and candid originator, Mr. Darwin himself. In particular, Mr. Wallace, who shares with Darwin, though in lesser degree, the honour of first propounding the hypothesis, thinks it inadequate to account for the highly developed and organized brain of the lowest savages—a brain so far in advance of any present needs to which they could apply it, and which therefore it should have been beyond the power of past needs to develop. And Hartmann, the pessimist philosopher, while admitting that natural selection and inheritance were made use of by the Unconscious Power in differentiating the species, and generally in developing the animal and plant world, still denies that these causes are adequate to account for the main part of the development in the organic sphere, which he ascribes to the direct action of the Unconscious, working on to its own special ends. But in my own opinion, the difficulty the hypothesis labours under is simply the tremendous and all but incredible range of effects of which natural selection is the only explanation offered, and which, if its pretensions are to be justified, it must actually have accomplished. For we are asked to believe that natural selection evolved or made the thousands and tens of thousands of species of plants and animals from one or a "few primordial forms;" that natural selection made not only the tree, but the bird that sings in it; not only the flower, but the bees that suck it; not only the man himself, but also, in great measure or altogether, his art, science, invention, language, institutions, civilizations, and all his special higher associations. Besides the species, natural selection made the music of the bird, the beauty of the flower, the thought of the man—for, beyond natural selection and the facts of adaptation and inheritance, no other causes are offered;—and all these different effects, when we view them in their totality, are so prodigious in comparison with the cause assigned, that the hypothesis seems wholly incredible. That natural selection, the seizing hold of an *accidental variation** useful to the individual, according favour to its possessor in the struggle for existence, and transmitting this advantage to the next generation; that a constant repetition of this simple process should alone have accomplished all the marvels of organic creation, and produced all the higher mental and moral peculiarities of the species, seems too futile an explanation to be seriously believed or entertained. The hypothesis of the spontaneous generation of elementary life by chemical combination seems a mere trifle in comparison with this tremendous hypothesis of the creation of all other living things merely by Nature's constant preference of individuals possessing an exceptional advantage which came at first by chance. And yet, when we read once again the *Origin of Species*, we see that natural selection must have done much, especially when supplemented by the subsidiary cause of sexual selection (itself, however, a species of natural selection). Between them, these agencies have done much: but have they accomplished all? Has natural selection been the sole cause of all from the scientific point of view, to say nothing now of the philosophical? I do not think so for the above reasons; but the reasons why I do not think natural selection a sufficient explanation of the development of man in particular will appear more fully in the following chapter. I shall only here say that, if natural selection be offered, not merely as a scientific hypothesis, which goes a considerable way in the explanation of the origin and differences of existing species, but also as a full scientific explanation, we cannot accept it without a larger reservation of doubt than belongs to the generality of scientific hypotheses; and if it be offered, not merely as a scientific, but also as a philo-

---

* *Origin of Species*, ch. iv. p. 63.

sophical explanation, which, together with its further developments, finally disposes of all questions of the beginning and present existence of things and species, and which frees the mind of man from all further need to ask questions, if, in short, it is to be a final philosophical as well as scientific explanation, we cannot accept it at all.

At the same time, the hypothesis is of the very greatest significance and importance in its philosophical reference. It opens out a new line of inquiry, and suggests a new train of arguments, which the materialist has long been in want of. It does more than this. It suggests new reflections and arguments to all classes of philosophical thinkers; so much so, that it will necessitate a fresh reconsideration of all philosophical and theological problems. Nay, what some may consider of possibly more consequence, it will necessitate an examination, from the very basis, of all our current theories of morals—possibly a fundamental reconstruction of them. The appearance of Darwin's *Origin of Species* in this century, like the appearance of Hume's *Essays* in the last century, makes and marks the beginning of a new epoch in the history of all philosophical, theological, and moral speculation; an epoch which, in the opinion of some evolutionists, is destined to simplify greatly all three of them, if not to remove two of them—theology and philosophy—wholly from the list of independent subjects of thought. This it is which makes the importance of the Darwinian hypothesis.

§ 7. Theology and philosophy, at least, will be simplified on evolution principles. For if the perfections of organs and their exquisite adaptations to their several ends and to each other were achieved by slow natural process, and only after many abortive and unskilful attempts had been made—the blunders and failures being necessarily dropped and hidden away from our sight—it would seem futile as well as useless to argue, from adaptations that have been slowly made and necessarily left, to a designing mind that conceived and constructed them all at once, as the old theologians argued. If all adaptations can be accounted for as *results* that came simply by natural process, why suppose *preconceptions* and special construction of them? More especially, if good results must have been reached by natural selection in any case, no matter on what road Nature started, why suppose them to have been specially conceived and planned in a mind that aimed at them? Not without reason, therefore, on evolution principles, have naturalists like Haeckel and Huxley so often repeated that the famous argument from Final Causes to prove the existence of a designing mind and maker is worthless. If Darwin's hypothesis contains the truth and the whole truth, all Theism is worthless, and we may burn our old *Natural Theologies* and *Bridgewater Treatises*. Even the qualified doctrine of Kant, that men must read teleology into organic Nature, whether there be warrant for it or no in her inmost structure and essence, is set aside by the new and startling suggestions of science and evolution. For we are shown that Nature had no special aims whatever in view; that she could not have had any such; that the only means employed by her, namely, natural selection, were capable of reaching almost any organic ends; that they did stray into uncouth and monstrous forms occasionally in geologic periods; that, in a word, Nature neither knew nor cared what forms should ultimately emerge from the general organic strife and the attempts of individuals to better their condition. We are shown that, though there were no aims in Nature, yet that some kind of order must have resulted, whatever course she took, if she only persevered sufficiently long in natural selection. As for the appearance of man, it was no more contemplated than that of any other species, nor were there any special preparations made for him on his arrival to ensure a lengthened stay. He came, as the rest, by the necessities of the case, in which, however, chance played a conspicuous part, and when he came he had to fit himself slowly, and with infinite pain and effort, to his by no means happy environment. There was no special Providence watching over his cradle, any more than a Creator which specially fashioned and instructed him.

Now, it is extremely difficult or wholly impossible to trace the operation of mind in this process. There is no room allowed for it. The more we read the story of Darwin, the further and further the notion and the possibility of mind recedes. The species in the organic worlds are brought into being in much the same fashion as the physical worlds in the system of Democritus, namely, by chance. In this system, after many unsuccessful trials and momentary adhesions of the atoms, after ephemeral worlds had been born and dissolved again in the course of a day,*—at length a particular combination of the atoms occurred, which, as the event turned out, had permanent cohesion in it, from which resulted the solid universe, and, in a like fashion, all that is therein. In a manner not dissimilar the species of animals and plants were begun and survived, while some quickly disappeared, on Darwin's theory; and there seems on the whole as little room left for a shaping intelligence (according to our old notions) in the origin of species according to

* Cicero, "De Finibus:" "Innumerabiles mundi, qui et oriantur, et intereant quotidie."

Darwin, or rather Darwinism, as in the origin of the worlds according to Democritus.

There is only intelligence which results, not previous thought or power which produces it. The first intelligence that appears is a faint glimmer that emerges mysteriously—a variation that offers itself, of advantage to the creature, but not the effect of superior intelligence outside. A rude sentience first comes by chance, it quickly manifests itself in its shapeless possessor by a blind instinctive groping for food, or by efforts to escape destruction, or to suit itself to its conditions. There is certainly no room for a Creator who planned and executed organisms with their adaptations according to men's old conception; there is scarcely room even for mind, in the most extended sense of the word; and there appears in the long process no trace of a guiding purpose. Chance, and unimaginable years which favoured it (for natural selection is but a phrase for the endless operation of chance), are the two shadowy and impalpable agents that alone appear as the authors of the protracted world-drama called evolution, from which both we and the worlds have come. These alone have produced the life, variety, adaptation, and beauty of the organic world.

§ 8 Again, on the moral side, theology and philosophy, after weighing Darwin's story—so strange and terrible and hopeful by turns—must look to and reconsider their first principles. For the old question of the origin and continuance of evil in this universe of strife, is once more raised up vividly before us; and this time it receives a new and simple, though sinister, solution. Formerly the knot which puzzled the philosophers was to reconcile the existence of benevolence in the Deity with so much evil and pain which was so antagonistic to it; now this part of the problem vanishes with the conscious personality of the Deity. No one, it seems, is to blame for all the evil that man and the other species have suffered. The evil lies in the nature of things which brought about conscious life, and finally in the properties of matter, according to the materialist. Nature, being impersonal and unconscious, is not to blame; at least it is useless to blame her. Were she conscious, and had she laboured with any connected and persistent purposes, she would be a criminal, as the pessimist argues. But in reality, she had no more a malevolent than a good intention in view; and so she stands acquitted.

The evil that exists, and the evil that has always existed, is rather the result of imperfect organization or of the strife for life between the units, necessarily too numerous for the supply of food. But this evil, in the human species at least, is a steadily diminishing factor, and in time, according to Mr. Herbert Spencer, though it be a long time, it will totally disappear. We men, particularly in civilized societies, have come well out of the long and bloody struggle of the past. The fortunes of our species, as appears from its best specimens in civilized nations, are steadily on the rise; and already great things have been attained, giving a promise of still greater. There has been from the infancy of the species a great and astonishing progress made; and there shall be yet further progress, and that too at a constantly accelerating rate of speed, so as to carry us further in shorter time. Thus Science, speaking through the mouth of her sanguine apostles, speaks and prophesies. And thus the faith of Science is optimistic, in spite of her painful knowledge of the past, and to some extent also the present, state of things in the world.

Science, indeed, must be *optimist*, both from her knowledge, her pretensions, and her actual work in helping men to subdue their evils. She shows us a great rise in our species from a low and unpromising origin, and moreover she has indirectly much mitigated the ills and multiplied the comforts of men through many and great inventions made by her suggestions. Looking backwards, she discerns that there has been an extraordinary expansion of man's nature, and a consequent increase of happiness; looking forward, she feels justified by her own inductive logic in prophesying a much higher and happier future for men. She not only prophesies it, but she will herself be the chief agency in the fulfilment of her prophecy—she will bring about the happier future and also fit men for it.

But though Science cannot despair of men and their prospects without stultifying herself and all her pretensions, and though the facts and results of evolution, in the hands of Darwin himself, as well as in those of Herbert Spencer, Huxley, Haeckel, and other savants as well as thinkers, lend themselves to a more or less pronounced optimism, nevertheless, we see from the new school of German pessimists that a quite different interpretation may be put both on the process of evolution, as well as upon its final result up to the present. The universe, according to Schopenhauer, the founder of the new school of thought, could not well have been worse without ceasing to exist altogether; life, and above all, consciousness, the great outcome of it, is itself the grand mistake; and even if our species has made the best of its unfortunate circumstances, which may be doubted; even if it has come out the conqueror crowned from the general battle-field of existence, yet bad has been the best, and the crown only covers the greater cares. According to Hartmann, who writes with a full knowledge of Darwin's doctrines, man pays a heavy price for this questionable superiority to the lower animals; for his widened consciousness has only enlarged the circle of his sufferings, his greater knowledge eminently multiplied his sorrows, except in so far as it may one day teach the species to end itself and them together. As for our much-vaunted progress, perhaps if it were well looked into, it might equally well deserve a very different or opposite name. For the evil of all kinds, physical and moral, ever increases as well as the good, or in a greater ratio than the good, while our nerves grow more sensitive to the former— which is the same thing as an increase in its amount. But it is the ratio between the two factors of evil and good, and not their absolute amounts, that should determine whether we are really making progress or the reverse.

It does not here concern us to estimate the weight of the pessimist's argument. Let it suffice to say for the present that pessimism has a case, and that the issue raised is not to be dismissed as an unpractical or a profitless one, on the ground that, whether life be an evil or no, man must submit to it. The rise and spread of pessimism is a fact of great interest and significance, which cannot be ignored when an estimate of the results of evolution is being made; and I shall have occasion to refer to the subject again at the proper place. For the present I am only concerned to notice an important difference between the Darwinian account of the origin and evolution of organized beings, and that of Hartmann, the great chief, after Schopenhauer, of the pessimist school of philosophy. In both Darwinism and the system of Hartmann, the universe now looks as if it had been planned by a conscious intelligence, though in reality it was not. So far the two philosophers are agreed, but only so far. For, according to Hartmann, the Unconscious Will which produced the world laboured without preconception, indeed, but still with a consummate art and skill in seeking its ends in the case of organized beings, and with a most persistent, though as the event proved a fatal and perverse, purpose in the evolution of life and consciousness. There was intelligence at work, though blind and unconscious, according to our modes of thinking; and there was will and intention, though they were not accompanied with a consciousness or shaped in a mind in the remotest degree like ours. The universe is not without an end and a purpose; far otherwise; but the misfortune was that the Unconscious, to reach its final aim, found it necessary to pass through consciousness on the road—a fatal and all but irretrievable blunder, for which all conscious beings, and we men in particular who suffer most in consciousness, are now paying the smart.

The point to which we wish to direct attention is that in the system of Hartmann there is will and purpose and skill manifested in the universe and its course of evolution. Not so in Darwinism, or apparently in the Philosophy of Evolution of Herbert Spencer, which contains the most systematic presentation of Darwin's doctrines. Here Natural Selection, or the "survival of the fittest," is offered to us as the sole shaping agency. This it was that, after endless ages, gave us law and beauty and adaptations in organic life. But natural selection irresistibly raises before our minds the agency of Chance, the opposite of purpose; and in natural selection, which takes ages to accomplish its chance results the conception of a single continuing and controlling Will is necessarily set aside, since such, if it existed and could only manifest itself through natural selection, would necessarily show itself as broken, disconnected, and contradictory. And on this point it is that the system of Hartmann seems to me to contain a deeper thought, a more fundamental truth.

The existence of purpose in the universe, Science must herself admit,—a purpose manifested in the fixed and rigid laws in the physical world, as well as in the uniform laws that govern vital processes, and the relations of parts to each other in all organisms, nay, even in the actions of men in societies, which are now found to be subject to laws of evolution and coexistence. In fact, wherever Science discovers the reign of law, whether in physical, physiological, or social phenomena, there too reigns purpose; and wherever she discovers powerful tendencies that will yet become facts and future laws, there the delayed purpose of the universe is still manifested, while awaiting fulfilment.

It is said, however, by Professor Haeckel that there is not any overruling purpose, and that there never was a purpose, in the sense of an intelligent one that aimed at special ends in the evolution of organized beings; that neither Nature nor any Power behind or immanent in Nature ever knew or cared what should come eventually out of the course of evolution; for to this extreme goes his total proscription of Final Causes and of the doctrine " of Providence or vague idealist pantheisms of Hegel, Schopenhauer, and Hartmann." And to this we can only reply that in that case, if there was no purpose, then all was the result of chance, and a blind mechanical necessity. It was chance that brought about the meeting of the right atoms, even if the inherent properties of matter were competent to evolve life from them. And even if necessity and physico-chemical laws produced the organs of animals, it was chance again which determined the "favourable variations" that were seized upon by natural selection; and it was only as the result of a thousand fortunate chances that man eventually emerged from the prolonged organic strife and hurly-burly. It was chance that presided over his cradle, and that favoured his further development; and, in a word, if we do not allow some principle, with Hartmann, that was ever powerfully pushing towards a goal—some power that, though not conscious as we are, yet had a most decided end to attain, and took the sure road to attain it,—then it was chance that stumbled upon every living thing, as well as that unique thing, the human consciousness, with all its wonderful content—Art, Science, Morality, and the thoughts that wander through eternity. And this conclusion the human mind refuses to receive. Thus, while chance is the only possible alternative offered, our reason necessarily falls back upon purpose, as in some sense the determining principle in the world-process, and into this notion it will be the business of Philosophy to throw the best meaning she can.

§ 9. We have been considering Darwinism in its essential principles, and as a philosophical system which has been developed by others rather than by its distinguished founder. And we are entitled to consider the system, whether Darwin himself would accept all the consequences involved in it or no. For it is the system as a whole that really concerns us; it is there that the important and far-reaching consequences of the whole doctrine of Natural Selection and Evolution are most clearly manifested. But Darwin himself is only responsible for the conclusions drawn by other evolution philosophers so far as they are logically contained in his principles and methods of reasoning.

Now, in Darwin's *Origin of Species* a Creator is placed at the commencement of the process of organic evolution—and an intelligent Creator other than the plastic powers of Nature—which, however, his most eminent followers have since set aside. The question arises—Are they justified in so doing on Darwinian principles? and the still graver question—Are they justified on true and universal and philosophical principles? The former question I am inclined to answer in the affirmative. For the Creator in the *Origin of Species* seems introduced more for ornament than for any serious work that He has to do; or at least, rather to conciliate the mass of hostile theological prejudice certain to be aroused by the other doctrines, than to satisfy any logical demands in the system. He has nothing to do at the beginning, save to endow "one or a few primordial forms" with the lowest degree of elementary life, leaving the rest of the work to natural selection and the ordeal of battle; and He has had nothing to do ever since (on the earth at least) but to sit passively by and watch laws which execute themselves without need of any interference on His part. He is "a monarch that reigns but does not govern," like the sovereigns under our parliamentary *régime;* and accordingly, in the evolutionary monism of Haeckel, the passive, Personal, Supernatural Creator is dethroned, and the real ruling and efficient agency, Matter, eternal and governed by its own laws, is placed on the vacant throne. There is no need to suppose creative agency either at the beginning or since, because "physico-chemical laws," which now regulate the behaviour of matter and all the processes of life, were quite competent to introduce life at first.

But is God denied entirely in the system of Haeckel? Apparently not. Apparently it is only the Personal Creator, if we are to judge from the following passage:—" The more developed man of the present day is capable of, and justified in, conceiving that infinitely nobler and sublimer idea of God, which alone is compatible with the monistic conception of the universe, and which recognizes God's Spirit and power in all phenomena without exception. This monistic idea of God, which belongs to the future, has already been expressed by Giordano Bruno, in the following words:—'A spirit exists in all things, and no body is so small but contains a part of the divine substance within itself, by which it is animated.'"

But the sublime conception here put forth of a Nature filled with the Spirit of God, seems in no way to consist with an explanation of the universe from mere matter and its laws. If a spirit exist in all things, it is clearly different from matter, and then it is impossible to explain the universe from matter alone, so long as the existence of this spirit in and under matter is acknowledged. The very admission destroys all materialistic systems. For possibly this immanent and universally diffused spirit is the real First Cause and principle of all things; and what, then, becomes of your materialism, which, if it have any significance, always means and must mean the derivation of all from, and the explanation of all by, matter? Even if this spirit were only another ultimate principle, coeternal and coefficient with matter in the evolution and present support of things, still, there it is, admitted as a second principle, and what becomes of your monism? "If, in short," we say to Professor Haeckel, "spirit is at the bottom and the most fundamental thing, the final word in your system should be spiritualism and not materialism; if only a second principle is admitted, not superior to matter, but also not resolvable into it, then your system is dualism and not monism."

But, however the conception of a Nature filled with the Spirit of God consists with Haeckel's materialism, the conception is admitted by him, and is a truly great one. It is the conception which Spinoza developed into such great proportions, with such memorable consequences to theology; and it seems to want only one thing to make it at once reconcilable with the needs of science, theology, poetry, and the imperious cravings of human nature. It wants only one thing, but that very important, the recognition of a purpose in this universal spirit; as otherwise we cannot conceive any explanation of the past course of evolution save chance; and we can have no guarantee that the future course of development will be controlled otherwise than by chance. Without purpose in the inmost essence of Nature, or the spirit diffused through Nature, there is only chance and mechanical necessity to determine what will take place anywhere in the universe, and this conclusion never has been accepted and never can be made acceptable to the human mind.

§ 10. We repeat—the fatal defect in Darwinism, and in all the more or less systematic presentments that have lately been given of the whole doctrine of Evolution, whether by Spencer, Haeckel, Huxley, or Strauss,[*] is the denial, express or by implication, of all and any purpose or Final Cause in the universe. For in purpose, in some sense of the word, and, moreover, in a rational purpose, however difficult it be to define the conception in human language or to assimilate it to our notions of purpose, the human mind, nevertheless, obstinately

[*] Strauss, *The New Faith and the Old.*

continues to believe. All men believe in it—the mass of mankind guided by common sense, as well as the masters of thought who have meditated most deeply on this all-important question. The greatest names in philosophy from Aristotle and Plato to Descartes and Leibnitz, to Kant and Hegel, even to Schopenhauer and Hartmann, have believed in purpose in some sense of the word; the only thinkers opposed being Democritus and Epicurus in ancient times, perhaps Spinoza and Hume in modern times, together with the present representatives of these. And apart from the balance of philosophical authority in its favour, can any rational and candid mind doubt that there was a purpose in the course of evolution of the universe? Can any one really doubt that the human consciousness on our earth was not meant and intended to come finally out of the whole evolutionary process and struggle for existence? At least, can any one doubt that the eye and the ear, which open out the world to all the animals, were not, somehow, in Nature's aims; or can they believe the other alternative, that the first rudimentary eye came one day as the result of a lucky chance, a fortunate meeting of the atoms,—that it only appeared after infinite impotent combinations had in vain been tried, at one happy moment when the right number and due arrangement of particles were hit upon? Is this credible? And then the same origin must be assigned for the ear, and for all the other organs of sense, as well as for all the mutually adapted organs of the body—the origin of chance, a perpetual shifting and rearrangement of the atoms by chance and mechanical necessity till the new and startling phenomena appeared. We say by chance, since they were not themselves endowed with any self-moving power, nor was any concert possible amongst them, nor any general marshalling agency supposed. Now, it is faintly conceivable, though incredible, that chance might produce the physical organ, which, it must be allowed, is resolvable into cells and nerves and finally into a collocation of atoms. Given endless time to exhaust all wrong arrangements, an instrument like the eye might in the end result; but it would clearly require an incredible period of time, by the laws of probability, before the right combination of atoms resulted from chance alone. But even if the right arrangement which gave the physical organ at last did result, there is still a gulf from the organ to the seeing power. What is this new phenomenon, the fact of vision, which opens out a new world, which one day or one moment came, having been non-existent just before? Is this new thing not something like creation? It is the product of the atoms, the effect of molecular changes, says the materialist. Then the atoms are literally creative—they have produced from nothing a most wonderful thing; they have evolved or evoked this unique power from no pre-existing materials; for the fact of vision is wholly different from the material particles which compose the organ—it is a thing not made up of them, nor of anything but itself, which one moment was not and the next moment was; and this is creation,—call it evolution, if you please. It is creation, and, moreover, it is very like creation *ex nihilo*, pronounced so absurd,—only that the blind atoms have accomplished the miracle, according to the materialist.

In short, we say to the materialist: you believe in creation after all, under the name of evolution; only it was matter which effected the creation; and you believe in the miracle of creation from nothing, only that the atoms, acting without intention or concert, accomplished the miracle. You believe in a creation by the atoms, only that the atoms did not know what they were about to do or what was about to happen. They had no intention of producing the result—nor could have had any; and the creation or evolution, first of the senses, then of consciousness, and last of the highest human reason, was the result of a long series of fortunate accidents. This is the real and most important issue raised to-day by Darwin, as in ancient times by Democritus—whether chance or purpose governs the world; and it is the issue raised by the thoughtful Evolution philosophy of Herbert Spencer as well as by the cruder atomistic materialism of some of the other expositors of Darwin's doctrines.

Now, for my own part, I am quite prepared to give up the old anthropomorphic Creator, who went to work in the construction of worlds and organisms as the architect and the machinist. I gladly deliver myself, by the aid of the scientific doctrine of the eternity and indestructibility of matter, from the old dogma of the creation *ex nihilo*, of the earth and planets by creative fiat. I am even ready, on the strength of the united demand of modern philosophy and thought, made by Spinoza, Fichte, Shelling, Hegel, Schopenhauer, and Hartmann, as thinkers; by Schliermacher as theologian, and by Goethe as poet, to surrender the human attributes of personality and consciousness in the Deity; and all the more readily as we are assured by philosophy that these attributes, which we find we can never, by the utmost effort of thought, connect in any way with the notion of God, are in clear contradiction to the notion of an Absolute Being, which, as such, cannot be subject to the limitations which consciousness implies. We can give up all these imperfect conceptions of God, one and all; but yet we cannot abandon all belief in a purpose, an intention, a finality of some sort, which has been and still is manifested in the universe, and in the evolution of human destiny.

We cannot give up belief in purpose, because the alternative belief is that the earth and the million spheres in space came from mechanical necessity and for no end, and that life and consciousness came from this same mechanical necessity, supplemented by chance as the active shaping agency and real divinity;—that all things came from chance and that the universe drifts at hazard towards no particular goal but final dissolution.

Men must postulate a purpose in the past, to control the course of evolution, to dispense with the hypothesis of "a fortuitous concourse of the atoms," to avoid the notion, shocking to the reason, of endless and abortive attempts of the atoms to frame a world and to produce life. We require a guiding inner principle; we even require to postulate creative agency where a new fact appeared, such as life, sensation, consciousness, unless these too existed from eternity as well as matter; but we do not require to postulate a personal Creator or special creations of the different species of plants and animals. We must have a purpose, and there must be creative power, at each new appearance between the chemically constituted cosmic vapour and the most developed human species. Evolution is granted, and the difference between creation and evolution is hardly worth disputing about. The first appearance of something wholly new, life-like,—is it to be called creation or evolution? This is a question that we care not how it be answered. There is, then, a purpose; it has been creative, and in a certain sense it is supernatural; for, as Herbert Spencer admits, there is a "power behind humanity and all things," which is not exhausted in any of its forms as shown in evolution. And this power behind Nature, and yet manifesting itself in Nature, might still be called supernatural as well as natural, were it not for the special association of the former word with miraculous interventions. But the power itself is admitted by all, excepting only those who, like Hume, maintain that phenomena alone, with nothing behind them, compose the universe.

The present is not the place to press further the inconsistency and insufficiency of the materialist explanation of the world. Let it here suffice to say that while purpose as well as wisdom is denied, power and even creative power is allowed, in the fact of evolution; while the further question, whether this power—which admittedly shows itself in Nature, though it is itself invisible, non-phenomenal, and so to speak behind Nature—should be described as supernatural or by some term of less equivocal meaning, is merely a question of words. The existence of the power is admitted by evolutionists themselves, as well as by so great a thinker as Kant, who is now in such special favour with them. Our belief goes further, for the reasons already assigned: we believe in a purpose, and we believe that purpose to be a good one. In holding this faith, we are at issue both with the evolutionist and the pessimist. In holding fast by purpose as the principle of the universe, we differ from the former; in holding that it is good, we differ from the latter. Both convictions are articles of faith that do not admit of perfect demonstration; neither are they always held with the same unwavering strength of conviction. Indeed, at times both are sorely tried. When we look around and see that justice is not yet enthroned in the world; when we see the terrible struggle for existence, in which virtue does *not* triumph; when we see the conditions, sometimes terrible as death itself, which the necessities of this struggle exact, not merely from the over-sensitive but from the best and bravest spirits; when we find the perpetual intervention of this formidable thing which we must call chance, in the crises of our own lives to make or mar them; and when, disturbed with these reflections, we look through history for support for our faith, and see that the truth has not always triumphed or the good cause prevailed, and that the crises of history, as well as of our own lives, have apparently turned upon a cast of the dice;—when we brood over all these things, then, indeed, the desperate suggestion sometimes rises within us, that there is and has been no power at the helm, that the universe drifts purposeless, or that some base and malignant power is a co-ordinate principle with the good, if not the chief controller of the course of things. In this mood, the stars seem to run blindly; the world is "an unweeded garden that runs to seed," where "things rank and gross in nature" alone have full and riotous possession; men are—

> The flies of later spring,
> That lay their eggs and sting and sing,
> And weave their petty cells and die.

But these are the dark moments of the trial of our faith, to which we ever return when the paroxysm of doubt and denial has passed. For if the social world, with its evils and miseries, thus sometimes shakes our belief, Nature, ever bountiful and beautiful, is all around us to restore it. And reason and reflection come to our aid also; for we find that truth after all is triumphing, and that the reign of justice is slowly extending. We find within ourselves that truth in its pursuit and possession is verily what Aristotle, what Plato, and what Bacon, following them, proclaimed it to be—"the sovereign good of human nature." And virtue, goodness, spite of appearances to the contrary, if the right tests are applied, is found to be progressing. Possibly not the heroic virtues, but at least sympathy, benevolence, pity, and a wider regard for justice. These social virtues are spreading over wider areas, and are diminishing the fell intensity of the conflict for existence, now no longer carried on without quarter to the vanquished. They are binding men together, and narrowing the range of the exclusively selfish regards, the old perennial spring of so much moral evil. And thus we support our faith in the good purpose of the universe.

It should also be confessed that we are to some extent fortified in it by considerations not altogether addressed to the reason, for no faith is solely rational. We close with it partly on account of the blank and frightful alternatives which the pessimist and the extreme materialist offer to us: the one pointing to a principle at the bottom of things, which, though without any evil intention, necessarily brings evil to us; and the other, scarcely less alarming, to a universe born of chance and mechanical necessity, and drifting aimlessly towards no goal but final dissolution from the same mechanical necessity.

CHAPTER II.

ON MAN AND HIS DEVELOPMENT.

§ 1. WE now approach the central and most important question of all—What is man himself?—a question in appearance sufficiently simple, and one, moreover, discussed from the dawn of speculation, but which, nevertheless, science holds to have been only rightly conceived and approached, and only truly answered in all its fulness and significance, for the first time in our day and generation.

The inquiry concerning the nature of man is evidently of fundamental importance, as all moralists, from the revival of independent moral speculation under Hobbes, two centuries ago, up to our own days, have fully perceived. On the answer to the question, What is man? clearly depends the answer to the three great questions of Kant, What can we know? What should we do? What may we hope? Nay, even the further question, What *can* we do? the great question of moral freedom, the ancient and still-agitated question whether our actions are the product of a secret material mechanism which ultimately sways our wills, or whether and how far man is the master of destiny and the ruler of circumstance, is evidently involved in the fundamental and all-comprehending one, What is man himself?

The full answer to this inquiry is, according to positive scientific thinkers, only to be obtained from a variety of sciences, from psychology, physiology, anthropology, sociology; though the great light that has been recently thrown upon the whole subject by the Darwinian discovery of man's animal descent, is of itself a revelation and a guiding clue of immense significance in all future speculations, producing as it does a total revolution in our point of view and in our methods of inquiry.

It is only in our day Professor Huxley* maintains that man has discovered his true place in Nature and his real relations to the rest of the animal kingdom, just as three hundred years ago the true position of the earth and its relations to the other heavenly bodies were discovered by Copernicus. It is only in our more favoured time Professor Haeckel† tells us that "the question of man's position in Nature, the highest of all problems," has been truly solved by Darwin's theory of descent, corroborated as it so strongly is by the facts of embryology and physiology. Indeed, it is only in our generation that the question could be even approached or rightly conceived, so thick a mass of fictions, illusions, and deep inborn prejudices had conspired together to draw an impenetrable veil round man's real nature, which effectually hid him from himself. The dogmas of theology and metaphysics, the vain imaginings of poetry, man's own pride and prejudices, had each in their several ways and degrees contributed to the one common result of placing a monstrous distorting mirror before him, which hindered him from seeing himself as he really was. They had made it impossible for him to get even on the right track to the

* Huxley, *Evidences as to Man's Place in Nature.*
† Haeckel, *History of Creation*, vol. i. p. 294; vol. ii. p. 368.

wise self-knowledge recommended by the old philosophers. He had fallen from an originally holy and god-like estate, theology assured him. His nature, once innocent, was now inherently vile, and he could do no good thing of himself, though infinite evil. In the other ear of man metaphysics whispered a far more flattering tale—in fact, a wholly opposite theory of man, and one much more soothing to his pride and encouraging to his hopes. His nature was innately grand and god-like, and shaded off on all sides without dividing boundary to the infinite. At the bottom of man's being lay his soul, of a character and composition very different from the theological representation of it. Far from being an essentially vicious thing, it was an ethereal substance, "a thing majestical," an indestructible diamond, that not the power of death or fate, hardly even that of omnipotence itself, could break. The soul, the ego, the inmost essence and core of the man, was an imperial thing on the earth, as demonstrated in its own free and uncaused will— uncaused by motive other than its own sovereign dictation ; and it was an immortal existence hereafter. Or if the soul was not of independent existence, as most of the metaphysicians argued, it was, according to others, a direct emanation of Deity, and to Him returned at death. So argued the metaphysicians in opposition to the theologians, asserting the innate rights and dignity of the soul, and of our essential human nature. Then followed poetry, at one time re-echoing the teaching of theology, at another that of metaphysics, in both cases mingling special fictions and fancies of her own, her Muse now bewailing man's hapless fall and hopeless state, anon chanting his lordly dignity and high future hopes. Thus poetry continued till the beginning of our century, when, having drunk deep the prevailing scepticism, and anticipated the coming pessimism, she separated herself definitively from theology, and, for a time, from philosophy and from hope; during which she struck those loud notes of lamentation over man's defeated hopes and mysterious isolation in the universe, which are still ringing in our ears.

§ 2. But now, stripped of fiction and illusion, what is the scientifically ascertained fact, the sober literal truth respecting human nature? We desire to know what man really is; we wish, if possible, to have the conjoint report of the several sciences concerned, and, that the account be the more reliable, from those authorities who have made a special side of man's nature a special subject of study.

And in response to this desire, we have the latest reports on human nature, as handed in from the several scientific sections, which, when put together, read to the following effect:—Man is the superior and highly developed animal, with intellectual, moral, social, æsthetic qualities, differing in degree but not in kind from similar qualities existing in some of the highest of the lower animals. From the point of view of comparative anatomy and physiology, man is of like bodily structure and organization with the anthropoids, so much so that, as Professor Huxley concludes, "The structural differences which separate man from the gorilla and chimpanzee, are not so great as those which separate the gorilla from the lower apes." Man closely resembles the most man-like apes, only that his structure is slightly more complex, and certain of his bodily organs are more highly and more delicately differentiated. The difference between the hand and foot is more pronounced in man than in the nearest resembling animals, his hand is more elaborately finished, his fingers finer and more flexible;

and from this superiority of hand, the brain suggesting the idea, he can make inventions,—tools, implements, weapons, complicated machines and appliances, to serve his ends. Moreover, through the higher differentiation of the larynx and tongue, he has the faculty of articulate speech in a much higher degree than any of the other animals, and he can thus communicate with his fellows to an extent that is quite impossible to them. Some of them, indeed, including his nearest relatives, possess the faculty of speech in a low degree; but man alone can convert the vocal sounds which he can make in the greatest variety, into signs of his inmost wishes and thoughts, and into general conceptions, by means of which he can think and reason about classes and universals, the highest prerogative of the scientific human intellect. Above all, the mass of man's brain is larger, its cells and fibres more numerous and complicated, and he can thence make greater mental acquisitions, which he can store away in the corpuscles of the brain, as in safe and secret closets, for future use. He is, from this comparatively greater size and finer structure of brain, a being of "larger discourse, looking before and after." He can think more clearly, he can see more deeply, he can feel more finely and variously, than any of his humbler brute brethren. He is presented with a clearer and fairer picture of the universe than the dull and confused apprehension of the brute can give. Moreover, his nerves are more numerous and more delicately strung, thereby giving him not only a wider area of pleasure and pain, but special emotional delights, in the cultivation and expression of which man has become an artist, as by his general brain superiority he had become an inventor and a thinker. Finally, man is the pre-eminently social animal, more essentially so than the bee, the ant, or any other; and to this fact of his nature, more than even to the special excellences of his hand and head, is to be attributed his great and successful career, and his completely outstripping all competing species in the struggle for existence. For without the social union, his other advantages would have been of little service; without it, indeed, they would have been but little developed; but by the social union, which makes division of labour possible, inventions and improvements are made, science and art become possible, and language, itself a necessary pre-requisite of society, becomes further perfected from the exigency of further social needs.

Man is a social animal, partly because his immediate animal progenitors were such in some low degree, but more because he speedily learned by painful experience the absolute necessity of union, for life itself on the one hand, and on the other, the great and ever-increasing advantages resulting from the union itself. Moreover, he found his pleasure as well as his profit in social life; being naturally of a sociable disposition, in spite of Hobbes's saying to the contrary. From being a social animal, man at length advanced till he became a moral being; that is, a being that not only seeks, as every individual created thing must seek, the conservation of its own existence, but which also, in order that others may be free to do the same and in order that society with its great advantages may be possible for all, manifests a regard for the rights of others as well as his own, and recognizes the necessity of obeying rules framed in the interest of all,—rules which limit the naturally excessive egotism of each to the fair amount which is compatible with that of all the rest. And man became a moral being all the sooner and more easily because he found within himself the germs of sympathy, as well as the undoubted fact of sociability attracting him to the company of his fellows; which two factors of sympathy and sociability at length between them begat the moral fact now known as benevolence,—something resembling a genuine regard for all the members of the tribe, and a consequent heartier disposition, not only to work more zealously with them for the common good and against the common dangers, but even to voluntarily restrict individual selfishness, and sometimes to surrender cheerfully some of his own share of satisfactions to the requirements of others; in which last case we have the beginnings of the self-sacrificing virtues.

Such man was in the past; in such ways and by such means he has been developed; and such as he was he still essentially is, according to the scientific account of him. He is both less and greater than his theological portrait had represented him: "not so happy, but much happier." Not so happy, because, though the race is to have an immortality and a great to-morrow, the individual will have none; there being no exceptional felicity reserved for him hereafter, any more than for the lower animals from whom he has been raised. Much happier, because there is a prosperous and progressive career marked out for the individual as for the species here on the earth; because his "homely nurse," the earth, has "filled her lap with pleasures of her own" to give him; because he may know assuredly that his nature has not degraded from a higher, but developed from a far lower level. He is not essentially vile and fallen, but neither is he on the other hand, Science assures him—lest he should boast—a being capable of any continued lofty heroism or transcendent excellence, or on the whole capable of more than very moderate and average virtues. Speaking generally, man is a being with an inherited leaning to both good and evil, to neither excessively, though, from pressure of circumstance, somewhat more given to the latter; not much, however, and the degree may be exaggerated, because there is of necessity much more attention called to his vices, which must be frequently punished, than to his virtues, which mostly pass without notice or external reward.

However this be, there is to be set against the existing evil the scientific promise of its future diminution, the assurance of a slow tendency to improvement. There is a slow, though admittedly a very slow, change in the relative proportions of the tendencies that make respectively for virtue and vice, and this alteration of the existing ratio is in favour of virtue, in the direction of the good. A reduction of evil, both physical and moral, is discoverable through the course of history, and a similar and still great reduction (as before remarked) is promised in the future, when man shall have more completely harmonized his nature with his physical and social environment.*

Thus, then, our species has not fallen from a perfect or paradisaical state; on the contrary, it has raised itself by its own efforts, by the favour of Nature, by the fact of natural selection, from a state low and terrible and precarious to its present comparatively enviable position. Man commenced his career with no very exceptional advantages; indeed, like our present "self-made man"—his nearest type and true representative—he commenced upon almost nothing; and the accumulated intellectual, emotional, and moral capital now possessed by the species is mainly an inherited bequest, the result of the patience, the persistent labour and energy, the unwearied ant-like industry of a thousand

* Spencer's *Data of Ethics*; also, *Principles of Biology*, ch. xiii.

generations—a result which natural selection has aided to produce, and which inheritance has handed on. Far from having fallen or retrograded, man has advanced very far indeed; his nature has been widened and deepened on all sides, and a yet further and more glorious development of his nature will take place. What he has done is but a promise of what he will do. What he is, is but as the statue in the rough compared to the finished man of the far future.

But human nature, though widened and deepened with the process of the suns, is not in any sense of the word infinite, as certain metaphysicians would have us believe. Man's mental, like his bodily constitution, is on all sides bounded and limited. Thought, emotion, volition, are all finite and conditioned; are subject to laws of regular and ascertained sequence; fall into the universal chain of cause and effect, as psychology and physiology teach. What, indeed, may be the ultimate or First Cause of the mental as of other phenomena, Science is unable to say—a First Cause, even if comprehensible, not being within the scope of her inquiries, and her only notion of causation being constantly recurring sequence—but so far as Science traces or follows the phenomena, so far as they are accessible to her most improved methods of search, they are in the last resort caused by states of the bodily organism, in particular by molecular changes in the brain and nervous system.* These are the invariable antecedents, the cause or conditions of consciousness in Hume's and Mill's sense of the word "cause." Without these no thought or consciousness is possible; with these they begin, and with these end. Here is the final fact, beyond which Science cannot go, finding no

* Huxley's *Life of Hume*, p. 79 ("English Men of Letters" series); also Bain's *Mind and Body*, pp. 11, 140.

firm foothold for the further speculations in which the metaphysicians are wont to indulge. Further inquiry or attempted explanation she prefers to leave to men of this class, who, however, she observes succeed but badly in their attempts to emancipate mind from its constant connection, from birth to death, with phenomenal matter, which connection she notes as the ultimate fact in this department of knowledge.

§ 3. Such are the universal and essential characteristics of our common human nature, as they manifest themselves to modern scientific inquiry. But now we must further observe, by way of supplement, or comment, that while human nature has its universal and necessary elements which appear in every individual, thereby producing that general sameness which makes it a fit subject for science, there are also the greatest possible differences amongst the human atoms, according as a greater or less degree or a different combination of the common elements enter into the mental and moral composition of each individual. Humanity is no homogeneous mass. The individuals composing it differ in intellectual, moral, and social qualities, in religious and æsthetic emotions, even more than they do in physical form and features. There is no identity of nature and no general equality amongst men, even confining the attention to the same society, or nation, or class. While the majority are average men, viewing human nature in its totality and from the point of view of science and of psychology, very many fall below, a considerable number rise above this general level line of humanity, and a select few rise to such exceptional and commanding heights that their fellow-men regard them as beings of a different nature from themselves, and history reserves for them the title of great. Into a few the common elements of our nature have entered in such pre-eminent degree and large amount, and they have thence been enabled to produce results so great and extraordinary for the rest of men—results so impossible of achievement or even of conception by the others, that they, with a sort of noble superstition, in former times credited these superior spirits with a divine nature, and reverenced their memory as of gods; and even still, with a lingering trace of this old hero-worship, with a survival of the old ennobling reverence, great men are called men of genius—a unique, indefinable thing, which marks off its possessor from the rest of mankind as of a different and higher nature. These spirits, specially touched to finer issues, seem even yet compact of finer clay and tempered with more ethereal fire than has gone to the composition of the generality; and if we remember the services which these select ones have rendered to humanity, in widening its range, in lifting it higher, in multiplying its power, in giving to it new and permanent realms of truth and beauty, in giving to it in their lives examples of its glorious possibilities of effort or achievement in virtue, we shall, in spite of the levelling doctrine of science and evolution, be inclined to deal tenderly with the still lingering and generous superstition that credits great men with being something peculiarly divine. In a sense so they still are, so they were, and so they must ever be.

In reality, great men are but the highest summits of that humanity which we all share; nevertheless, they have shown us what heights there are in humanity, from whence a grander horizon opens. They have shown us how we may climb nearer to those heights. In a certain sense they have been the true creators. They have increased and deepened human nature. They have shown us the truth and beauty we could not have seen save through their eyes. They have created the truth and beauty. They have given us the power we could not have had without their help; and if they have not created this power, they have given us the control over it. Great men have been the means of developing mankind far more directly and essentially than natural selection, assisted by heredity and adaptation, as even Darwin admits.* It was by means of the superior and original minds that the adaptation of the rest to their environment was brought about. The evolution of human societies and civilizations, the evolution of the arts, institutions, religions, philosophies, literatures, laws, has been accomplished by a series of loftier minds, the individuals of which took up successively and improved upon the thoughts and ideas of their predecessors, beginning with the first creative mind; and without such minds no fresh initiative or improvement, no originality or advance, no new creation or fresh suggestion appears. There is substantial truth in the view of a great writer that "the history of what man has accomplished in this world is at bottom the history of the great men who have worked there." † Herbert Spencer, it is true, lightly esteems the theory, and asks in reply—Whence comes the great man? What makes him possible? The great man, he tells us, must be made by his society before he can unmake or improve it. And this view is also,to a certain extent, true; but not in the most important or essential sense. For society makes only so much of the great man as goes to the composition of the average man, leaving an overplus which is not to be put to the credit of society or previous human

---

* *The Descent of Man.* † Carlyle, *Lectures on Heroes.*

acquisition, but which is a gift from Nature—from the Unknown. It makes all of the great man except his special genius, which is afterwards to improve society; all of Shakespeare except his extraordinary imagination and insight, by which he has for ever enriched the world. Even if we revert to the earliest stages of development, we can see that before natural selection got anything worth selecting in the most primitive societies, the creative spirit, the superior man, had first to appear. Before primitive man could make any decided step in advance, or could separate himself conspicuously from his lower animal relations, some inventive individual had to conceive and construct the first rude flint weapon, which gave men so great advantage in the combat with wild beasts or with their fellows; some prehistoric Prometheus first stole the secret of fire from Nature, and showed to the others its uses; some one discovered the fruitful corn amongst the common grasses, and taught the rest to plant it; to some one the idea first occurred that the skin of a slain beast, if deftly transferred and arranged, would warm himself as it did its original owner. Again, and later, some one invented spoken speech, some one before Cadmus invented the use of letters, some one before Tubalcain taught how to temper and shape the metals. But in all these and many other cases, the first seeds of fruitful thought or invention appeared in one mind; the subsequent important improvements have likewise come from one. And this has been true of the history of the arts of war as of peace; from the inventor of the bow, the spear, and the plough, to the inventor of the printing press and the steam-engine.

If we come to the historical stages of the course of evolution, we shall see the truth of this exemplified in still more important matters. We still see that all discovery, advance, and improvement depend on great men, and find their limits and arrest with the non-appearance of these. Civilizations became what they were by a series of great men; without these, they either would not have been at all, or their courses would have been wholly different. But in the absence of the particular great men, would not others have taken their places—other Columbuses, other Newtons? Possibly, in some cases; in others not; but even had others appeared in all, then these would have been the initiating spirits. So that the course of history and evolution would still have moved under the initiative and guidance of individuals.

§ 4. Our civilization and culture is what great men, as distinct from natural selection, have made it; what inventors and discoverers, what philosophers, founders of religions and lawgivers, what artists and poets, what even statesmen and conquerors, have made it; much more than what evolution, unaided by these, though with the full benefit of natural selection, heredity, and adaptation, has made it. The Homers and Dantes and Shakespeares have enlarged our human nature by revealing to it what was before invisible in itself, by teaching it to read and truly to know itself. They have brought from non-existence into being, and have annexed for ever to man's spiritual kingdom, a new and wonderful world of beauty and of truth, ever the twin bequest of the great poet. They have widened our consciousness of Nature and of ourselves, have added inexhaustible fields of spiritual delight for the soul to revel in in all her changing moods. They have supplied to our spirit its proper elements on which it lives, the nutriment on which it may feed, the air which it can respire. And have not the Beethovens and Mozarts, the Raphaels and Titians, artists of different types from the poets—the former who have struck a new and different shaft into the previously unsounded depths of the soul, and have found a language for its previously unexpressed but real emotions; and the latter who have made colours and lines instead of words and sounds, into a language that powerfully speaks to, ennobles, and stirs the soul;—have not these also enlarged our spiritual life?

And the Keplers and Newtons, the Lyells and Darwins, the labourers in one grand division of the field of truth, the wide and ever-increasing province of scientific knowledge; the men who, after prolonged thought, at length extorted from Nature, despite her many masks and disguises, the long-kept secrets of the laws of her mighty and mysterious movements, in the heavens above and in the earth beneath, in sustaining and moving the spheres, in sculpturing the outlines of the earth, in the production and differentiating the forms of life;—these men at least, the great geniuses in science—must not the apostles of science and evolution allow?—have aided in the development and elevation and civilization of mankind, apart from any operation of natural selection. And the Platos, and Spinozas, and Kants, and Hegels, the daring leaders of that ever-existing, never-disheartened company of searchers, sworn to fathom the secret of the universe, resultless as their labours have been as regards their final aim, have yet been of incalculable service in the culture and education of the race. Nay more, these lonely thinkers, after long beating against the bars of their own great minds, seem at last almost to break down the barrier between themselves and the Infinite; they actually seem to catch a glimpse, in some supreme moment of revelation—were it only for a moment—of the final secret of the world, which in a measure they can darkly symbolize to us. And at the lowest estimate of their services, the masters of thought, by their mining and quarrying in the secret subterranean regions of thought, not less than by their aspiring flights, if they have not revealed the whole mystery or opened out a tunnel between our world of phenomena and the unknown land beyond, they have, both by their labour and by their failure, shown to us why we cannot reach this transcendent world where repose the real essences of things. They have shown us that our faculties are bounded, even when themselves stretching them to the utmost, even when actually widening them, like Kant. They have shown us the utmost butt and sea-mark of our sail, even when trying to prove that the philosopher's thought is absolute knowledge, like Hegel. They have all confirmed the lesson of our philosopher Locke, to sit down in contented ignorance of knowledge denied to human faculties, even though other beings in the universe may possess it.

And there have been yet greater men than any of these; —men who have revealed the great possibilities of virtue latent in humanity, as these others its capacity for truth and beauty, and its aspirations to the Unknown. Besides the great discoverers of truth, there have been men who have shown to us what may be dared for truth when discovered —the men who have given for truth their blood, and bequeathed to humanity the great traditions which it cannot forget, and dare not fall wholly away from, without accepted dishonour and degradation. There have been the noble army of martyrs for truth, amongst whom science and philosophy are worthily represented. There have been martyrs who, like Socrates and Bruno, have shown that, even when humanity has sunk low, there ever exist individual spirits who redeem it and prevent it from sinking to still lower deeps; men who have shown the mighty power for virtue that lies even in one unbending will; and such suggest the reassuring thought that similar spirits exist at the worst of times, who will dare all—death itself, and worse, if fate has worse—rather than betray the sacred cause of Truth at a time critical for Humanity itself, when her life seems threatened.

And there has been a still more select and inimitable few;—spirits, awful, beautiful, all but divine, who, troubled at once by the mystery of life, and moved by the mighty miseries of men to an infinite love and pity for them, have turned aside from the joys of life that they might have had, if only they could have enjoyed them in the midst of the endless sorrow and with the infinite wail of the world ringing in their ears; men who have thought, and meditated, and fasted, and supplicated to find out some way of salvation for afflicted mankind, or some mitigation at least of all its miseries. There have been men who could find no peace or joy in life for themselves while the huge incarnate sorrow existed all around them; who were ready to die for men, if only they might thereby improve their lot; who like Buddha, resigned all that men call happiness, who like Mahomet, staked life, and like Christ, voluntarily sacrificed it, to save the rest of their fellows. What is more, these mighty spirits not only tried to discover, but actually found, a means of salvation—a way of righteousness for men. They did veritably discover and teach men the true way of life, and how they might bear or conquer the evils of life and of destiny. Each of them found a means, pointed out a way, as best suited the needs of their contemporary men, and these means and this way were in great measure applicable to all mankind. They found out truths, permanent and great truths—renunciation, resignation, duty, love of our fellows; only that these truths, great and important and eternal as they are, require to be further supplemented or qualified to make them suitable to the modern man's nature and circumstances, altered in some respects but still the same, with the same needs, spiritual and social, in others.

§ 5. Thus the development of the human species, the civilizations of humanity, have not been accomplished by natural selection, as the Darwinian doctrine implies. The development of the human spirit has come from an inner revelation to certain privileged individuals—a revelation of truth, of insight, of inventive power, of duty, of beauty; visiting the soul unsolicited; coming none can say whence, not even the possessors, further than that it is from the Unknown, from the Purpose of the universe, that thus means and wishes to declare and develop itself—from God and not from Chance. Natural selection has clearly had nothing to do with the origin, with the deposition of the first germs of morality, art, invention, science, or religion; and it has really had extremely little to do with the further development of any of these, or, by consequence, of mankind. It has been through great individuals, men of higher, deeper, finer, nobler natures, in mind, or soul, or moral purpose, that our human species has been developed and lifted up to its present proud heights. It has not been by natural selection that man's soul has been differentiated and perfected, however this be true of his bodily organization. It has been through the superior single souls, and where none such have appeared, as amongst the savage races, man has still remained but a few removes from the brute. It has been by the help of these great ones, formerly held as demigods and heroes, that all the progress and development which science rightly refers to as the special characteristic of our favoured species, has been made possible. The accidental variation or departure from the average, that occasionally occurs in the individuals of a species, and which gives to its possessor an advantage in the struggle of life, which, according to Darwin, is transmitted to posterity by inheritance, so as to become in time an attribute of the whole species by natural selection,— this accidental variation corresponds to the appearance of the man of genius, of superior insight, in the human species, save only that the rare differential quality is scarcely ever transmitted by inheritance, and does *not* usually give its possessor the victory in the combat of existence.

Human societies, then, have not been raised by natural selection. It has not been in the manner implied in the doctrine of Darwin and evolution that man's mental and moral constitution has been developed, whatever be the truth as regards his physical. It has not been by the superior man winning in the battle of life, and then transmitting his genius to his children, who thus became the origin of a chosen race, that the great man has profited either his species or himself. He has served his kind by the communication of his special secret, new truth, superior insight, higher quality of soul, to some of his brother men the likest himself, and these again to others, till in time the whole mass of men becomes possessed of his idea, and leavened with his spirit. He served men not by the hereditary transmission, but by the direct communication, of his soul. Often the man of genius or hero did not win in the battle of life, rarely or never he transmitted his genius to his children, even if he had any. He did better; he gave the benefit of it at once to all who could profit by it, and ultimately to the human race. At least this is what the real and greatest benefactors of their kind have done—the discoverers, inventors, philosophers, poets, lawgivers, and founders of religions, if not the warrior-kings and conquerors. Neither Plato, nor Mahomet, nor Columbus, nor Shakespeare, nor Newton, produced appreciable effect on the world through the transmission of their peculiar qualities by heredity. They did not thus distribute the germs of their genius at last through their countrymen and mankind. The manner of their action on men was different; but the result was more speedy as well as more effectual. They delivered their message, did their work, and the others found it directly profitable and acceptable to them. They lifted up the others nearer to their own sublime heights; and by such a process it has ever been that real progress has been made—by the species as a whole endeavouring to expand itself to the dimensions of these kingly spirits, who have been its true educators, improvers, and benefactors.

§ 6. It is to be further observed that all these great men have expanded human nature on those sides in which we differ chiefly from the lower animals—in our capacities for invention, art, thought, morality, religion, which constitute our properly human as distinct from our merely animal nature. They have developed the higher and mental side, comprehending the intellect, the soul, the social and moral sentiments, as distinguished from the self-regarding and sensual side of our nature, the animal impulses and dispositions, which the brutes possess as well as we.

And yet these other sides, the self-regarding and the sensual, can never be got rid of, as science unmistakably reminds us. They can never be left wholly behind us, as useless and troublesome incumbrances on our march to perfection, while man remains on the earth. However far man may leave behind his animal and put on angelic nature, still the animal remains in the depths of his being, sleeping but not dead, combated it may be and reduced within bounds, but never wholly conquered or subdued. However desirable it might appear that men should die to sense, and live only to the better life of the intellect and the soul, when once they have tasted it; however good it would be for the world that they should put off the old Adam of self, and put on the new life of self-renouncement in behalf of others and of love and labour for them; however these were to be wished, yet science and experience teach that, considering the inmost nature of man and his inevitable conditions on this earth, this is vain to expect and impossible of achievement, beyond a certain limited extent, determined by these same unchangeable conditions of man, and unchangeable elements of his nature. Man's nature can indeed be changed, and it has been improved; but there remains something at the base, and particularly the senses and the self-conserving instincts, which cannot be changed. While man remains an animal, susceptible of pleasure and pain, who lives by food, and must be born of woman, so long we may be sure—and Nature has taken especial care upon this point—he shall be powerfully moved by his appetites and passions, and so long the advice and prescriptions of Buddha and Schopenhauer to quench them will remain unfollowed or inoperative; and so long, again, as life continues, as in some respect it must ever continue, a competition—if not always for material divisible goods, yet for ever for certain indivisible satisfactions that must remain the monopoly of individuals—so long must the self-asserting and competitive side of man's nature exist and assert itself. Like the sensual side, this too is capable of reduction, and of a greater corresponding reduction in its exclusively selfish form, through the growth of sympathy and benevolence; but as in the former, so in this case, there are determinable limits fixed by the nature of things, which can never be passed.

Sense and self can never be set aside or annihilated, But it is conceivable and possible that, though narrowed in certain directions, unprofitable to society as well as to the individual, they may find the means of a better life, may become ennobled by entering into alliance with the higher parts of our nature; sense finding the advantage of a union with the affections and the soul, and the self-regarding instincts finding their best and highest life and sustentation from a certain incorporation of the social, or altruistic, sentiments. Sense, in short, may rise to soul, and the life for others might be the best life of self. This is possible, this is the true ideal, and undoubtedly there is some tendency in this happy and beneficial direction. The coarsely sensual and the narrowly selfish life is being slowly left behind us; but the process is slow, slow as all evolutionary processes, and the history of mankind makes us aware of fatal lapses and retrogressions. For twice before in the history of morals and religion—once under Buddhism, and again under Christianity—this very idea of love and labour for others has emerged, and twice it again became submerged by a strong return and reassertion of the old selfish and violent impulses. Once again, and for the third time, this sentiment has appeared, and seems slowly struggling to assert itself in the hearts and moral consciousness of men. Shall it this time succeed and triumph, as the one surest means of bringing in righteousness and securing the salvation of man on the earth? We cannot be sure; we can only hope it will advance; but the question how far men's hearts are really fitted for the reception of the sentiment of love for others or for their species, is one upon which something will be said in the following chapter.

§ 7. Meantime, before concluding the present chapter, on man's development, let us come to a provisional understanding with the pessimist, who denies the worth of conscious life, however variously or widely developed.

According to the true pessimist, life is so ingeniously adapted to ensure misery—and the greatest possible sum of misery,—that if it had been expressly and malignly contrived by a designing mind to that very end, there could have been no greater success. The maximum of misery is what is really produced in "this best of all possible worlds," so much admired of Leibnitz. For with just a little more evil added on, the world could not continue to exist at all. Men at least could no longer endure existence, if any sudden and general increase were made to the sum of sorrows, which they now so stolidly bear much more from custom and a mere animal clinging to life, blind and instinctive, than from any rational or well-grounded conviction of its worth. Development is itself an evil, and the more the greater. The more conscious evolution there is, the more the contents of consciousness are widened in range or deepened in degree, the worse for the conscious individual. It is rather the business of the wise man to despise progress, and in his own person to resist an expanded development, by narrowing the range of his desires, by denial of the will to live; or to assist the course of progress, only as an evil in itself, which may, however, lead the sooner to the saving truth that all is hopeless, and should have an end.

Now, without going the extreme length of the pessimists, some of whom, however, seem after all to find life far from being the melancholy and terrible thing which their masters have painted it, this much we must concede to the genuine pessimist—that up to the present hour, although human nature has been widened and deepened on all sides sufficient (as we who are not pessimists contend) to give promises and glimpses of its glorious further possibilities, which a fortunate few seem even now to realize, yet it must be confessed that the net result in happiness realized by our species is somehow disappointingly small. Though a few in whom the elements have been more genially mixed find a high flavour in life, yet men in general, even men of the selecter races and nations, nay, even the most highly gifted specimens of men, do not seem to find a large overbalance of happiness or satisfaction in life. For the most part, men have not yet been able to live and enjoy the higher, or to secure the happier life which has been promised and shown to be possible. They have not yet been permitted by destiny to enter in and take possession of the land of promise foreshadowed by Science, which it now seems, according to Herbert Spencer, the prophet of evolution, is to be reserved for our happier but remote posterity—the elect of a more prolonged natural selection.

However the prophecy may turn out, certain it is that we in the mean time have most of us largely missed an amount of happiness that was possible to us, nay, that was near to us and within our grasp. As Bishop Butler suggests, perhaps every one has missed a degree of happiness that he might have attained. How far this fatal result may be owing to the obstinate and over-large claims of sense and self, already alluded to; how far to the cares and crosses and shocks of chance, incidental to all individual life; how far it may be due to some deep and essential and irrevocable contradictions in things, or to some fatal misapprehension on our own part of the real laws and conditions which govern our life, and which our wise men and philosophers have not yet discovered for us;—how far the final fact be due to these singly or in combination, and how far we may hope to escape from the consequences of some of them, are questions which will engage our attention hereafter. For the present, it need only be said that probably all the above-named causes, in addition to the weakness of our nerves and the want of firmness and solidity in the physical texture and basis, have co-operated in the final result. Together, if not in turn, they have assisted to "put rancours in the vessel of our peace," and to greatly spoil our chance of earthly happiness.

These adverse things have drawn a strange mist before our eyes, which blots out the divine beauty which is else so evident, and spread so lavishly over the whole face of Nature; they have shrouded the beauty, and quenched the gladness which beauty should bring; they have broken the contented calm, and the deep and satisfying peace—the peace which the sage enjoys, but which it is the special promise of the life in intellect to give to all her votaries, and which, when realized, is the fairest reward of the devoted pursuit of truth. These things, which between them would almost alone make a heaven on earth, the joy and the peace from the presence and contemplation of beauty and truth, we have lost them, though near them. For this veil, which hides alike from us the beauty of Nature and of Art, is only drawn aside at certain happy holiday moments, to tantalize us with a great but suddenly vanishing vision of universal beauty, of a heaven revealed near us and all around us, and then suddenly closing upon us again; a vision most real for the moment, which we would fain prolong for years —a moment so fair that, Faust-like, we would fain arrest it for ever, but which nevertheless some fatal or malign power without us or within us prevents us from grasping and making permanently ours. In like manner, our pleasure in the pursuit of truth is broken and fragmentary, though here happily something is always given to the resolute spirit. But its pursuit postulates a preliminary instalment of that peace which it promises to deepen and to make sweeter, and this preliminary amount we usually lack to begin with. If we do not conquer this necessary peace at the point of the sword almost; if we do not violently take it by force; that is to say, if we do not shut our eyes to all lesser attractions, and steel our hearts to all competing demands, as only a Spinoza, a Bruno, or a Goethe,—as only men great or resolute or possibly devoid of heart can do, then we are scarcely likely to become the devoted followers of truth, and we cannot hope to have the peculiar peace and satisfaction which its pursuit and possession brings.

Finally, our disappointed species has not often as yet found on the earth, but only in the realms of the fancy, that other great and good thing—the abiding joy and content from a real communion of soul and affection, the high though different delights of love and friendship. Even here, besides the blight of evanescence, there is the formidable interference of Fate. There is loss total, there is separation, there is estrangement. We can hardly hope to have, or to have for long, that high felicity which our poet describes as the prerogative of spirits in a higher and serener sphere than our earthly one. We cannot here experience

> Such love as spirits feel
> In worlds whose course is equable and pure.;
> No fears to beat away, no strife to heal,
> The past unsighed for, and the future sure.

Love, truth, and beauty are the chief needs of the higher nature of man. Of all we may have more and of better quality, from our more developed capacity of soul, than was possible to men in ruder ages; but yet we feel that of all we are in some way stinted, and that Nature is niggard to a degree, with all her occasional intimations of boundless wealth. These great and good things are all around us; the capacities to feel and to enjoy them are within us; what hinders us, then, that we cannot get them? It sometimes seems as if we had but to open our eyes to see everywhere beauty; to think boldly and honestly for an hour to stand in the very presence of Truth; to stretch forth merely our hand to make love and friendship and happiness our own; and yet how we manage for the most part to miss them all—nay, worse, to lose them often when within our very hands! What fatality or malign power, we ask, is at work against us, that the most great and glorious things should be without us, within us, and all around us, and yet that they fly us, as water the lip of Tantalus? What may be the cause, we must again ask, of our so frequent failure to secure the good, and of our fatality to incur the evil? May it be, after all, that the cause lies greatly in us, and is removable; that the fault lies not in our evil stars, nor in things, but in ourselves, that so much amiss happens to us; that a truer estimate of ourselves and of the inevitable conditions of life, a correcter knowledge of the terms of what Butler calls our Natural Government, and which Science has for a long time been engaged in ascertaining more clearly for us, might place us in a better position for securing happiness, or at least give us a more commanding ground of vantage for ascertaining what amount and degree of happiness is possible and legitimate to aim at, and what, on the other side, is impossible and must be renounced with resignation? This is, indeed, possible. There is, indeed, some hope in this quarter, the amount and nature of which we shall make some attempt to indicate hereafter in the proper place.* In the mean time, the reader is not to conclude, from what has been said in this section, that we attach much significance to the pessimist's valuation of life, which, in reality, we regard as a very erroneous estimate; nor yet that we have been indulging in a digression from the proper subject of our chapter, which relates to the development of man. What has been here said will be found to have its place in our exposition and argument, as it has its significance in any correct portrait of man or true account of his nature and history.

See Book II. ch. i. and ii.

CHAPTER III.

ON HUMAN NATURE AND ITS CAPACITIES FOR VIRTUE.

§ 1. THE conclusions of psychology, of physiology, of the science of society and of the natural history of man as given by Darwin, place the whole subject of conduct, and particularly of moral conduct—vast and complicated as it is—in a new and more intelligible light; and they will serve to place all future systems of ethics that duly regard them on a more comprehensive and stable basis than any former systems.

After the revival, two centuries ago, of independent ethical speculation, which had been suspended for the previous sixteen centuries, all our English moralists, following the example of Hobbes, the initiator of the ethical Renaissance—Locke, Shaftesbury, Hutcheson, Butler, Hume, Adam Smith, Bentham—with the natural instinct for facts as opposed to theories, which has ever since distinguished the English as compared with Continental thinkers, disregarding the current theological and metaphysical dogmas respecting the nature of man and his soul, endeavoured to anchor their moral systems on the solid foundation of human nature as it really is. Each one tried to base his system upon some principle which he thought the most fundamental and permanent, upon some fact which he thought the most central and universal, from which he attempted to explain all the variety of human conduct; one tracing all moral facts to self-love, another to sympathy, a third to benevolence, another again to a union of self-love and benevolence. But with the best of aims, and sometimes with extraordinary genius, unfortunately none of the celebrated line of English ethical constructors possessed, nor was it possible in their time that they could possess, that full and comprehensive knowledge of man's real nature which the conjoint conclusions of the several sciences—mostly in their infancy when these men wrote—have only recently disclosed to us. The important contributory sciences of psychology and physiology scarcely existed a century ago; sociology and anthropology have only been admitted into the rank of sciences in the present generation; and the reformed natural history of Darwin, which includes man in the circle of the animal kingdom, with all the ethical consequences which flow from that fact, is only a thing of yesterday;—from all which it follows that a science of human nature, the indispensable foundation for any stable system of ethics, was not possible to any of our eighteenth-century thinkers.

There was no psychology before the appearance of Locke's great *Essay on the Human Understanding*, nor for a considerable time after was there further attempt to apply scientific methods to the investigation of mental phenomena. The foundation for a science of physiology was, indeed, laid by Harvey's discovery of the circulation of the blood, even before Locke's time, but there was little further development of that science for more than a century, and certainly none in connection with psychology till we come to Hartley. It is true that Hobbes, with the divination of genius, had early apprehended the general and deep connection between our mental and bodily states—a connection which he has expressed with that unrivalled point and perspicuity which is characteristic of all his writings. But Hobbes had only divined the general fact of the dependence of psychical on physiological conditions; he did not know the subordinate laws which govern the union and mutual dependence of body and mind; and he had not reached his general conviction by mounting through lower laws and facts scientifically established. In another direction, Hobbes had also perceived the general truth, without knowing the details which would have justified it. He had perceived the truth, of great and fundamental importance in morals, that most of our social and disinterested sentiments are traceable in large measure (if not, as he believed, wholly) to a self-regarding root; above all, he saw that moral obligation originally owed and still owes much of its binding force to the imperative of the sovereign authority, furthering the ends of the general social weal. These central facts of the sciences of ethics and of society, Hobbes apprehended with the clearest mental vision, and he expressed them with wonderful clearness and brevity of language. But here also he lacked our later knowledge. He wanted the light which recent research has shed upon the composition of primitive societies, and the real primitive condition of men, so different from his hypothesis of mutual repulsion. In short, Hobbes wanted the conclusions of science, of physiology, of natural history, of civil history, in order to free the great and profound guesses of genius from the accompanying admixture of fiction and hypothesis thrown out at hazard, and to connect his truthful and penetrating but partial glances with the real and scientifically established facts and laws of human nature. But still, what Hobbes, what Butler, the most original thinker after Hobbes, and what the other moralists of the eighteenth century have left to us, considering the imperfect state of contemporary science, is wonderful indeed, and would appear still more wonderful if we did not remember that they had the ancient ethics to draw upon—the ethics of Aristotle and Plato, the systems of the Stoics and the Epicureans; and if we did not reflect that, conduct being at all times a necessity for man, some recognized rules of conduct, if not scientific theories, must have at all times existed, whether expressed in current maxims, or drawn from sacred books, or embodied in laws which guarded the general interest of society.

Our past moralists have left us a series of systems of conduct, each one containing some special or important truth overlooked by the others, the later generally embodying the unquestioned truths of the earlier, and being, generally speaking, less open to objection; but nevertheless, none of the systems, nor yet all together, contain the whole truth nor the fundamental truth, either on the subject of morality or the final ground of our obligation to its practice. From none of them could we obtain a code of ethics suitable for our guidance; for besides that the writers are often at variance with themselves within the limits of their single systems, the systems are wholly opposed to each other with regard to moral obligation, even with regard to the reality of virtue whenever we pass beyond the very elementary virtues which society insists upon as a condition of its own existence. In short, of the many theories of morality and of moral obligation that have been produced in the past, none of them are quite satisfactory to us to-day; and their rules are of little service to us in the way of guidance in critical, or conflicting, or delicate cases of conduct.

§ 2. The masters of morals in the past failed to construct abiding systems because they had an imperfect knowledge of the human subject; they failed to create a science and a code of ethics because, even if human conduct can be reduced to rule and system—a point not without doubt—still the subordinate sciences had not been created or sufficiently far developed to furnish solid principles and reliable clues through the complexities of human nature and human affairs.

They did not know the human subject: they did not know, as we do to-day from the principles of physiology, the close dependence of our mental and even of our moral life upon the bodily material basis—a truth which finds its chief weight and application in the free-will controversy, and the apportionment of moral responsibility, but which is not without its significance or importance here, where the nature and limits of virtue are under consideration. They did not know that thought, emotion, and volition, the trinity in unity that on the inner side make the man and compose the contents of his consciousness, are all, in a certain extremely important though not definitely measurable sense, functions of the brain and nervous system, of the general bodily health and finally of the quality of the blood; that they vary both in degree of perfection and in amount with our varying bodily states,—so much so that an impoverishment of the blood will starve simultaneously the thought and emotions, and will weaken or paralyze the strongest will; that a prolonged and sustained strain on the brain and nervous system will make "all the uses of this world" seem "weary, stale, flat, and unprofitable," may convert the whole circle and content of consciousness into a perpetual sea of troubles, where virtue and vice are scarcely distinguishable, or seem only matter of opinion, where "nothing is either good or bad, but thinking makes it so;" and that finally, if the nerve exhaustion be pushed sufficiently far, there may result the permanent perverted function of the cerebral organs, which is at once the cause and the physical correlate of that chaos in consciousness which we call insanity—the state where reason and virtue are alike unthroned. Our moralists did not know or did not sufficiently ponder the fact that virtue, as well as reason, may be attacked and destroyed by disorder in the cerebral atoms, or that both may be perverted long before they are destroyed, by prolonged disorder even in the general bodily machinery,—truths which are now becoming the commonplaces of mental physiology, but which have not even yet been taken up by the moralist and assigned their proper place and weight in the sphere of ethical speculation or construction.

Our past philosophers did, indeed, know that man was an animal. This was a very old proposition, that did much service in the various treatises on the school logic; nevertheless, the philosophers by no means dreamt of the full truth and significance of this well-worn and universally accepted proposition. Man is an animal, as Science teaches, and nothing more; and an animal he remains till the latest day of his earthly sojourn. He is an animal all too surely, and descended from a long line of animal ancestors, stretching backwards to the very dawn of life; and however far he may appear in certain directions to have transcended his animal origin, and to have put on spiritual or angelic nature; whatever height he has reached in thought, or art, or virtue;—still the animal sleeps at the bottom of his being, a fundamental, heavy thing, never to be got rid of, which ever and anon wakes into aggressive and unreasoning life, and which ever pulls him down again to the earth after his most aspiring spiritual flights. There still exists in all of us, as in the Lucretius of Tennyson, " the brute brain within the man's," whose aroused activity troubled the materialist poet and thinker. There are still resident, even within the best, the two natures, each striving for mastery, of which Faust complains; one clinging with clumsy tendrils

> To all the fleshly joys the coarse earth yields;

and one that would rise to the contemplation of truth and beauty, and ever aspires to the infinite and the unknown. There is in every man that warfare between the flesh and the spirit, in which the latter is often brought into bondage, as deplored by St. Paul; and this degrading dualism and antagonism must remain a permanent fact in human nature, however much the latter be developed. It is true that evolution philosophers promise a diminished antagonism in the future; and Herbert Spencer in particular—here as elsewhere an optimist for the far future—relying on the general physiological truth of the increase of all organs in proportion to their use, promises a great lessening of the discord between soul and sense by the relatively greater exercise of the brain, the organs of thought, than of those related to the senses and appetites, not to speak of the ever-continuing action of natural selection in picking out, for preferment and for the perpetuation of the species, those individuals with the highest-developed brains. But besides that this alleviation of the strife between the lower and higher natures is only to come at a very distant date, as all evolutionary improvements; and moreover, so long as man is subject to hunger, and desire must always have its limits, and can never be very complete;—we do not find that there is much consolation in these assurances for our generation or for the two or three immediately following ours, with which alone science and philosophy, on their practical sides, are concerned. There are, indeed, many and strong reasons to conclude, even on the principles of Herbert Spencer's own philosophy, that the organs which have reference to the continuance of the species will never become rudimentary through disuse, whatever others have become or may yet become so in the course of man's strange metamorphoses. There is every reason to think that the instincts related to the preservation of the individual as well as of the species, as they are the first and strongest, as they are at the bottom of the universal life, so they will continue in nearly undiminished force to the end of man's career. Man will remain an animal with appetites and desires, as well as with affections and a conscience, and the former fact must be accepted and made the best of by the mass of men who can accept it, as well as by economists and philosophers who so much deplore it. Any reduction of the sensual side of our nature that is possible or desirable, must be looked for in a different direction from that indicated by Spencer, or Mill, or Schopenhauer. Meantime, the fact itself of the war between the flesh and the spirit, between the body and the soul, is not without its utility. It is a part of our probation, which disciplines the character like all probation, as it has its wider and deeper uses in the aims and total economy of Nature, even in the promotion and spread of civilization, according to Spencer himself. But so much at least is certain : that it will long continue, in spite of the prescriptions of all the philosophers from Buddha to Schopenhauer, and of all political economists from Malthus to Mill, to cure or to mitigate it. And it will continue notwithstanding the promises of evolution, which, even under the most favourable circumstances, asks for a long time to effect a change, and a much longer time—almost a geological period—to effect any fundamental change in human nature. For that such changes are infinitesimally slow is the one chief lesson of the evolution philosophy.

§ 3. Further, man is not only an animal, he is moreover, as all living beings, necessarily a self-regarding, albeit that he is likewise, as Darwin tells us, a social, animal. He is self-regarding as well as social; but the former in a more deep and abiding sense than the latter. The truth clearly laid down so long ago by Epicurus, revived by Hobbes, and assented to by a moralist in many respects so different from both as Butler, that man, in common with every living creature, seeks first and before all else the conservation of his own being and the greatest sum of well-being, remains an eternal and necessary truth, which has received in our day a fresh emphasis from biological science, and a new significance in its bearings upon ethical theory.

Every human being, however sociable, or sympathetic, or capable of sacrifice he may be, yet resident necessarily in his own isolated consciousness, which acquaints him with pleasure and pain, happiness and misery, necessarily seeks to minimize the one and to increase the other. It is no objection to the doctrine, that the wise man sometimes accepts or even voluntarily incurs a pain that he might have avoided; for he does so for the sake of a higher satisfaction or to avoid a greater pain. It is no objection that he often rejects the nearer pleasure, fearing the distant and larger pain. Nor is it an objection that the virtuous man often acts from conscience or a sense of duty, which must bring direct and foreseen pain, without any other future pleasure to set against it save the feeling and satisfaction of right doing; for even in this case he would have suffered greater pain from a contrary course of action, in the stings of his outraged conscience. Still less is there any objection in the fact that a benevolent man often foregoes the means of happiness for the sake of others, since, as Butler has shown, there is in this case a distinct and positive pleasure secured much greater than the possible amount foregone,—benevolence, both as a frame of mind and in the accomplishment of its aims, bringing its own satisfaction and reward more surely than any other active principle. In all these seemingly exceptional cases, as in all other cases, man follows pleasure, satisfaction, happiness of some species; whether or no his happiness is inclusive or exclusive of that of others; whether he prefers the near and sure, or the distant and larger but more doubtful satisfaction; whether he pursues it directly or circuitously; and whether, finally, he does or does not secure this invariable end of his pursuit and aim of his being. He follows pleasure, happiness, well-being, let us call it by what names we please, and be the happiness certain or doubtful, near or far off, narrowly and entirely selfish or including in it the happiness of others; and all this remains true, though, owing to the severe conditions of existence and the evils of his environment, man must more frequently direct his efforts to the diminution of his pains than to the increase of his positive happiness.

Each individual, then, necessarily seeks his own well-being; and within limits set by law and conscience, which prescribe that he shall not lessen in certain cases the well-being of others, he is justified, nay, further, he is to a large extent compelled to seek it by the strongest compulsion, or cease to exist. And often, in seeking our own legitimate life and happiness, we are further compelled to act in ways that must inevitably subtract from the happiness of others—those in competition or in collision with us; worse, even our friends. The conditions of existence force upon man, as upon all the lower animals, this self-regarding course of action, whatever disagreeable results may follow to others from it; and some such is sure to result. In a word, the exigencies of life compel men to act in a prescribed way as respects their own interest. We must in certain cases put self-interest in the narrow sense first. But what we must do, that we ought to do; or at least so to do is legitimate and cannot be shown to be immoral. There is, in fact, an "ought" which comes from strict physical necessity, as well as an "ought" which comes from conscience, and the former carries the first obligation with it.

Life for self, then, as Herbert Spencer and many moralists before him have concluded, comes first; life for others, or for humanity—if the latter be a practicable as it is a noble ideal—can only come second. The truth that man is necessarily a self-regarding animal first, and a social or a sympathetic one afterwards, is forced upon our attention by the facts of experience, by the universal *régime* of competition all around. But it has been brought before us in a more deep and comprehensive manner by the teaching of evolution in the writings of Darwin, Spencer, Haeckel, all of whom show us that the struggle for existence is the all-pervading law throughout the whole animal kingdom. Everywhere they point out to us this universal trial by battle, in some sense of the word. Darwin, it is true, in the case of man, is somewhat inclined to draw a veil over the

disagreeable facts of this seemingly selfish struggle; but this veil, Haeckel, dissatisfied with the present course of things and social arrangements, would boldly tear aside. He affirms the everywhere selfish, pitiless, and immoral or non-moral character of the whole contest, and this not less in the case of man than of any other species. Thus he tells us, in bold and brusque language, that only "the idealist scholar who closes his eyes to the real truth, or the priest who tries to keep his spiritual flock in ecclesiastical leading-strings, can any longer tell the fable of the 'moral ordering of the world.' It exists neither in nature nor in human life, neither in natural history nor the history of civilization. The terrible and ceaseless 'struggle for existence' gives the real impulse to the blind course of the world. A moral ordering and a purposed plan of the world can only be visible if the prevalence of an immoral rule of the strongest and undesigned organization is entirely ignored." *
The picture here drawn is darkly coloured, and, in fact, is not true; for, as we have maintained elsewhere, there is a purpose and also a morality discernible in the facts of life and the structure of society; there is, moreover, a progress visible and a tendency to a higher morality, though not quite through the agency of natural selection; nevertheless there remains an important truth in the view of Haeckel which our "benevolence" moralists of the past century did not perceive or found it convenient to overlook; and which our humanitarians and utilitarians of to-day, the followers of Bentham, Mill, and Comte, would do well to remember. There is a struggle for existence still going on, which tends to bring out the self-asserting and selfish side

* *The Evolution of Man*, vol. i. p. 112; also *History of Creation*, vol. i. p. 19, where the like sentiments are expressed.

of our nature into undue prominence; the fierceness and fellness of the struggle is indeed considerably mitigated, as compared with that of former ages, and some quarter is usually shown to the conquered; nevertheless, the struggle still goes on, and, though with mitigated fury, its consequences are sufficiently terrible, for our nerves are now more sensitive, we have less toughness of fibre, possibly less courage of heart, than our fathers,—all which weakness in the physical base make the consequences of defeat and failure in the contest the more dreadful in our apprehension.

The struggle continues; and while it lasts, and in proportion to its intensity, it tends to keep the social virtues, which undoubtedly exist, from further development. It keeps them down to that moderate minimum which society exacts, and indeed absolutely requires, as a condition even of carrying on the competitive struggle within some recognized lines of honour and fair play.

§ 4. Happily, however, man is naturally, as Darwin maintains,* a social animal. He is such, both by long-inherited instincts and the numerous necessities of his life. And men have devised the means of pursuing their own advantage and happiness, in very many cases not only without interfering with that of others, but in some cases all the more effectually in association, actual or virtual, with others; while advancing a great step, by a happy and fortunate development in man's nature, the greatest in the entire history of our species, they have even come to include the happiness of others as a distinct and important part of their own.

Men have discovered that many of the materials of well-being and happiness can be best secured by acting in

* *Descent of Man*, ch. iii., "On a Moral Sense."

company with others; that the result of united efforts secures a much greater proportion for each when divided than could have been realized by each one acting in isolation; that their interests are very often harmonious and not antagonistic. But what is of far greater significance and importance, they have found a still surer way of conciliating in many cases the old antagonism between the claims of self and others, namely, by the abolition of the antagonism —by the distinct evolution in the individual breast, in the very theatre of self, of the social impulses of benevolence, sympathy, and pity, which powerfully urge their plea in behalf of others, compel us to regard the pleasure, happiness, and satisfaction of others as a part of our own, and which even make us pursue others' happiness as a considerable contribution to our own.

This fact, the evolution of benevolence or love for others, may fairly be regarded as the happiest feat of evolution. Amongst all the new phenomena which it has turned up, there is none so important as this one, and none promises more in the future to mankind. What may have been the first origin of this feeling of love for others, of this wonderful guest within the rude primitive breast, it is difficult to say, as the first appearance of every pleasurable fact of consciousness—the feeling of beauty and the gratification from it, the feeling of curiosity and the pleasure from knowledge—is involved in mystery. They came we know not whence or why. They did not appear in the plants, or stones, or lower animals, at least not in the latter in high degree; they appeared in the theatre of man's consciousness, and he found them pleasant, and was thus encouraged to develop them more. But although the first cause of the fact and feeling of love or sympathy is a mystery, there is no doubt of the immense importance of the new feeling for the future of the species, nor of the further historical fact that it owed much of its development to the teaching of the great founders of religions—to Buddha, and above all to Christ. Love for man was taught by the former, but it was inculcated with new and more intense emphasis by Jesus five hundred years later. It was the "new commandment" for men, and by his teaching and great example, the sentiment received an extension and a deepening in the consciousness of humanity that it never had before. And in very truth, could this sentiment only have taken possession of all men's hearts, the kingdom of heaven had been at hand, and the salvation of man on earth assured. Unfortunately, though the feeling of love and brotherhood did spread amongst the early Christians, it was yet too noble a sentiment to fill men generally; it spent its strength in converting the barbarous nations, and the old selfishness in man's heart returned, or it had never been rooted out of the hearts of these rude races who found life a struggle for existence in the extremest sense. Christianity, and the love of others which it teaches, however, kept the struggle from being more fell and deadly; and a few good spirits ever were found who made the religion of Christ what he intended it to be—one of love and good deeds to others. At the end of the long struggle of the strongest in the dark and Middle Ages, the principle of love to others again emerged in Europe; it was proclaimed as the principle of morality by the amiable eighteenth-century moralists, Hutcheson, Hartley, Priestley, and in great measure by Butler and Hume; it even battled fiercely for wider existence under the form of "fraternity" of the French revolutionists; while in our own days, it is once more pressed upon our regard and attention under the formula of the "love of humanity" of the Comtist, and of "the greatest happiness of the greatest number" of the Benthamite, while it is an indispensable postulate in all socialist programmes. But whether this old revived principle of love for others may be expected to regenerate society and abolish or abate the struggle for existence, we shall be in a better position to see presently, when we have glanced briefly at the scientific account of its origin and development.

§ 5. The light of scientific research and reasoning has lately been thrown far back upon the condition of our half-human progenitors in pre-historic times; and the picture which we have been thence assisted to summon up in imagination of our ancestors, is one strange and wonderful and not altogether agreeable to contemplate. It is with mingled feelings of pity and wonder, and aversion, and yet with a strange sympathy and fascination, that we are drawn to the portrait, which scientific inquirers have sketched for us, of the primitive man. He appears extremely selfish, in the narrow animal sense of the word, ferociously cruel, visited at moments with a gleam of terror and superstition which may one day develop into religion, and with an occasional touch of the faint elements of pity which may hereafter facilitate moral development; yet in the main, a creature destitute of sympathy, affection, or pity, and with nothing that could be properly regarded as religion, or morality; in fact, in a state far below that of the lowest savages of to-day, and scarcely one remove from the brute from whom he had become separated thousands of years previously. But happily, the light of historical research first falls upon him in a state of society, which, indeed, may have been his natural state, as it is that of some species of apes, according to Darwin; or he may have been forced into it from necessity, from experiencing the danger of living alone, then infinitely greater than after the invention of weapons. Natural selection certainly would favour the social life; at all events, whether he had previously existed in the isolation of the family or no, at the moment that science takes him up, man is shown to us as a member of a community, and a community in the widest conceivable sense, in which property, women, and children pertained to all. It is, however, all but certain that our repulsive but most pitiable and forlorn progenitors possessed one redeeming quality, that of sociability, from which everything might be hoped in the future, and from which, in fact, all moral improvement did actually afterwards come.

Aboriginal man was a social animal; he had in him the germs of the quality of sociability, which attracted him to his fellows, and made him dissatisfied and uncomfortable when long alone. Man inherited this quality probably from the man-like apes, his immediate ancestors,[*] since we find some of the existing species of apes are social, if not sociable; at all events, however acquired, our Caliban ancestors early possessed sociability, and by degrees they developed it more and more. The rude primitive man, moreover, became in time attracted to some rather than others of his half-human brothers, within his own horde or tribe; a conscious, and in itself an agreeable, feeling of liking for some rather than others of his forlorn fellows, was born in his rugged breast—perhaps for one only who had been more useful to him, or particularly pleasant, or even likeable without known reason. From this rude beginning was born friendship; the feeling of affection and love for others, though in

---

[*] Darwin's *Descent of Man*, vol. i. pp. 74, 85.

faint and elementary degree. But where there is love for one, love for several is always possible; and from sociability and a feeling of common interest and common danger, a general and diffused feeling of good-will to all the members would result. It is probable also that, together with sociability, the faint germs of sympathy existed in aboriginal man, which would make easier the evolution of all the subsequent virtues, including love and pity and justice.*

According to Darwin, the social instincts in animals generally are the result mainly of natural selection. Thus he says, "the feeling of pleasure from society is probably an extension of the parental or filial affections; and this extension may be in chief part attributed to natural selection, but perhaps in part to mere habit. For with those animals which were benefited by living in close association, the individuals which took the greatest pleasure in society would best escape various dangers; whilst those that cared least for their comrades, and lived solitary, would perish in greater numbers." And not only the social feelings, but parental and filial affections were thus largely developed. "With respect to the origin of the parental and filial affections, which apparently lie at the basis of the social affections, it is hopeless to speculate; but we may infer that they have been to a large extent gained through natural selection. So it has almost certainly been with the unusual and opposite feeling of hatred between the nearest relations, as with the worker bees, which kill their brother drones, and with the queen bees, which kill their daughter queens; the desire to destroy instead of loving their nearest relations having been here of service to the community."† Natural selection doubtless tended to im-

* Darwin's *Descent of Man*, vol. i. p. 78.   † Ibid., pp. 80, 81.

prove the social affections by preserving those societies which had them most developed; but, as in all other cases, natural selection does not account for the first appearance of the inward conscious feeling of satisfaction or pleasure in the presence of another being of the species, in which the feeling of sociability consists, still less does natural selection account for the origin of the feeling of love of its young by the parent animal, or of the latter reciprocally by them. It is a more natural explanation to suppose that the appearance of the mother is the sign and symbol of pleasure, of food, and protection from danger to the young animal from the earliest moment, and that thus association from the earliest dawn of sensation, following upon inherited predisposition, is the true explanation of the filial affections;—the parental being grounded on original instinct, strongly assisted by pity and the principle of association.

But whatever its origin, the sentiment of sociability was the real internal cement of the primitive societies and communities, and the true source of morality from the inner and conscious side, just as the exigencies and needs of all, the necessity of union against other hostile tribes competing with them for limited food, against formidable wild beasts, or for the purposes of procuring food and shelter, constituted the external pressure conspiring to the same end of social coherence and consequent social morality. The principle of sociability drew aboriginal men together without compulsion, but the necessities of their position would have forced them together, even without any such principle. In short, they found a pleasure in each other's society; they found the greatest profit in union, and they had further discovered by a painful experience the absolute necessity for it. But all this implies the primary virtues and moral rules. There could not be union at all, and still less pleasure and profit in the union, without mutual trust and confidence, without an equitable arrangement and fair division of acquisitions—in other words, without the essentials of truth and justice; and there could be no prosperity without some regard for the general weal, and some at first interested, but afterwards disinterested, efforts to promote it.

And this principle of sociability or attraction in man to his fellows appeared earlier than the feeling of fear and hostility, which Hobbes assumed, without proof, to be the primitive natural feeling in man. But it must be admitted that the friendly feeling was strictly confined to members of the tribe, and was compatible with hostility to all outside competing tribes, together with aversion to all their individual members. The researches of Lubbock, Tylor, and others reveal to us the primitive man, not in the state of solitary isolation, where fear and distrust of others would indeed be the natural feeling, but in communities of more or less size and coherence, inside the circle of which a certain amount of sociability and mutual confidence existed, while the feelings of repulsion and of hostility, and sometimes of fear, were only roused by the outside tribes, the possible competitors for food and possessions.

§ 6. The feeling of liking for the average man as such, merely on the ground of his common humanity, of his being one of the same species linked in a common brotherhood, is a product of much later evolution; a sentiment developed in the course of civilization, which owes much of whatever strength it possesses to the inculcations of the great religions, and in particular to those of Christianity. But this sentiment has never been very deep or general; is liable even where it really exists, to be set aside or temporarily extinguished by various antagonistic principles; and has never yet really extended to all men and nations with the same degree of force. It is true, in modern times there have appeared philanthropists who professedly love their species as such, and who have laboured in its behalf; yet these estimable and distinguished men have usually not come into prolonged or close contact with many individual specimens of their kind—an experience which might have severely tried the strength of their love and patience, or even demonstrated that a general good disposition towards mankind was compatible with an aversion to many individuals composing it.

There are also in our own day some who, following the teaching of Comte, would put before us as a moral ideal the love of humanity, and life and labour in its general interest —a noble aim and goal, if it were only practicable by the human units; and there are those in still greater numbers who, adopting the creed of Bentham and the elder and younger Mill, tell us that the "greatest happiness of the greatest number" is the right moral aim for men—the true ethical aim for all men, and not merely for those in influential or commanding positions, as autocratic rulers, statesmen, legislators, philosophers, for whom the maxim is true and on whom it is obligatory, though in different degrees. The only thing we are here concerned to note with respect to these several systems—the humanitarianism of the philanthropist, the love of humanity of the Comtist, and the utilitarianism of the Benthamite—is that all alike disregard some of the facts of our actual human nature as far as it has yet been developed, and all ignore not merely the present facts of human nature, but the eternal and necessary conditions of human life and of all life on the earth, at least as disclosed by the latest teaching of science and natural history. They are at variance with science, as interpreted to us by Darwin, Haeckel, and Spencer, and though this is not decisive, it is a presumption against them. My own objection to them is that they are impracticable; they make a demand upon our virtue which it has not strength to sustain; they postulate a force of enthusiasm which exists only here and there in individuals, and which even in them is only an intermittent fire and force. To aim at the happiness of others, at that of the greatest number, is so far from being the right goal of moral action, that if we set about it with all the skill and wisdom and resource at our command, we should scarcely succeed in effecting much happiness, or even a balance of happiness, for one solitary individual. For how ill most of us succeed in promoting the happiness of the one individual with whose case and aspirations we are best acquainted! how lamentably in general we succeed in securing our own happiness! How little, then, could we do for others if we tried our utmost; how little for the happiness of all by directly aiming at it, or in any other way than by first trying to secure a moderate amount for ourselves and those directly dependent on us, and then, or subsidiary to this, by filling some function generally useful to mankind.

The scientific objection to the utilitarianism of Bentham, and the love and labour for humanity, is somewhat different, being grounded on the fact that these systems ignore the most generalized conclusions of history and experience. They ignore the facts and conditions of modern life and society; further, the fundamental facts of all life and of all conceivable societies as disclosed by the sciences of biology and sociology;* and, further yet, the obvious facts of human nature, of which we are all conscious, but which are only systematically brought before us in the science of psychology.

And, first, " the love of humanity " in any wide and real sense is opposed to the permanent facts of human nature—to facts, at least, which have remained in the species since the days of our rugged primitive ancestors, and which, to all appearance, have still a long vitality in them. For there exist in our nature, together with the undoubted fact of benevolence and love of others, the opposite facts of anger, resentment, an instinctive dislike and antipathy to certain persons, together with something very like the seeds of what Professor Bain calls a principle of malevolence. This eminent authority on questions of psychology is inclined to believe, from the hate that may long burn " with almost unremitted glow " in men, as well as for other reasons, that there exists an original principle of malevolence in our imperfect nature; and certainly, whether it be original or no, none can shut their eyes to the facts of anger, resentment, hatred, envy, and instinctive dislike existing all around us in the world. Besides the benevolent affections, there are also the malevolent; as well as philanthropy, there exists in germ the principle of misanthropy—a dislike instead of a love of humanity, and not uncommonly something resembling a contempt for human nature; and, unhappily, these last sentiments are quite as likely to be developed in our contact with men, by the scorching probation of life, by the

* See Spencer, *Data of Ethics*, ch. xi. and xiii.; also *The Study of Sociology*, p. 185.

terrible battle for existence, in which, at times, we are inclined to think, it is the unfit who chiefly survive and the unheroic who succeed. There are always amongst men, as the master of the human heart and the sounder of all experience knew, spirits of the stamp of Timon—

> With his noble heart,
> That, strongly loathing, greatly broke.

There are still men like him, generous, magnanimous, open and true, whose loving dispositions and noble natures become poisoned by their life experience, who are stung to madness and universal dislike by the selfishness and heartlessness of men, by the wrongs received, by the treachery of seeming friends, by the general meanness and baseness of their human environment. There are still survivors of the species of Swift, whose proud natures become converted to universal gall, less by the crosses and disappointments of life than from their painful experience of their kind; and such, not the worst specimens of their species, having received many of the evils they suffer directly from their fellows, and reasoning from the part to the whole of humanity, under the smart of their sufferings, which perverts their judgment, though it gives venom to their satire, come at last, like Swift, to feel contempt and scorn, rising at times to hatred, for their species, and to doubt or deny the possibility of any real virtue or goodness in man or in woman.

And at certain moments of funereal hue, do we not all take sides with the cynics and contemners of our species? How else explain the pleasure felt in the dark and malignant portrait of man drawn by Swift; the higher pleasure in the splendid cynicism which breaks forth from some of Shakespeare's nobler characters, the Hamlets, Lears,

Macbeths, and Timons; nay, the lurking satisfaction at the terrible denial of virtue by his baser ones, his Iagos and Falstaffs? "Works of art," it will be said, "and art, catholic in her selection of subject, pleases by the portraiture of an Iago as well as of a Brutus, the pleasure coming from the superiority of the art displayed." But still, our engaged sympathies with these denunciations of men and this denial of goodness, testify to something deeper, to some flaw in human nature, or defect or taint in human virtue; to this and to a secret consciousness of our weakness as well as scorn of it, the last feeling being the one redeeming fact which the mental analysis discloses.

And, indeed, what poor stuff our vaunted virtues, as they commonly manifest themselves in men and women, really appear to be to all of us in our cynical or desponding moments! How prudent and calculating; how safe; how little sacrificing! How feeble and timorous of heart their possessors; how little risk they will run; how little hardship suffer! At such moments, be they of deep delusion or of sinister illumination, the masks fall momentarily off from the faces of virtue and vice alike, with the startling revelation that there is little essential difference between the two;— an error, indeed, and quickly corrected by the healthy mind, the difference between virtue and vice being real and eternal; but not so great an error of judgment when applied to conventional virtue and vice, where at times we think that the advantage is in favour of what passes under the name of vice; nor when applied to that mixture, in various proportions, of the two ingredients with which we are most commonly presented under either name. Not surely, like ours, we think at these moments, were the virtues of past ages, in the days of the martyrs, the heroes, even the fighting men. They were more boldly pronounced, they were more clearly outlined from vice than our nineteenth-century virtues, "neither cold nor hot," though happily in the course of further improvement, under the fostering care of natural selection, and the breaking in of man to his environment! Surely, we think, the virtues of our fathers were more virile and more genuine, even if their vices were grosser than ours. They, at least, believed in the duty of sacrifice. For a cause which they had at heart they would precipitate a quarrel, in which they were ready to spend their lives and fortunes. For what cause, in these days, will men do as much? Our virtues are often varnished vices; even those produced by natural selection are merely a calculating prudence, "the reptile virtue" stigmatized by Burke, or else a mere coarse self-assertion or cunning to outwit our competitors in the modern form of the struggle for existence; qualities contemptible and degrading to human nature, and the opposite of virtues, however necessary their evolution may be shown to be.

Thus argues the cynical spirit within us all, not without some reason. And indeed, in this mood, the facts and conditions of life assume such sombre and sinister hue that a pessimist view of life the most pronounced alone recommends itself to us. Surely, we say, there is something ineradicably evil in this thing called human nature; some serpent drop of venom was originally imbibed in the infancy of the species, which has been circulating in the system ever since, and which, until eliminated from the blood, of which there appears no hope, will for ever prevent mankind from attaining to any high goal of virtue or happiness. They cannot attain the first; they do not deserve the second. Human nature is hopelessly and incorrigibly evil or weak in all men, as theology describes it, and as we feel it in ourselves.

Shall it be said, in reply, that this spirit speaks too severely, and condemns without discrimination; that it confounds under one sweeping denunciation, the real and undoubted moral differences between one man and another, as well as all the different shades and degrees of virtue and vice which really show themselves; and that such cynicism, true to its profession, tends in the individual to act as if there were no distinction between good and evil, and in the species tends to the fulfilment of its own prophecy that man will never attain to good? May it be said that the cynicism, such as manifests itself in the great writers, Shakespeare, Pascal, Swift, is a quality good for producing literary effect, and useful as affording a vent for the gloomy side of the souls of men of genius, which they have further invested with a strange attractiveness, but that, nevertheless, all delineations of man, conceived in that spirit, are understood to be too darkly coloured; that, finally, the cases of the haters and contemners of their species are extreme and exceptional, just as madmen are exceptional? All this may be said, and with a degree of truth; nevertheless, there is a certain truth in the other views also; and the last-named cases do really represent a very considerable fraction of mankind similarly affected, though not to the extreme or insane degree. Still more, they represent all of us at certain moments; for as it has been said that all men are more or less insane and irrational, so it may be said with greater truth, that all men at times are more or less cynical. The character of man, in fact, is no fixed, unchanging thing; his views are not always the same or under the yoke of one system of opinions, as philosophers fancy. His opinions vary; he holds one set of views under one mood, another under a different mood of mind; and at certain moments, in a particular mood, under a certain light, the cynical account of man seems the truest expression of the facts, and the pessimist's the most correct portrait of human nature.

§ 7. But what has all this to do with the question of the love of our kind? Something; for if they be even partially true, such accounts abate so far our power of loving such a being as man; and the existence of such portraits when taken in conjunction with such undoubted facts as anger, instinctive dislike, indignation, envy, rivalry, go to prove that we are not yet ripe for the religion of the love of humanity, and that we are not yet inwardly ready to strike for the greatest happiness of the greatest number, even if we knew how, amidst the complexities, and chances, and uncertainties, and contradictions of things, to proceed to secure the happiness of even the smallest number, nay, even, as Butler argues, of one single human individual, for whom we were most deeply concerned.

Still further: the love and service of humanity is an impossible and Utopian ideal, so long as antagonism exists between nation and nation, ever and anon breaking out into deadly wars; so long as civilized nations destroy contiguous savage ones under natural selection; so long as, within the same nation and within all modern society, there exists envy and enmity scarce concealed and ever deepening between class and class, to say nothing of the differences produced by party spirit or religious rancour; so long, finally, as the social struggle for existence lasts which necessitates competition and rivalry between man and man for place, possession, power, reputation. In particular, the love of humanity, the aim at the greatest happiness, must be postponed for some considerable time to come, as evidently incompatible with the state of growing antagonism between the two main sections of modern society—an antagonism threatening civil war or social revolution in all modern civilized nations, although in our own it has only assumed the milder form of a struggle, legal and seemingly peaceful, but really of a most disastrous character, between employers and employed, and in which not the combatants alone but the whole community suffers. When the whole existing frame of society is being shaken; when there are signs that great social changes are impending; when, in short, we are in the midst of an age of social revolution rather than of social evolution;—the moral creed of Comte, of Bentham, and of Mill is specially out of place and inapplicable to men's guidance. When the time of struggle is over, if that time ever comes; when men have recognized their general brotherhood, whoever may live to see it;—then the happiness of others might, it is just conceivable, be an aim for men in general, and the equal happiness of all an aim for the statesman. But even then the average man would do well to limit his aim and his efforts to the happiness of a few, and the statesman to that of his own nation.

To sum up this part of our argument: The facts and conditions of modern social and civilized life are not favourable to the cultivation of the virtues required in the love and service of humanity; and they are possibly still less favourable to the growth of those postulated by the utilitarian ethics of Bentham and Mill, aiming at the greatest happiness of the greatest number. The armed peace, as well as the actual wars, of nations forbid such virtues; the internal antagonisms of social classes, the struggle for existence between the social individuals, forbid them; the facts of anger, hatred, repulsion, dislike, which necessarily exist, as well as the opposite and because of the opposite facts of love and good will,—all these, added to the innate contradictions of life, as well as to its eternal evil conditions which make it to a certain extent an instinctively selfish struggle as of men in shipwreck; nay, our own imperfect virtues in evil sympathy with the general imperfect humanity around us, to which they have reference, forbid them; and show that the ideal of Bentham and Comte has been pitched too high for our humanity, so far as yet developed; as also that the systems are in other respects ill-timed and unsuited to the social and political condition of modern nations in a state of great change and agitation.

§ 8. And yet we allow that, in a certain sense, love of our species, taken as a whole, is possible, and that admiration is justly excited by what it has done and suffered. For all that is great, and worthy, and meritorious, and sacrificing has been done by man, and by man alone. If these words have still any meaning, as undoubtedly they have, they refer exclusively and truly only to the actions of man, and not to those of brutes, angels, or gods. If only man is vile, the converse is equally true—only man is noble. The two propositions stand or fall together. Love of our species, then, is possible, and therefore actions may be asked of individuals, so far as it is in their power, in furtherance of the best interests of the species. But let us be clearly understood. Love for man, for the species is possible, though it is not possible for all the individuals composing it; and love for the species, because its higher specimens have redeemed the rest of it and cause us to forget them, or, if we think of its inferior atoms, to forgive them. The whole becomes lovely and sacred because of the better parts, because there have been and there are sparks of celestial fire mingled in the general mass of dull and heavy human earth. We love mankind because great men have in very truth loved it, and have lived and laboured and died for it; we love it in the persons of these men, and because we can love these who were the best part of it. These and their nearest living representatives make humanity, in many respects an unlovable thing, lovely in our eyes.

We can love man for the great and good men of the past, or of the present when we are assured of their existence; and also, let it be particularly noted, because the dearest and most lovable, as well as most beautiful things that our earth has to show to us, are some of the human spirits that we meet in it on our passage—spirits generous, and brave, and true, and loving, though great perhaps only in our eyes, in mind, or soul, or heart. Unfortunate he whose life experience has not shown him some of these spirits touched to these good or noble issues; and unhappy, for in the admission of the fact would lie his own condemnation—the implicit confession that there was nothing of analogous nature in himself; that he himself was neither generous, nor true, nor brave; that he himself was of those of whom our poet speaks, who shut love out, and "who in turn shall be shut out from Love, and on her threshold lie howling in outer darkness."

For to the noble and generous and true natures, men naturally turn whatever there is of the like in themselves, ashamed to confess or show an utter penury of the higher human graces in the presence of those richly endowed with them, and who freely and without calculation of cost manifest them in action. To the true and good, men show their best and truest sides as they did to Brutus. Their "better self" comes forward, the baser recedes; one of the reassuring things which prove, should we feel ever inclined to doubt, the reality and efficacy of truth and goodness. Nor is there a deeper knowledge of human nature anywhere shown, a finer insight into the deepest springs of noble character in their rarer and subtler movements anywhere displayed, a more touching tribute to the reality and potency of virtue anywhere paid, than where Brutus—the same Brutus who, according to Plutarch, once asked, in a despairing moment, whether virtue were other than a name—is made by Shakespeare to utter on the final day at Philippi, and at the supreme hour when men's hearts speak the deepest truth and feeling that is in them, the great and proud and satisfied acknowledgment—

> Countrymen,
> My heart doth joy that yet, in all my life,
> I found no man but he was true to me.

To resume, then: a few have sanctified the many for us; a few superior specimens of humanity, the general mass of human clay and frailty; the past and present illustrious ones, and the beautiful characters that happily all have met as well as their opposites. These raise humanity in our eyes; and to these must be added a certain select company —happily not a few, of whose existence we are certainly assured, though we know them not—that noble band whose case touches our hearts, whose praise has not been widely sounded either by others or themselves, but who nevertheless remain ever the salt of the earth, upon whom the greater ones calculate; that noble company of unconscious heroes who do their duty—aye, and we are tempted to say more than their duty—without asking reward or taking any special credit to themselves for so doing. Honour to these, to the many unknown heroes, to the latent virtue of the world, to the men who do their duty and speak not of it, almost know not of it. If we too have spoken evil things of our species, in the instances of these men and women, and in the reverent and admiring recognition of their worth and merit in the moral order of the world, we would make reparation and acknowledgment of error to our kind. For these are they who in every nation keep up the standard of duty, who maintain the honour of humanity unsullied, who preserve the distinction of virtue and vice from being obscured or wholly obliterated.

These last, our friends, the few great ones existing, and the many great ones dead but whose work still lives, are the real reconcilers of us to our species, the real redeemers of mankind, the real representatives of what is lovable in humanity. Through them only the "love of humanity" becomes possible, and the phrase receives whatever practical significance it has.

§ 9. Such then, finally, is human nature, and moral systems must be founded on, as well as addressed to, human nature. If they undertake to guide it, they must begin by taking account of its moral forces and capacities, of what it can do, of what it can only approximately do, of what it cannot do at all. If moral systems are to furnish us with rules of conduct, they must be such as we can follow, and they must be such, moreover, as it will be generally profitable to follow. Above all, they must not be hopelessly above our power, else we shall be disheartened by their impracticability, no matter what the promises attached to obedience may be; and we shall end by neglecting them, having thrown them over in despair of fulfilment.

This is the defect and the danger in the ethical system of Kant. This great thinker and master of system has presented to mankind a wonderful system of morals, internally articulated, rigidly deduced from first principles, and wanting only one thing—but that a most important thing—to make the system perfect. It has no special reference to human nature. He has founded his system on principles, which are not principles of human nature, not even as shown in the choicest moral specimens of our species. Kant, indeed, avowedly did not build his system on any psychological basis, on any theory of man's actual mental and moral constitution. He did not build it on "empirical," that is, actual human nature. He built it upon a wholly hypothetical human nature, possessed of a free, autonomous will, undetermined, as ours is, by the stress of circumstances, by the strength of internal impulses and forces, by the imperious coercion of society; upon a human nature whose asserted free-will is not conceivable, as he himself admits, within the sphere of phenomena, but only in the mysterious region of "things-in-themselves"; upon a human nature that feels the unconditional imperative of duty, even when duties are mutually conflicting; in a word, upon a hypothetical human nature, that, far from approximately coinciding with our actual human nature, scarcely touches it at a single point of contact. And the result has been that human nature, and what science has shown to be its general properties, being disregarded, while a heavy and impossible burden of logically deduced duties and precepts is imposed upon it,—human nature has refused to consider the moral message of Kant as specially intended for it, and men have declined to be bound by so logically perfect but humanly inapplicable a system.

In his anxiety to place the moral law quite outside and

above human nature; in his laudable desire to give it a more sacred authority by detaching it wholly from men's interests and inclinations, he has overshot his mark, and made it impossible for men to apply or to follow it. In this last attempt to make fast to heaven the moral law, which Kant, in spider fashion, had educed from his own breast, the great modern moralist and law-giver has only cut its special connection with men on earth; and his wonderful ethical system has in consequence as completely missed its mark in being addressed to men, as if it had been sent to the wrong planet by mistake. It should have gone elsewhere—to some other world, to Jupiter or Uranus, where, according to another speculation of the same philosopher, the inhabitants are of a more ethereal and virtuous temper than we are. "For the Earth" must have been written by mistake on the transcendental tablets containing the new message of the law which Kant received from the Absolute in the *terra incognita* of the noumenal world.

In conclusion, let me further add that the system of ethics suitable for man, if any such system be possible, remains to be written. Neither utilitarianism, nor transcendentalism, nor our ordinary intuitional morality, nor any other system, will suit. We could not regulate our life for a single day by any of them. And certain it is, if any satisfactory ethical system be ever given to men, it must take account of human nature, both as it now shows itself to psychology, physiology, and the social sciences, and as it has grown, as proved by historical research; in a word, it must first consider, and that carefully, what Science has to say on the subject. And Science has at least something very pertinent, if not something decisive, to say upon one old and very important question, on which every possible system of ethics or theory of human conduct must embrace a side. She has something to say worth hearing on the question of free-will and necessity—a subject so large and so important as to merit a chapter to itself.

CHAPTER IV.

ON FREE-WILL, AND MAN'S AUTOMATISM.

§ 1. UNDERLYING the whole question of man's capacity for virtue or for improvement in virtue, affecting the question of his moral responsibility, that of the justice or injustice of civil punishments, and in some degree affecting the question of the reality of virtue itself on the central point of the merit or demerit of our characters and actions, is the deeper question of moral freedom or free-agency; the old and still-debated controversy of free-will, which has ever divided philosophers and theologians, which was discussed resultlessly by the metaphysical fallen angels, on the "hill retired" in the infernal abodes; the great question whether we or our wills have any directive control over our volitions and actions, or whether these are not in all cases the proper resultant of motive forces within us which produce them independently of ourselves or our wills, which are merged—the one as part and the other as total—in the forces themselves. The latter is the conclusion of Science, of psychological as distinct from physical science; the arguments in support of which theory, as well as the necessary qualifications, we propose to give in what follows.

And, happily, in treating the subject we may now, in great degree, keep clear of its old accompanying metaphysical snares and perplexities; the bottomless vortices into which the mind was formerly sucked, may now be avoided, thanks to the light thrown upon man's nature by the modern sciences of psychology and physiology, which enable us to clear the issues and to ascertain the facts really pertinent to the question.

§ 2. There has been an old theory of man lately brought forward by certain eminent physicists and naturalists, notably by Professor Huxley, which, if satisfactorily established, would finally and effectually close the free-will controversy. We mean the theory of man's automatism, according to which man, equally with all animals lower in the scale of being, is merely a machine, though a most skilfully constructed one; a machine in which all mental as well as bodily actions and states, all volitions, emotions, thoughts, as well as bodily movements and functions, are really determined by mechanical forces, irrespective of an imaginary ruling and directing entity called Self, or of any exercise of a supposed independent faculty called Will, which last, so far as it has a real existence in the shape of conscious volitions, merely registers and assents to a decision already reached by the other and only powers at work— the physical—merely symbolizes a state of the cerebral atoms, a condition of the physical and chemical energies, the only real and all-sufficient causative forces.

A volition is not the product of a "masterful ego," or of an independent faculty called will, according to Professor Huxley. The volition is caused by hidden mechanical forces, by cerebral molecular movements, just as, when the volition is carried into outward visible effect, the resulting action is obviously due to muscular or mechanical forces. Conscious volition, thought, or emotion is always produced by unconscious physico-chemical energies. True, the effects are unlike the causes; a volition, a thought, an impulse is wholly unlike its physico-chemical cause. But the same might be said in every case of cause and effect; and just as oxygen and hydrogen produce water—a wholly unlike phenomenon; just as a special combination of atoms may have the unlike phenomenon of life annexed to them; so particular arrangements and movements of the cerebral cells and fibres may have, as product or resultant, the wholly unlike phenomenon, an emotion, volition, or thought.

Man is, in fact, a machine, an automaton. Descartes was right in affirming this of the brutes; he was only wrong in arbitrarily severing them from men—a position no longer tenable since Darwin's discoveries. Man, too, is a machine, only the most skilfully constructed of all that Nature has produced. He is a machine, and, moreover, a locomotive machine, moved by the internal mechanical forces generated within from the fuel supplied by the food consumed. He is not moved hither and thither by the directive agency of a spiritual entity called self, supposed to be different from the material forces, yet to be in some indescribable local relation to them, and also to be capable of moving and wielding them. There is, indeed, no such self discoverable, no such directing spiritual agency. There is a thing called consciousness; there is a mass of conscious impulses and principles of action; but all these are themselves products of the physical energies. When we think we have made a prudential resolve as to a line of action, our resolve and our prudence are alike products of a particular position of the cerebral atoms—the final source and seat of prudence and resolution, as of all other conscious facts.

The human animal is also the human machine, and in strictness is only a machine. There are no facts discoverable that cannot be expressed in mechanical terms. Man is a machine in which there is a quantity of disposable energy locked up—chemical, mechanical, electrical, thermal energy,—which may be transmuted, but which seeks a vent either in muscular movement, in locomotive effort, in the play of consciousness, or in the production of the severer effort of thought. To produce these conscious states, energy is expended, the inner fire and fuel is burnt as well as in physical exertion. There is a certain quantity of the physical energy required for all mental work, which may express itself in a drama, a philosophical system, a scientific discovery, as well as in the construction of a railway tunnel. In all cases alike energy is merely transformed, and the work done may be conceivably reduced to a common measure in foot-pounds. An hour's labour with the brain, an hour's muscular exertion may be conceivably compared together, even though the products be so different; in either case it is the same stock of energy that is drawn upon, and this may be drafted, in the same individual, now into the service of the brain, and now directed to muscular effort. It is true that the energy which passes into conscious states or permanent mental products addressed to consciousness, is no longer available for further use, nor can any of it be retransformed in any case into the original physical factors; a fact which possibly constitutes an exception to the generality of the law of the transformation and conservation of energy. Or possibly, as an eminent physicist asserts, consciousness is not the proper or primary product of the physical energies in the man-machine, which must always remain physico-chemical. Possibly consciousness is only, as Professor Tyndall has termed it, an accidental "bye-product"—something over and above the full and fair physical result, which by an accident, fortunate or otherwise, appeared to watch over and register the whole series of physical processes, though these would have gone on just as well in its absence. In this case, thought or consciousness would not consume any of the stock of energy; the law of conservation of energy would not be threatened in its generality; and man would be a true automaton, with consciousness added as a spectator, but not as a director of the machinery.

The theory of the man-machine which thus emerges, culminates in Professor Huxley's comparison of man to a clock very cunningly constructed, whose face, with the information upon it, corresponds to consciousness, which presents us with thoughts, emotions, volitions; and just as we know that the hour and minute hand of the clock, which mark the time, are obedient to and caused by hidden forces and inner movements, whose action they serve to measure and visibly symbolize, so our consciousness but symbolizes and expresses the mysterious springs and inner movements of the machinery of the brain and nerves, by which, in like manner, states of consciousness are finally caused. Every mental state of which we are conscious is thus at once the symbol and product of a particular position of the cerebral atoms, of which we are unconscious. The former, according to Professor Huxley, is the effect of the latter, not merely as a "bye-product," but a true product in the scientific sense of the word, because it is an effect which follows from the other as an invariable antecedent. It is an effect, but on the theory of automatism it can scarcely be considered the proper primary effect; for consciousness might conceivably have been absent altogether (as it now occasionally is in our strictly automatic states and actions), and yet the man-machine might have existed. He might have existed, and, according to Lange and Nägeli, have performed all outward bodily actions, have walked, uttered speech, made music, possibly mechanical inventions, and all this without the present accidental adjunct of consciousness. He would have been then a perfect walking and moving automaton, seemingly skilful and with a certain method, as he is now essentially all this,—only with consciousness superadded.

§ 3. This theory of the essentially mechanical nature of man, it need scarcely be stated, is also materialism of the extremest character. It expels everything from man except matter and its properties. The "dominion in the head and breast," the proud characteristic of man, is explained by the properties of matter, by the greater number and finer organization of the cerebral atoms and fibres. There is evidently, on this view of man, not only no free-will, but there is not even any possible power of controlling or guiding conduct. If every volition, as well as every action, is determined by the physical energies, there is nothing left for the moral man to do. In the reduction of everything in man to physical forces, their interaction and results, the moral man is entirely lost, and the power of self-direction—which all moralists and all men, including even the automatonists themselves, admit—becomes impossible of explanation. Our guidance by the mental light of consciousness, as by the moral light of conscience, is alike incapable of explanation. But as this theory has not received the general sanction even of scientific philosophers; and moreover, even if, as Professor Huxley contends, molecular movements and mechanical forces cause our conscious volitions and cause our conduct, still, as for purposes of science we must accept the conscious symbols which we do feel and know as the only measures of the unconscious atomic changes said to cause them, which we do not know and cannot hope to reach; since, as Mill on this subject argues, of the two corresponding series we take the clear and the better known for purposes of further explanation, rather than the obscure or worse known;—then, it would seem that, as regards our present question of man's moral freedom, neither the theory of man's automatism nor any other theory which professes to explain mental phenomena solely by physiological or physical causes need be here considered at any great length.*

We do not argue against the undoubted influence of the body over the mind; nor dispute that there is a certain amount of truth in the theory of the mechanical causation of all our mental states, including our volitions. It must be freely granted to the materialists that the mind is powerfully influenced by the states of the body, or by what are called states of the body, though what subtle and mysterious elements are here at work none can say. At all events, we are all well aware from experience, if science had not placed the matter beyond the reach of doubt, that what is called the mind is healthy or diseased according to the condition of the brain and nerves, according even to the general health of the body. The total contents of consciousness, thoughts, emotions, and volitions, rise or fall in quantity and quality with the general bodily tone. Even the moral character may become affected, the perception of beauty and

* The theory of man's automatism is maintained by Huxley; by Nägeli (see Report of the Munich Congress of the German Association: *Nature*, October 4, 1877); by Lange, *History of Materialism*. The theory is in its essentials the same as that advanced more than a century ago in La Mettrie's *L'Homme Machine*.

truth may become dull or perverted, from some cause connected with possibly only a slight disturbance in the general health of the system. Such considerations show that there are physical causes at work in the production and alteration of mental phenomena; but whether these are the sole and ultimate causes is quite another question, and one which, even if the materialist's answer be the true one, need not further concern us here.* We contend, so far as regards this question of moral freedom, that to argue that the will cannot be free because all volitions are determined by molecular changes, is to bring this very old controversy into a darker and more hopeless region of discussion than ever. It is to leave light just when the science of psychology (assisted, no doubt, by biology) had given it to us, after infinite vain wrangling and logomachy, prosecuted in the dark.

§ 4. Science, at least psychological science, is not committed to the theory of man's automatism; a theory which is only a fresh and exaggerated instance of the strong tendency in men and philosophers in all ages to try to explain all phenomena, however different, by the particular class of phenomena with which they are habitually conversant; an instance of the same kind as that of the musical philosopher who explained the soul as a species of harmony, as that of the Pythagorean, whose mathematical meditations allowed him only to discern number as the essential fact and principle in all things. Man is, indeed, a machine, moreover a living and moving one; but he is also something more, and this additional something,—an accident merely,

---

* For a full consideration of the materialism resting on the doctrine of the conservation of energy, from which the theory of man's automatism is considered to be a corollary, the reader is referred to Book III. ch. i.

according to the true automatonist philosopher,—constitutes, in fact, man's differential feature and his true human nature; though, to estimate it properly, is beyond the reach of biological and still more of merely physical science. To read and measure human nature, and consciousness which reflects it, belongs to psychology—to psychology, aided by the sciences which are ministrant and subsidiary to it; and to psychology, consequently, we are referred by Bain and Mill for a true theory of human nature, as well as to know the opinion of science on the question of the freedom of the will.

From the point of view of psychology, we have a picture of man different from the physicist's or naturalist's; and we have a more satisfactory application of scientific method to investigate and explain his actions. According to Bain and Mill, the most eminent psychologists who have discussed the present question, our volitions are determined by conscious motives, by prospective pleasures and pains, even though there always is a physical counterpart to each consciously felt fact. There is that uniformity of sequence between motive and volition, if not between character and conduct, which, wherever it exists, marks a proper field for scientific inquiry. According to Mill, "a volition is a moral effect which follows the corresponding moral causes as certainly and as invariably as physical effects follow their physical causes." And the moral antecedents or causes are, he tells us, " desires, aversions, habits, and dispositions, combined with outward circumstances suited to call those internal incentives into action. All these, again, are effects of causes, those of them which are mental being consequences of education and of other moral and physical influences." And the same doctrine of the uniformity of sequence between motive and action is laid down with much clearness, accompanied by a masterly psychological analysis, in the writings of Professor Bain. According to this eminent authority, "the same motive in the same circumstances will be followed by the same action."* The doctrine of the uniform sequence of motive and action explains all the mental facts of choice, deliberation, self-determination, moral agency, responsibility, "without the mysticism of free-will." Moreover, the practice of mankind assumes the uniformity of motive and action. It does not assume the opposite theory. "No one ever supposes either that human actions arise without motive, or that the same motives operate differently in the same circumstances." Hunger always impels us to seek for food, the tender feeling seeks objects of affection, anger prompts to revenge, the desire of fame to live laborious days. Or, if these expected sequences fail to arise, we ascribe it, not to the failure of the motives, but to their counteraction by other and more powerful motives.

Further, our expectation of men's behaviour depends on the assumed regularity of sequence between motive and action. All government which makes laws threatening penalties for disobedience, assumes that motives are the sole causes of actions, and that the regular operation of motives may be relied on. All theories of education, of political economy, of society, all operations of trade and all the intercourse of life postulate the reign of law in the human mind; and all statistics confirm the assumption on the large scale,

* The sequence is between motive and *volition* according to Mill, between motive and *action* according to Bain; but as the volition is only an interposed link between the motive and the action which it contemplates, there is no substantial difference between the two views. The controversy, however, usually has to do with the first sequence, which alone falls under the internal consciousness.

just as our accurate prediction of the behaviour of those whose characters we know, confirms it in individual cases. In fact, man can be said to have a character only on the assumption that the same motives addressed to him will cause him to act always in the same constant manner.

§ 5. Such, in brief, is the theory of the determination of the will by motives, as given by Mill and Bain. In substance we accept it. But it requires a deeper and more comprehensive statement to connect it with the truths of evolution and physiology, with the facts of heredity, and with present physiological facts, both of which influence largely the motives, and are thus causes of our actions. The theory requires qualification, both from the point of view of physiology and from that of evolution; for we are assured that unconscious motives, be they materialistic and mechanical or no, have an influence, mysterious but potent, in the determination of the conscious ones, which alone are recognized by Mill and Bain as the causes of volition. We know, too, how much of our action passes into the automatic, the habitual, the mechanical, where we are as unconscious of volitions as the merest machines. Further, in the world of conscious motives we are certain that what outwardly appears the same motive is not inwardly judged by us to be so, from some change in us; that our conscious feelings, by which we must measure all motives, are treacherous and uncertain scales in many cases; that there may be such a thing as a change in character, amounting to revolution, in a comparatively short time; and that such change may affect our old motives in very unequal degrees, annihilating some and intensifying others; that besides revolution in character, there is always evolution or development up to a certain time of life; and that in age a reverse process of decay sets in. We feel at times like Lucretius, as if some mighty and malign but invisible hand had seized our will (or what we call our will), "wrenching it backward into his;" again, as if the uses of the world had become weary and unprofitable; as if all our old motives had lost their efficacy and influence over us;—all which facts and considerations, though they do not contradict the theory that the will is governed by motives, yet show that the reign of law in the human subject is much less uniform than it is in the physical world, and that the theory of Mill requires qualification, if not a new presentation from a more comprehensive point of view.

§ 6. Our whole moral character—the conscious mass of dispositions, impulses, sentiments from which we act—is a product that can be analyzed. While conscious motives can mostly be discovered for each separate action, the strength of the motives themselves can be traced backward to larger and more permanent moral forces which Science can investigate and ascertain something about, quite irrespective of the particular state and properties of the physical molecules of the brain and body.

According to evolution, the cerebral atoms themselves, with their inherent moral properties, were derived from parents and ancestors with like moral properties; so that even if they are at present ultimate, they are not true first causes, but themselves results of more comprehensive and controlling causes, which can only be explained by the laws of heredity.

Again, in addition to inherited organization containing in it the germs of the future moral as well as intellectual qualities and dispositions, we have been subject from the first dawn of consciousness, from even our mothers' arms, to education, an external and long-continued influence, which co-operates powerfully with inherited organization to give us our principles of action, and to shape our future character. Later still, we became units in the social body, for which our education was in great part a training, and our society with all but omnipotent strength has compelled us to accept and act upon its most accredited principles of action under penalty of its displeasure—a most formidable sanction. Besides compelling us to obey its laws, it forces upon us a conformity with its beliefs, sentiments, opinions, so far as these are necessary for the preservation of its own existence; while the subordinate sections of society with which we may be connected in different relations, in like manner have compelled us to a conformity with their laws and usages and principles. And concurrently with education and the pressure of society, there has been all the time the never-ceasing, ever-changing pressure of circumstances co-operating in the evolution and fixing of our moral character; and so great has been the total influence of these various forces, heredity, education, the social imperative, and the constant pressure of circumstance, that an extremely narrow margin indeed is left at any time for the operation of the free autonomous will of Kant and the transcendental metaphysicians. These various factors amongst them make up so much of the moral man that they almost justify the aphorism (quoted by Professor Huxley) that "our moral character is woven for us, not by us."

At all events, they show that our wills are not free. Our volitions, our actions, are determined by motives, as Mill and Bain contend; and the motives owe their strength to our character thus shaped under the forces above described.

It is true that men imagine they are free to act or not to act, to decide one way or the other, in a given case, because, as Spinoza has said, we know our actions, but not always the motives from which they spring and which really determine them. In reality, our actions, in our maturer years, and after our character has acquired fixity, follow with mechanical regularity from it, and in particular from one or other of the bundle of habits which, in great measure, our character has become. Action from habit is economy of force, a saving of conscious reflection and deliberation; but it is mechanical and automatic, there is no intervention of the faculty of will, any more than there is the weighing of motives. And whenever, as occasionally happens in maturer life, in cases of importance, novel action must be taken, where conscious deliberation does actually precede the decision of the best course of action, our decisions, our volitions, as well as our actions, follow from the motives which are strongest, which are no others than those which promise on the whole the most satisfactory results. It is the strongest motive which determines volition; there is no arbitrary volition made by a free will in the teeth of the strongest motives or in total disregard of them. Or, if there ever seems to be a case of this description, as where a man affirms that he will act in a particular manner, be the motives on the other side what they may, the fact is that the adverse conscious motives visible or possible, are dominated by the strength of the rival ones, supplemented by a substratum of unconscious motives referrable to the general moral character and dispositions, but never to a free will. The man knows how strong are the motives which influence him; he does not expect that any so strong can possibly appear on the other side; and his will seems arbitrarily to decide what his character has really determined.

The case of mechanical action from habit, the case of conscious deliberation, and the case where we are not able to state precisely the motives really influencing us, exhaust all cases. But they also leave no scope for the exercise of free-will. In the first case the action is determined mechanically, and in the second and third, by the strength of the motives at work. There is literally no work left for a free will to do, even if the existence of the supposed independent entity called the free self could be proved. There is no work for it to do which is not already taken in hand by other agencies. There is only the case, more conceivable than ever actual, of which the free-will metaphysicians have made so much use—the case where the motives seem exactly balanced, as in the example of the ass of Buridanus between the two identical bundles of hay. Here, it is argued, on the motive theory there could be no decision according to the strongest motive, from whence it follows the ass must starve; but he does not: therefore there is some faculty which arbitrarily elects for one or the other, *i.e.* there exists a free will. But even in this extreme case, one or other alternative at a particular moment seems to present the stronger inducement, and the volition, rightly or wrongly, is carried with it. Moreover, if the individual could not properly be said to act from the stronger motive in such a case, but rather from a mechanical and unreasoning impulse, just as little could this impulse be ascribed to the action of a free will.

§ 7. If it were possible to uncoil from the completely formed character one by one the various factors which have gone to compose it, so as to lay bare the pure nucleus or inner core of self which is supposed to lie at the root of character, and which it is further supposed can act irrespective of motives, or even in opposition to their strongest momentum, how much, we might ask of the free-will metaphysician, would remain to represent our proper self, and what range would be left for its free will to operate in? Indeed, is it not clear that the more superinduced moral influences, such as the effect of education or the imperative of society, are withdrawn, as we sometimes witness in certain forms of insanity or other diseases, the nearer we should come, not to the supposed underlying pure self endowed with a power of free-will, but either to a moral chaos or simply to the underlying animal, governed, as other animals, by the most elementary instincts and impulses? We should not find an independent self, because none such exists independent of the several elements of character. And should we attempt to dive, like Kant, beneath the circle of phenomenal motives, we should not come any nearer to the free imperial ego of the transcendental philosopher; we should not find it located out of space, but rather in our attempts we should strike the hard bottom of the material atoms of Professor Huxley, which, though we have not been able to regard them as omnipotent nor yet as first causes, nevertheless do exist, and as experience together with science assures us, do exert a very potent though somewhat occult influence over our lives.

Still more, if there were this mysterious self lodged at the bottom of our being, endowed with the power of free volition, whether it issues its mandates from out the indescribable sphere of the noumenal world, as Kant maintains, or whether it lives and governs amongst the circle of phenomenal motives in our ordinary phenomenal world, as other metaphysicians hold, in either case a consequence very serious for Science would result. The self, or ego, would be a first cause; its exercise of free-will would be a miracle, and something extremely like the miracle of creation *ex nihilo*. It would be the production and exercise of a force or energy underived from any prior energy or from other source than itself, which, so far as we can attempt to conceive an inconceivable and impossible thing, would be the mysterious and inexplicable process of creation from nothing. It would be the accomplishment of the feat which Kant himself declared impossible within the field of Nature, and which accordingly he can represent as possible only by shutting the ego out of phenomenal nature as he has done.

If we grant free-will, we must be prepared for further consequences. We shall have once more the return of the miracle, everywhere else expelled from the field of science and history; and this time all the more dangerous if the power of working it be lodged within the man's breast to be daily exercised. Let us but once grant this mysterious self endowed with this power of free volition, and the miracle becomes everywhere else credible, as required by theological or metaphysical needs. For what is a miracle but the interruption of the regularity of natural sequence by the sudden irruption and interference of a foreign and superior power? And what is the exercise of a free will but the like arbitrary appearance and interference of a foreign power in the circle of natural phenomenal motives for the purpose of breaking the natural sequence of motive and volition? It is not the appearance of a new motive, but of a power different in kind, a thing *per se*, of whose existence, moreover, we have no evidence. Indeed, if we admit this miracle to be performed within ourselves and by ourselves, we are only obstinate as well as illogical in affirming its impossibility in other cases where it seems more urgently called for.

But Science cannot without self-destruction allow either the miracle in general or the special one of creation *ex nihilo*; and least of all can she allow that both take place within the theatre of man's breast in the production of something from nothing, as in the supposed exercise of a free uncaused will. Science explains the facts and phenomena of Nature from second causes, which are invariably, as Mill tells us, phenomenal causes. To do so is the business of Science. She is not concerned either with ontologic or with first causes; but the existence of a free will, or ego, is either an ontologic cause with which Science is not concerned, or it is a phenomenal one for whose existence she finds no evidence, while it would contradict her two highest generalizations, the law of universal causation and the law of the conservation of energy. The doctrine of a free will would enthrone the man himself as Deity, would make the ego a true creator—a result consistent possibly with most forms of German transcendental philosophy, but not with the conclusions of psychology and of modern science generally.

§ 8. But is it not an admitted fact that men can alter their character for the better? and does not this imply a power of free will? Not so; a power of improving the character to a certain limited extent is granted; but this power, limited at best, is one that steadily decreases with years, and a time comes when it ceases altogether. The old cannot change their character for the better. In fact, a time comes in our mature years, different though it be for different persons, when the character has acquired such rigidity, such uniformity in its actions, and it has become so near to an impossibility for its possessor to change it for the better, that some theologians bring in a special miracle to get over the otherwise insuperable difficulty—the miracle of sudden conversion, represented as a change of heart, of soul, and of life. But this very necessity for a supernatural intervention is in effect, as it is in the express words of those who believe in it, an admission of the impotence of the free autonomous will of Kant and the metaphysicians to do the work of change. According to these last, the self, or ego, is free, free to fulfil the law of duty, but it is not free to alter itself greatly. It is free to do what it is its nature to do; in other words, it is free to produce its natural effects, as it is to a plant to grow and to flower, though by the same reasoning it is evidently not free to do other than it does, or other than it is its nature to do. It is not free for the bramble to bring forth grapes, or for any tree or man to produce other than its natural fruit—a consideration which may show how little the alleged freedom really amounts to.

According to the necessitarian, like Mill, a power of improving the character to an extent is allowed; if we really strongly wish to do so, we can; the wish itself being an important motive force in the case, and one depending probably on the original inherited basis of character. But while this power really remains, we can apply it only by perceiving and pressing into our service sufficiently powerful motives to conquer the rival and inferior motives. We must endeavour to make the better motives effect a lodgment in our breast; we must make them become a part of our character; and this we can only do on the two conditions that their germs are already within us, and also that they promise a certain balance and reward of pleasurable result. Before a drunkard can be got to make an effort for his reformation, he must have strong motives put before him. If he sees his health, fortune, and family in danger of being ruined, here are strongly deterring motives to the further indulgence of his vice. The only question is— Can these and the opposite class of pleasurable motives counteract the imperious craving of his bad habit. By trying to press good motives into our service, by incorporating them into our character and trying to work under them, we may succeed in permanently improving the character; but in order to a continued perseverance and a final victory, these good motives and inducements must continue with us as constant forces in the hour of temptation, and they must be so powerful as to conquer and subdue the old competing inducements and army of lower motives which still, though in diminishing strength, besiege the will. Thus, even in the change of character for the better, and still more clearly in the far commoner change for the worse, we do not get beyond the sway and sphere of motives. We are still within the circle of known, natural, phenomenal causes. We do not reach or perceive the operation of a free will, which, did it indeed exist, we should imagine could have no difficulty in improving the character. In the change of character here described, we find neither the miraculous agency of free-will nor the still more miraculous sudden conversion of the character by supernatural agency. Every way regarded, the alleged fact of free-will turns out to be an unmeaning figment, an inconceivable and impossible thing. It was a fiction invented by the older metaphysicians anxious for the dignity of man and for the interests of morality, both of which, in the opinion of the necessitarian, can very well dispense with it; and a fiction sometimes countenanced by theology, in the same interests of morality, sometimes discountenanced, because opposed to the general theological doctrines of original sin and of grace, as well as to the particular doctrine of predestination.

§ 9. Does not this theory of the determination of the will by motives take away all merit and demerit from our characters and actions? and does it not destroy all moral responsibility or accountability for the consequences of our actions? If the strongest motive prevails and really determines action, where lies the merit if the action be what is called a good one? where the demerit if it be the reverse? Is there any more merit or demerit in human actions on this theory than in the actions of lions or tigers which in like manner obey the strongest motive? Is not the murderer's act assimilated to that of the tiger who kills a man? Is not the most heroic action due to the accidental presence and strength of a good motive in the breast, to a happy grace from Nature? In answer to this it must be confessed that the merit and demerit of actions is, on the necessitarian theory, considerably diminished, though not the praise or blame, the admiration or detestation which they may arouse. The merit or demerit of our actions is diminished when we remember that it follows necessarily from motives, that the motives come from character, and that character is in great measure determined for us by heredity, education, and circumstance. Still, it is not wholly so determined, and we are meritorious so far as we endeavour to make it better, so far as we endeavour to make a good conscience our strongest motive force, even though here again we cannot greatly succeed unless, by the grace of Nature, the germs of good have already been deposited within us. But to raise the question of merit or demerit is to raise a vain and misleading issue. Our merits at the best are slight, as others besides the Calvinist theologians have discovered, and, undoubtedly, the demerit goes with the merit. If all got their deserts it might not be just to say with Hamlet that "few should escape a whipping;" but certainly few should get any extra reward; and the best, like St. Paul, are those who would lay the least claim to any. It is true we cannot help attributing merit to the men who have stood firm even unto death for truth and right. We attribute merit to them because they have served and saved the world, although the best of them knew and felt how little in truth was their own merit or desert, that they but did what it was in their nature and given impulse to do, and what on the whole they were obliged by the forces within them to do. They felt that they acted from forces lent to them, and that they deserved little credit for so doing. But the further reason why we on our part are inclined to attribute real and extraordinary merit to the great servers of their species is, that we know there was a war of motives, a conflict between good and evil, going on within the breast, and we persist in representing the good man, the Socrates or Buddha, as having arbitrarily made election for the good by his own free-will and choice, as having closed once for all with the right side, and determined to follow it, though it brought his own extinction from the world. We represent it thus, and in a general way not erroneously. The great man did all this, and so far as to justly excite the admiration and reverence, the love and gratitude, of his fellows and of posterity; but when we speak scientifically, and from the result of psychological analysis, we see that even the hero or martyr made his memorable decisions by the strength of the motives resident in his breast, as he kept to them by the continuing strength of these same inner moral forces, which were only a happy and glorious grace of Nature or God vouchsafed to him. He felt as Luther—this he must do and no other;—from the strength of the motive within, but not from the strength of his own free-will. This *he* felt, though *we*, on the other hand, cannot help having feelings of reverence, gratitude, admiration, which implicitly acknowledge a merit in him; feelings which, however, are ennobling to the possessor, as they were part of the sustaining motives to the hero's action itself.

§ 10. Why, then, are men punished for actions injurious to others or to society, when they only act from the strongest motives? If the strongest motive or sum of motives invariably prevails and carries the volition with it, it is still a matter of chance whether the motives are good or bad ones, though, if bad or anti-social, we must necessarily act from them. Am I not compelled to act from the strongest motive as irresistibly as a steam-engine is urged forward by the mechanical forces animating it? and if compelled, are not merit and demerit alike removed? Why, then, should I be punished if the consequences of my action should happen to harm others? Why on any ground except the superior might of society and not on grounds of justice?

And the answer to such an objection usually urged against the motive theory is as follows:—"Doubtless you must always decide and act according to the strongest motive which for the time being is before you, unless you postpone your decision in order to allow other motives to rise to view; but in either case there was supposed to have been present and included in your general circle of motives sitting in council, some degree of conscience, some regard for the rights, and if not also some small desire for the good of others, at least no wish to do them harm. Further, even if all these good motives were absent, still a fear of punishment was very confidently calculated upon by society as being present in your case, as in all cases, amongst the other motives, to warn you off from actions hurtful to society. Some of these motives, prohibitory of injurious action to others, and very particularly the dread of punishment, were assumed as having been present to your mind as to all properly constituted minds; and if unhappily they were not present in due strength, if they were present but were not felt sufficiently strongly to deter you from wrong doing, society, also governed by motives directed to its own preservation and weal, is justified, through its arm of justice guarding its interests, in punishing you, so as to make the deterring motives stronger in future in you and others similar." In order to show the falseness of the theory, a burglar or murderer of a metaphysical turn of mind, who has adopted the necessitarian creed, is sometimes represented as urging:—"But is the punishment really just? How can it be just to punish me if my will has been coerced by the strength of the motives which were unfortunately present to me?" And the answer provided by Bishop Butler still holds good, even from the necessitarian point of view. "As if," says Butler, "the necessity which is supposed to destroy the injustice of murder would not also destroy the injustice of punishing it." But the burglar may be answered more fully from the point of view of his own creed, from the principles of Edwards and Priestley, of

Mill and Bain. We may suppose a necessitarian judge to have tried the necessitarian house-breaker, and to reply to his objection :—" It appears from the event that respect for the rights of others, for the just rights of property, were very feebly deterring motives with you when you committed this crime; further, that the fear of punishment was not so strong as it is desirable it should have been; it was calculated that, if not as a moral being, yet at least as a prudent one, mindful of your own interest and self-preservation you would have had the latter motive before you; it was even confidently assumed that you would have it before you in some degree, since you were forewarned of the penalty attached to your offence against the law; it now appears that, though you doubtless had it before you, you had it not in sufficient degree. This is unfortunate for you, especially since you have been convicted of the crime; and society in self-defence must make the fear of punishment stronger in your apprehension in future, as well as in others resembling you; and there is no other way in which this can be so effectually done as by making you experience punishment in severe and unpleasant form. You have attacked society in one of its essential foundations, the rights of property, and society is justified in repelling such attacks. It is just to defend just rights, and to do so by means of punishment, which is society's means of defence, is just. Further, it is not only just, but the general weal absolutely requires it; for all which reasons I, as the representative of society, and moved by considerations for its security, must pass such a sentence of punishment on you as the gravity of your offence justly deserves."

So much by way of answer to the metaphysical burglar. And most of the argument applies to the case of him who has taken life; only that here the further and more special question of the justice of capital punishment enters—a question which, however, does not concern us at present.

Thus punishment may be defended as just on the motive theory as well as on the rival theory of free-will. Mill goes even further, maintaining that it is only on the motive theory that punishment has any true significance or justification; that it would miss its aim if the will were not determined by motives. Punishment, in his opinion, owes its sole efficacy to its being a motive which will certainly have an influence amongst the others at work, which will certainly be taken into more or less serious account by all who meditate crime against society. "Punishment," he says, "proceeds on the assumption that the will is governed by motives. If punishment had no power of acting on the will, it would be illegitimate, however natural might be the inclination to inflict it. Just so far as the will is supposed free, that is, capable of acting *against* motives, punishment is disappointed of its object and deprived of justification."*

The final justification of punishment is the greater good to be attained, only by its infliction. It cannot be justified on grounds of vengeance, or of retaliation, or of a desire to inflict pain. The reformation of the individual and the larger good of society are the aims of punishment, but the latter is so much the more important that the former must give way to it in all cases where the two are incompatible, as in the case of the murderer, whose life is dangerous to the community. The aim of punishment is the prevention of crime, sometimes the improvement of

* *Examination of Sir W. Hamilton's Philosophy*, p. 576.

the individual. The further question arises before it can be justified—Is it efficacious to its end? Does it prevent crime or improve the offender? And there can be no doubt what the answer should be. There is no doubt of the efficacy of punishment in general, sometimes for the improvement of the individual, but far more for the prevention of future crimes. There can be no question that the fear of punishment prevents innumerable crimes of all kinds which nothing but such fear would prevent. Without going the length of Professor Bain, who affirms that "punishment or retribution in some form is one-half the motive power to virtue in the very best of human beings, while it is more than three-fourths in the mass of mankind," we have no doubt at least that the fear of punishment sits as a constant monitor and motive force in the general assembly of the criminal's motives. There can be no question that the dread of punishment is "very potent with such spirits," and that its monitions prevail to such an extent as not only to prevent many potential burglars, swindlers, and murderers, from becoming actual ones; but also that amongst actual criminals, the fear of consequences acting in the place of a conscience, in many cases turns away the current of the criminal's thought from the premeditated crime; so that the cunningly conceived fraud will not be carried out, the meditated murder will be only in imagination, the contemplated burglarious "enterprise of great pith and moment" will remain only a great idea which will never merit the name of action.

Responsibility, then, is not destroyed by the theory of motives. On the contrary, a practical sense of it is only to be brought home to the individual who has no conscience or regard for the rights of others, by punishment, that is, by a motive. And this punishment must, in the general interest of society, be made sufficiently severe to effect its proper aim of repressing crime within due limits, which it can never hope by excessive severity to wholly extirpate so long as the imperfect constitution of society itself, as well as the imperfect constitution of human nature, are two large producing causes. Punishment by society should not be vengeance, it should not be cruel or excessive, it should be tempered with a judicious mercy, and allowance made where possible for the pressure of temptation, for the stress of circumstance, for the compulsion of actual want which sometimes drives to crime. It should be remembered by society that, though we know the temptation which has proved too strong, we do not know how much has been successfully resisted, the amount of which, in the opinion of all moralists, is a chief factor in appraising the moral worth of character. Finally, it should be remembered that besides a compulsion scarcely short of physical, which want may bring—and for which none should be held accountable morally—the sum total of the conditions of society itself may be one of the larger causes of the compulsion to crime, on which account also a plea for mercy and leniency is allowed in all cases where it can be exercised without danger to the general social interests.

§ 11. And yet, after all, in spite of the speculative conclusion that the will is not a free causal agency, but itself determined by causes, is there not the equally clear practical conviction that man can control the course of his life and actions to some considerable degree? Are we not assured that man is not only the master of Nature, but more the master of his own destiny to-day than he was in any former period of his history? I think we must admit it. And still more; man in civilized communities feels assured that he is not the slave of any fatalistic necessity; that he is less the sport of chance than man in former ages or in ruder nations; that he can not only direct and shape the outward physical facts and forces of Nature in his favour, but that he can even, if he wishes it, to an important extent, reshape his own character, in which is implicitly contained so much, if not as Schopenhauer contends the whole, of his future destiny. The *Man* has, if his *Will* has not, a certain directive power. Even the believers in his automatism are obliged to grant so much, however little their principles would explain it. He can to a large extent control his conduct; he has an undoubted and a great capacity of working towards distant aims, which he strongly desires to reach, and of foreseeing and directing the intermediate steps towards these ends. We thus possess a practical freedom, the freedom of working towards a desired end, the only freedom of any value; and we have this freedom the greater in proportion to our native force of character and wisdom. That we have such freedom, the fact of our labouring for distant ends, and of our power of choosing the appropriate means to reach foreseen goals, decisively prove, even though it can be shown that each step of our actions falls under the sway of mechanical necessity, and that each item of our deliberations was controlled by motives. There is now less of chance pressing on us; more of choice allowed us;—less of the fatalistic necessity where we can only bow our heads, and with Stoic or Islamite resignation passively await the event which neither effort nor thought can prevent. There is more room in our age of Science for our thought and will, for purpose and design, to influence the known course of things in our favour. The mighty machinery of the universe, vast and complicated as it is, permits man, through the knowledge of it, which Science gives, to turn to profit the very invariability of the working of the machinery, the rigid uniformity of the laws, which at first sight would seem to crush him under the weight of helpless necessity. By his knowledge of the uniform behaviour of Nature, he regains the practical freedom which the universal reign of invariable law seems at first to take away. For by this regularity of natural law, and by his knowledge of it, man is able to press the laws into his service so as to aid in the accomplishment of his designs and desires; and the more completely all Nature, including his own bodily and mental states, passes under the dominion of established scientific laws, the more fully man can avail himself of them, and recover his freedom within their bounds and by their means. The more he knows them and takes account of them, the fuller he secures his own practical freedom. We are free,—and the condition of our freedom is this very rigidity of Nature's laws, joined to our knowledge of the several laws themselves. We are free, and knowledge is the true emancipator. To know the physical law, and to make use of it, to know the physiological, or mental, or economic law, and to take account of it, is to make the law our servant and not our master.

Nature is unchanging; it is for us to know her, and after knowing to obey her, in obeying to obtain the dominion over her. But knowledge is the first condition of empire. Knowledge—which positive science as distinct from hypothesis provides—is thus the true deliverer of man both from the tyranny and seeming caprice of external natural forces, blind and powerful, as well as from the maleficent forces moral, or organic, resident within. Ever it is the truth which makes man free, so far as freedom can be predicated of a being subject to external and internal conditions, which can be indefinitely modified and made to serve his most intimate desire and purpose, but which in themselves are unalterable.

We are free, in the sense explained; but there is no autonomous will. There is no absolute sovereignty of the will, but only a constitutional rule subject to many checks and conditions. The will is limited by laws and conditions, physical, organic, mental, social, which must be accepted in any case; but which, if accepted and made the best of, man can control his destiny in their despite, and even by their means. We can thus *act* as if we were free, in spite of the doctrine of speculative necessity, as Butler argues; we are free to pursue our most desired ends—the only freedom that any need care to have; and we shall obtain all the more of this kind of freedom, the more all Nature passes under the yoke of invariable and unchanging laws.

CHAPTER V.

ON IMMORTALITY.

§ 1. AND now, what is the scientific doctrine on the great theme of immortality? Is there any hope for men? In one word, no. For any such hope, if men must continue to indulge in it after hearing the scientific arguments, they must go elsewhere—to the theologian, the metaphysician, the mystic, the poet. These men, habitually dwelling in their several spheres of illusion and unreality, may find suggestions of the phantasy which they persuade themselves are arguments in favour of a future life; the man of science, for his part, and the positive thinker, building on science—who keep within the solid land of inductive truth and positive knowledge, where proof is possible, and where short of absolute proof, analogy should guide the judgment—consider no proposition more certain than that the soul is mortal as well as the body which supported it, and of which it was merely the final flower and product.

Our modern naturalist, following Darwin, has satisfied himself that man is only the superior animal derived from the inferior; why should he not die as the others? Our modern physiologist has ascertained that thought is but a function of the brain and nerves; why should it not perish with these? Our most advanced physicists have discovered that man is a machine first, an animal afterwards, and a conscious being by an inexplicable accident only in the third instance; a machine in which the various physical agencies are mysteriously transmuted and utilized to repair the parts, and to propel the whole, with consciousness super-added as spectator, but not as director or controller of the machine;—why should it not collapse with the general break-up of the machinery? why should it not cease when no longer supported by the various physical energies whose transformations within the bodily machine alone made its existence possible?

Yes, indeed; our modern savants, and what is of still more consequence, our positive scientific thinkers, reasoning independently from the verified conclusions of science, have, with few exceptions, come to the conclusion that the belief in a future life so long prevalent amongst men must be finally given up. While only partially assenting to Hamlet's great eulogium on man,* with his nobility of reason, his infinity of faculty, his "express and admirable" mechanism, they have, with all but unanimous voice, accepted Hamlet's cynical conclusion in its most strict and literal and serious sense, that all is but the "quintessence of dust." For man, though the acknowledged "beauty of the world and the paragon of animals," is still only an animal, subject to the common doom of the rest. The dust is the end; and this is the conclusion even of those who do not accept the remainder of the materialist's creed,—that the cunning arrangements of the atoms was the beginning, and their mysterious

---

* The whole wonderful passage is well worth comparing with the Darwinian doctrine of man, standing as it does so much opposed to it at all points save the conclusion:—"What a piece of work is man! how noble in reason! how infinite in faculty! in form and moving, how express and admirable! in action, how like an angel! in apprehension, how like a god! the beauty of the world! the paragon of animals! And yet to me what is this quintessence of dust?"

marshallings and combinations the underlying essence and cause of the whole life-drama of man.

§ 2. Such is the conclusion of science; but before exhibiting in detail the arguments on which it depends, it is desirable to revert to, and briefly to consider, the theological and metaphysical theories of the soul, together with the arguments for a future existence founded upon them. We shall then be in a better position to estimate the comparative weight of these on the one side, and those advanced by science on the other.

The metaphysicians of the seventeenth and eighteenth centuries—Descartes, Leibnitz, Wolf, Clarke—with minor and unimportant differences, had agreed and laid down that the soul was an independent entity, separate from the body, and of wholly dissimilar nature. It was a thinking substance, of its own nature, and of necessity an immaterial and an immortal thing. But as a further security and protection in the great shock of death, in order to shield it from all harm at that great transition, so suggestive to the imagination of fateful possibilities, they had made it one and indivisible. In short, it was a thinking substance, simple, indivisible, immaterial, and immortal. It could not be broken up or dissolved by death, for death could find no avenue of assault, no vulnerable point in a thing so carefully guarded. It could not be touched by any power short of Omnipotence, and not even by Him after an irrevocable existence had once been granted. True, the metaphysicians did not really prove that the soul possessed the alleged attributes, including immortality; they had only covertly assumed them in their definitions of the soul, and afterwards, according to the fashion of skilful conjurors, merely shook out of their definitions the desired conclusions which they had already secretly placed there, or which at least they could scarcely avoid knowing were already implicitly folded up in the hypotheses they started with. And it was one of the great tasks which Kant imposed upon himself to unmask and discredit all these pretended proofs of the soul's necessary immortality—a work accomplished by him so very effectually as for ever to discredit this line of argument for a future life. But strange to say, this great destroyer of other metaphysical constructions, having completely demolished the old theories of the soul and destroyed the old proofs of its immortality, raised up a theory of his own, which, though more profound and possibly more invulnerable to logical or metaphysical assault, is, for all practical purposes, and to those not versed in the subtleties of metaphysical speculations, substantially the same as the theories destroyed, and open to hardly less weighty objections than lay against them. For, after all, there was a self, or ego, underlying our phenomenal consciousness, though, dive we never so deep with introverted psychological eyes, we could not find it or come into contact with it in any way. There was a real self, though completely and effectually shrouded from our view. There was a real ego, different from the merely empirical ego, from the common ego of our ordinary acquaintance, such as our consciousness shows it to us; but of this real ego we can only know the existence and nothing more. Hume was consequently right when he said, "We never find what is called self, but only a conscious impression when we look inward." He was only wrong in denying that there was any self, an error corrected by Kant. The ego exists beneath, or rather outside, consciousness. It is a noumenon, a *ding-an-sich*, an indescribable something, safely located out of space and time, and as such, not subject to the mutabilities of these phenomenal spheres.

The soul, according to Kant, is an unconditional existence, a thing *per se*, a noumenon, residing *out* of consciousness, of whose ontologic existence we are made aware by its phenomenal projections or effects *in* consciousness. It lives, so to speak, beneath the waters of consciousness, but by its sub-conscious activity it produces the ripples and agitations which appear on the surface. It is true that we cannot prove the existence of this real self in the common scientific, but only in a transcendental, sense. The existence of the ego, in the strictest sense of experienced existence, we cannot prove, because we can have no intuition of it on the one hand; and on the other, the categories of the understanding, Substance, Cause, and the like, which are necessary to make our experience, do not legitimately apply to noumena, which lie quite beyond the frontiers of all possible experience. In reality, the soul is beyond the bounds, though it lies at the bottom, of all our experience. But we must grant its existence, both from the side of the Speculative Reason as explained above, as a cause or source of the phenomena of consciousness; and again we must grant its existence from the side of the Practical Reason as a moral will. Moreover, as moral will, and from the point of view of action, the ego is free, since we feel the imperative of duty demanding unconditional fulfilment from us, which would be a mockery or practical contradiction on the part of its Author if we had no power to obey its behests. We *ought*, therefore we *can*. In this famous argument Kant secures our moral freedom. And finally immortality must be also postulated, though, like the freedom of the will and the existence of God, it is confessedly not proved speculatively. A future life, and that an immortal one, must be granted us to reach that perfection, whose pursuit reason prescribes as the true end of our being, but which on earth is never reached by even the most virtuous, and which in even any time short of eternity can only be indefinitely approximated to without being ever fully attained.

Thus the metaphysicians in general, and Kant in particular, had tried to ground their beliefs in the soul's immortality. The theologians had reached the same conclusion by a different route. The future life was a revelation from God Himself. It could not confessedly have been deduced with any certainty from reason alone. Nor was it an invariable element in every revelation, since there appears no trace of it in the Mosaic, and little in the Old Testament revelation taken generally. In the Christian revelation, however, the doctrine of the resurrection to a future life is, as St. Paul assures us, the most central and vital point. According to the Christian theology, an immortal soul is lodged in every man,—not immortal in its own essence, as the metaphysicians had made it, but as the gift of God, who has so bade it and declared it to us. The soul existing in every one is, however, impure and sinful in its own nature, owing to the original sin of Adam which all his posterity has inherited, and requires the blood of Christ to purify it, the action of the Holy Spirit to sanctify it. It has ingrained spots and essential taints, which ever tend to deepen and to develop into worse evil as life proceeds, and it must be inevitably and irrevocably lost unless its further corruption be arrested, unless it be wholly regenerated by the grace of God, the efficacy of the Spirit, and the merits of the Redeemer, according to the Christian scheme of salvation, as generally understood. But even in the worst cases (except, indeed, under the Calvinistic theology), the soul, so far lost, can be recovered by the appropriate means of grace. Who are the depositaries of the means is a question, it is true, which divides Christian Churches and sects; but still it is a consolation held out by all forms of Christianity except Calvinism, that the old vessel of self, after disastrous voyage and seemingly total wreck on earth, can yet be repaired and refitted for another and a happier venture, if not for a final, sure, and certain haven of rest; but whether, on quitting the earth and leaving this life, the soul launches on prosperous or perilous seas, whether it reaches the islands of the blest or is pent with "those whom lawless and uncertain thoughts imagine howling," the soul, according to all theologians, is immortal, and will preserve its individuality and its present consciousness for ever.

§ 3. But Science, for her part, finds no grounds for the beliefs of theology or metaphysics in a future life—beliefs, moreover, which she regards as little comforting at the best. If her instruments and methods of research, so successful in other fields of inquiry, can be relied upon when applied to man himself, as adequate to measure the full range and to sound the lowest depths of his nature; and if, moreover, the report handed in respecting that nature is accurate and exhaustive, which assures us that man is only the higher and more developed animal, whose mental nature is only a function of his bodily organism;—then the final conclusion seems to follow irresistibly, that immortality, the eternal prolongation of the mental individuality after the dissolution of the associated organism, is an inconceivable and an incredible thing. This is, indeed, the distinct conclusion of all merely scientific thought when directed to the question; and here the arguments advanced demand our greatest and most serious attention. Let us proceed to unfold them more fully.

Thought, emotion, volition, the psycho-physiologist tells us, the three things which make up consciousness, or the mental side of the man, are inseparably bound up with the brain and nervous system, whose functions they are, just as it is the function of the heart to pump up the blood, and of the lungs to aërate it; and as all functions one day evidently cease their work together—the heart to beat, the eye to see, the lungs to breathe—by what logic, it is demanded, can an exception be made in favour of thinking, the function of the brain, which as palpably ceases as all the rest? Can thought go on after the dissolution of the brain, the thinking organ? Indeed, if thought, if consciousness be only a function of the brain, to put the question thus is to show the absurdity of the doctrine of a future life. For can a function be even imagined to exist without the organ whose action in fact constituted its sole existence? The soul, of whose future existence you speak, is nothing but our consciousness composed of its threefold contents, and these are only functions of the bodily organism—the highest functions, it is allowed, but still only functions, all of which must cease together with the body. Is not the power of muscular movement palpably arrested when the limbs become rigid; and the power of thought, is it not to all appearance as palpably? why should the appearance be deceptive in the one case rather than in the other? It is not a case of an independent entity temporarily lodged in the body which merely changes its residence at death, or of an entity which could exist without any bodily residence, as Plato and Butler and the metaphysicians generally conceived it; it is the case of a power, or function, or faculty, which ceases with its appropriate bodily organ. Or, if you prefer it, it is the case of an effect which ceases, like every effect, with its proper cause; for the brain is the cause of thought in the strict scientific sense, that the former is the sum of the antecedent conditions, in the absence of which thought is never produced, but which, being given, carries the power of thought invariably with it. And that thought is fully and adequately described as the function of the brain; that it is nothing more, and nothing other (for to regard it as a case of causation amounts to the same thing), is proved, according to physiologists, by abundant and increasing evidence.* It is proved by our own varied experience in the effort of thinking, as well as by the report of the most competent psychologists and physiologists who have studied the subject, and who show us in proof of the statement the constant concomitant variations in the state of the brain, and in the faculty of thought, in youth and in age, in sickness and in health. In short, thought grows with the growth of the brain, it strengthens with its strength, it varies with its health, declines with its general vigour, and, must we not conclude, by the canons of inductive logic, that it finally dies, as it appears to do, with its dissolution?

Add to this what embryology shows us, that consciousness came by slow degrees from unconsciousness. Once there was absolutely no thought, no consciousness, which was gradually evolved from the growing organism as the final outcome and flower of it. We are sure from this circumstance that the relation between the body and soul is

* Bain's *Mind and Body*.

of the most intimate and essential nature. The soul was evolved out of the body, as the flower from the plant; it came with the body, and must it not go with the body, as Haeckel argues?*

§ 4. Moreover, there is a wholly new argument now adduced by naturalists as a result of the Darwinian doctrine of descent, which, it is thought, should finally lay this question of man's immortality for ever at rest.

According to this argument, which is wholly independent of the physiological ones just considered, man is only the higher animal slowly evolved from the lower, with intellectual and moral qualities differing only in degree, and not in kind, from the lower; why, then, should he not share the common final fate of all the animals? He is not an infinitely superior being, separated, as he once fondly supposed, by an impassable gulf from the rest of living beings; the very attributes which he possesses only in higher degree, and in virtue of which the claim to immortality has been preferred in his behalf, the other animals possess in some degree, and, indeed, together with intellectual qualities not inconsiderable, in the possession of some of the highest moral attributes—courage, fidelity, patience, self-sacrifice, affection—some of the lower animals, the dog, the horse, the ant, far surpass him; while in the human species itself, as is well known, these same higher qualities, mental and moral, exist in all degrees, from their almost total absence in the savage whether untutored or civilized, up to the intellectual height of a Shakespeare or a Newton, and to the moral splendour of a Socrates or a Buddha;—is it, then, to be contended that every man, from the saint, the sage, and the

* *History of Creation*, vol. ii. p. 361.

martyr, to the savage, the fool, and the man "more brutish than the brute," and still more that every animal, from the man down to the mollusc, is to possess the dread and extraordinary attribute of immortality? No, certainly; not every animal; only the man, we are told. But even with this sharp separation of man, there would be abundant difficulties in admitting all men equally to immortality, as we have just seen. Unfortunately, however, this separation, this arbitrary exclusion of the lower animals, can no longer be made, if once the Darwinian doctrine of man's descent be admitted. And, indeed, long before Darwin's doctrine had been heard of, Bishop Butler almost admitted that the arguments for man's immortality apply equally to the case of the brutes; all of them except one, specified as peculiar to mankind, namely, our capacity for intellectual life independent of the body, after ideas had been once gained through the senses;—an exception which he would scarce have made if he had known all that Science, after the research of a century and a half, has since revealed to us in physiology, psychology, and natural history;—if he had only fully realized the truth that the very highest life of the intellect and the soul is, at bottom, conditioned by physiological processes, and that the intelligence as well as the moral qualities of the brutes differs not in nature, but only in degree from our own.*

But the doctrine of man's descent once granted, there can be no arbitrary exclusion of the brutes, and no special

* See Butler's *Analogy*, ch. i., "On a Future Life;" in which he speaks of the "natural immortality of brutes," and even of the possibility of their being endowed with latent mental and moral capacities, though it does not seem to have occurred to him that they have actual faculties of this sort, both of which are clearly manifested in all social communities, as the ants, bees, and many others (see Darwin's *Descent of Man*, vol. i. ch. ii. and iii.).

elevation of man to the privilege of a future life. And that man is, indeed, descended from the lower animals, in particular from some extinct variety of the ape species, is the undoubting conviction of all biologists, who alone are competent to pronounce an opinion on the question; a conclusion, moreover, which, though deducible from Darwin's theory of development as an evident corollary, is also supported by so much independent evidence drawn from comparative anatomy and embryology, that it would remain unaffected by any future qualifications or corrections that may be made in that theory.

That man is an animal is the great and special discovery of natural science in our generation. He is only an animal, though the highest of the animals, who has been raised to his pre-eminence partly by the long-continued favour of fortune, partly by his own efforts, but not by any means by special creation or special favour shown him after his supposed creation. He but started his career with a slightly better capital of physical and mental endowment than any of his original competitors, and this slight mental advantage it was which, supplemented by a long run of good fortune, enabled him at length so far to surpass all the rest, that he actually came in time to believe he was of an infinitely superior nature to any of them.

He had far surpassed the lower animals in the race; he had conquered them, and subjected some to his service; and as he was really ignorant of his true origin, and also as his naturally vain and presumptuous disposition had been further stimulated by his successful career, he began, after the manner of parvenus, to take on grand airs, and at length succeeded in persuading himself that he had a far other and nobler origin than his humbler brute brethren, and was made of more ethereal elements than entered into their composition; that he was entitled to another life succeeding this; and finally, as the climax of madness and presumption, to a never-ending life. As Alexander, drunk with the fumes of flattery and pride, assumed the god, and suffered divine honours to be paid to him by the priests in Egypt, so our poor presumptuous man at last persuaded himself that he was a god,—for to such a height does the belief in a life interminable virtually amount.

A strange and extravagant fancy that arose one day in the breast of one more aspiring than the rest, became soon afterwards a wish; the wish became a fixed idea, that drew round itself vain and spurious arguments in its favour; and at length the fancy, the wish, the idea, was erected into an established doctrine of belief. Such, in sum, is the natural history of the famous dogma of a future life. Not by any means, however, was it a primitive and universal belief of all nations. Arising probably at first with the Egyptians, it was only after a long time taken up by the Jews, then, or possibly earlier, by the Greeks, with whom, however, the life held out, thin and unsubstantial even at best, was far from being desirable. It was only in the Christian and Mohammedan religions that the notion of a future and eternal life was fully developed, and that the doctrine was erected into a central and essential article of belief.

But now, if man be derived by insensible stages of development from the lower animals, then, unless they also are immortal, the question is irresistibly forced upon us, when and how man became immortal. When did he first become separated so decisively from all lower forms of life? and when did he become differentiated from his nearest of kin by so prodigious an attribute as immortality? Shall it be said that he was immortal from the beginning of his career?—then so must also have been the brutes, for at the beginning he was indistinguishable from them. On the other hand, if he only became immortal later on, he must have either slowly acquired the gift or else it was suddenly conferred upon him. In either case, there must have been a particular moment or day when he became immortal. And is it possible to conceive that the species was mortal one day or moment, and immortal the next? And then the question *how* he became immortal is still more difficult; as the question *why*, or for what merit or demerit, having been previously mortal like the brutes, and not more moral, he became liable to an eternity of happiness or misery, is wholly unanswerable. Possibly, however, only superior spirits, and those who strongly desired it, were privileged with the boon of immortality. But in that case, it is not an attribute of the species, and all pretence at constructing a universal argument in favour of it is given up. Indeed, these very questions that we must nevertheless raise, for they force themselves upon us, sufficiently show the absurd notion of the whole doctrine; as a moment's reflection on the kind of future life that religions offer us shows how little desirable it would be, even if a thing so tremendous were at all within the scope of possibility.

It is, nevertheless, the secret hope and aspiration of man's heart that he shall have another life, and in spite of his religions, that that life shall be a happier one; and to this the reply of Science is that the thing is incredible and impossible. The origin of man abundantly demonstrates the groundless nature of this special claim and hope; and of this origin he must be reminded when he manifests such aspiring blood. He must be told that he is only the higher animal, who has distanced the others in the struggle for existence, and that it is not clear how he has acquired any title to an immortal future merely by his successful efforts to advance himself—efforts, too, which would scarcely have been so successful had not fortune favoured him much beyond his merits. In short, he should rest satisfied with his earthly superiority; and when he aspires to immortality he must be emphatically reminded that he is only, with all his pride and after all his success, the superior social animal, scarcely even so much in some important particulars; that he is animal, and descended from the animals; of like bodily structure with some of them, and nourished as they upon earthly elements; that he sleeps and feeds and continues his kind even as they; and finally, his functions fulfilled, that he, as they, falls back upon the breast of the earth, the common nourisher and mother, for his final and eternal rest. The energy locked up in his frame, as in theirs, is let loose;— the energy which was only borrowed, but never created, and which in the wondrous bodily machine was transmuted into chemical, mechanical, electrical, vital, and mental forms, is now restored to the vast and universal reservoir of Nature, thence to be redistributed, and to cycle again in new or old forms of life, in man, or bird, or beast, or flower. The man dies as the brute; the imprisoned physical and chemical forces escape; but there is no imprisoned soul set free, that goes forth (as in the dream of Shakespeare's Clarence) to "seek the empty, vast, and wandering air." He dies, and there is an end; and, were he only wise, he should be thankful indeed that it is so determined. While grateful to Nature for the life he has had, he should, if happily constituted and circumstanced, be more grateful for this her crowning act of grace and indemnity shown in affording a secure final harbour of perfect rest and peace, an escape from the strife and turmoil of life, into the quiet regions of non-existence—the peaceful shores of Nirvâna, that Buddha promised as special reward only to the wise and good who had earned it on earth by severest virtue. Above all, he should be thankful to Science for having at last, but only in our days, finished the work of Lucretius and Epicurus, by delivering men from the superstitions and vain terrors, the fear of the gods and of death, that so long had tormented and oppressed them; for showing us what Nature's behaviour in the past to man has really been, what her good and peaceful intentions to him when he quits this life really are.

We are assured, indeed, by Bishop Butler that there is no true analogy in all Nature which would lead us to think that death will prove the destruction of a living creature;[*] none, save the delusive semblance of analogy, furnished by the decay and dissolution of the vegetables. But, we must ask, is not the life of the vegetable, the plant, palpably arrested and destroyed at its dissolution; and is not the life of the animal, including man, as palpably? And as the plant dies for ever as an individual plant, as all that goes to constitute it a plant is dissolved and scattered at the consummation of the event called death, so dies the animal in like manner. The phenomenon, whether to the eye of sense or of reason, is the same in both instances. Further still, there is no rigid line of separation between the plant and the animal; the naturalist cannot say when he has passed the boundaries of the one kingdom and entered

[*] *Analogy*, ch. i., "On a Future Life."

into the other; on this account also we must conclude that death, which destroys the one, destroys the other. As the plant dies, then, so dies the animal, and as the animal dies, so also the man, for in like manner there is no rigid line of separation between them, and no special reason to be urged why man is to have an exceptional immortality. But since the candid and philosophic bishop wrote more than a century ago, only too many analogies have been suggested by Science from her several regions of inquiry—astronomy, geology, physiology, natural history—all pointing to the one conclusion that all individual things must die, the animal as the vegetable, the man as the animal; nay, even the stars, the sun, the earth itself, with all that ever flourished upon it, including the human soul.

The earth herself shall perish; her energies exhausted, like those of the moon, her motion in space constantly impeded, and her orbit narrowed, she will finally become precipitated upon the parent sun. But long before that distant catastrophe, our species shall have vanished from off the earth. For Science shows us that man, though the most remarkable and brilliant phenomenon that has appeared, was only a comparatively late arrival on the stage of our planet, and she further clearly hints that he may have to depart comparatively soon. The records of geology show us the general law, that all species have their term of being. They appear, and after a period disappear. They have, as individuals, their exits and their entrances and their several stages. Man, too, will disappear, as other species have done. We can even foresee the possible causes which may lead to this result. His fuel, his food, his heart, or his virtue may fail him. His fuel may fail from exhaustion; his food from blight, from innumerable noxious insects, defying his means of destruction, from sterility in the earth induced by exhaustion, from the competition of lower animals; worse than all, his own heart may fail if the creed of the pessimist prevails. With all these is he threatened, and one would be sufficient to cause his extinction. But however it happen, and however long the end be delayed, the belief of science is that, as our species is not coeternal with the earth, as it came one day on the stage, so it will one day vanish. And the day may not be so remote, as our poet makes Lucretius say—

> That hour perhaps
> Is not so far when momentary man
> Shall seem no more a something to himself;
> But he, his hopes and hates, his homes and fanes,
> And even his bones long laid within the grave,
> The very sides of the grave itself, shall pass,
> Vanishing, atom and void, atom and void,
> Into the unseen forever.

How absurd, then, to raise a question as to the immortality of the countless myriads of a species that in time shall itself have utterly vanished, without leaving a trace; the very memory of which shall have passed out of the consciousness of the universe, if any such be left after the disappearance of man! How presumptuous to suppose that Nature so values these countless individuals as to think it worth her pains to preserve their souls for ever! Immortality was a doctrine begotten of man's presumption, and suitable to his days of ignorance, when he believed that the earth was the central and only important body in the universe; that he himself was specially created, and wholly different from the animals; and that his soul was a most precious thing, which must at all hazards be saved in the economy of Nature. It is not a doctrine that harmonizes with the views of life and the universe that modern science discloses, still less with the more modest estimate of his own nature and merits, that the judgment of every rational man, in confirmation of the conclusions of science, must, if he is only fair and candid with himself, inevitably come to.

CHAPTER VI.

ON IMMORTALITY: COUNTERTHESIS.

§ 1. SUCH is the argument of Science, seemingly decisive against a future life. As we listen to her array of syllogisms, our hearts die within us. The hopes of men, placed in one scale to be weighed, seem to fly up against the massive weight of her evidence, placed in the other. It seems as if all our arguments were vain and unsubstantial, as if our future expectations were the foolish dreams of children, as if there could not be any other possible verdict arrived at upon the evidence brought forward.

Nevertheless, it is a remarkable fact that there still exist amongst us types of mind quite distinct from the theological, that remain wholly unconvinced by the scientific logic—men who cannot and will not accept the verdict as final. There are those who persist in believing, however seemingly rigorous the reasoning, however true the premises from which the conclusion is drawn, and however apparently exhaustive the whole series of scientific arguments, that still there is a hidden vice, an undetected flaw somewhere; there is something not yet taken into account in these arguments addressed to the logical understanding; a side or aspect of our nature omitted from the scientific map of the mind, the omission of which nullifies or vitiates the positive argument, the consideration of which would justify our title to immortality. The poet, the mystic, the spiritualist, the moral idealist, whoever has deeply loved, whoever has greatly suffered, will not hear of a conclusion which forbids the hope in a future of redress, of reunion, of happiness; and we should not be doing justice to our theme of debate if we did not grant a hearing to some of these dissidents, who moreover can put their objections into words, not merely founded on fancy, as the men of science are wont to affirm, but apparently founded on fact, appealing to the reasoning faculty, and sometimes carrying conviction with them. Let us, then, hear the reply of the spiritualist.

According to your argument, urges the latter, all thought is bound up with the bodily machine or organism, and disappears with it, and if all organisms disappear, as Science teaches they will, then all mind would also vanish from the universe. Either this must be, or mind can exist without the bodily machinery, which scientific materialism does not grant. And is this extreme scientific conclusion credible? Is it possible that mind,—the thing so splendid in its higher manifestations, with its vision of beauty, its depths of tender affection, its godlike apprehension of truth, its divine enthusiasm for right,—this subtle and wonderful essence, so slowly gathered and distilled through countless ages, as evolution teaches, should be thus recklessly spilt and lost again out of the universe? Is this wonderful and potent extract from matter, rising through life, through animal sensations, till, thrice sublimed, it became thought and spirit, which searches the secret of the universe, and through Philosophy and Science herself has partly found it,—is this wonderful quintessence, the inmost nerve and life of Philosophy, of Art, as well as of Science herself, to be thus finally wasted? Is Nature so blind and stupid, as well as so foolishly wasteful of her gathered gains, as to throw away the grandest thing—the only really great thing she had reached, and to throw it away just when she had perfected it? The thing, moreover, to attain to which it seems that all her efforts were bent, and towards which all her labours in all directions finally converged? And is it credible, or even thinkable, that all thought and consciousness should finally perish out of the universe?—for to this length the scientific argument really goes, maintaining, as it does, that not merely my individual consciousness, and all others resembling mine, must cease, but that the human species itself must perish in process of time, together with the earth, the sun, our system, and finally all the systems of the universe. Is it thinkable that all consciousness should perish, and that eternal night and nothingness should set in? that the universe should return once again to the cosmic vapour and the eternal silence from which it first proceeded? For this is the alternative; since science has not made the provision of philosophy or religion for the preservation of mind by the postulate of an Eternal Spirit, or, at least, of a great universal mind different from all individual ones. We might have become reconciled to the belief, however insufficient the evidence for it appears to be, that the earth, the sun, nay, even all the spheres of space, should die; we might have even accepted the extinction of our hopes of individual immortality; but when we find that the same argument which destroys all these and ourselves brings us in the end to a universe of death, we must conclude there is a vice in the reasoning which leads to a conclusion so desperate and absurd. For who could really believe that this marvellous thing called mind is but a brilliant meteor, that flashed for a brief moment in the infinite night, and then faded again into eternal darkness? that Nature, after her long, deep, unconscious sleep, should have a bright dream called consciousness, to be succeeded by her heavy slumber of death again?

We cannot accept this conclusion, so that if immortality, the continued existence of the individual, be as science maintains, inconceivable and incredible; her own conclusion, which is bound up with, and a corollary from, her demonstrated impossibility of immortality, is still more incredible. The scientific argument leads to an inconceivable terminus, equally with the opposite argument for a future individual life. The mind, thus placed between seemingly contradictory conclusions, happily bethinks itself that it is after all only finite; that it cannot possibly exhaust the possibilities of being and of existence; that it does not even know, nor can Science say, what the conditions of consciousness, and still less of our own self-consciousness may be, so as to be in a position to conclude positively that the latter must cease at death. These things being borne in mind together with a final mystery unexplored and inexplorable at the bottom of the universe and of all existence, allow of the possibility of a state of mind, too much overlooked by the dogmatists of science, called doubt, or suspense of judgment; and this suspense permits a breathing space for the higher and healthier state called hope, a thing which even a positive thinker like Mill, building his philosophy on the data of positive science, would not wholly take away from men. Thus, in the final mystery of the universe, great, black, and unsounded by scientific plummet, uninterrogated by experiment or observation, now lies our hope; in the great sphere of the possible, which Science should know is great, and which scientific thinkers like Herbert Spencer assure us is very great indeed, there is ground for our hope of further life ; and this hope, as it has ample room to live, so it resides in a region, it is fed from a source, which is perfectly secure from all possible assaults or check by positive science.

And the answer of the positive scientific thinker to this line of argument is something to the following effect:—

Whether consciousness is to be finally lost out of the universe is a question that might be discussed, and on the whole Science leans to the opinion that it will be lost; but at least there is no question about the final extinction of our particular consciousness. It goes with its old physical basis, the body, and in particular with the brain, the organ of memory, without which there is no consciousness. And we are asked—Is Nature so wasteful and so blind as to throw away consciousness after painfully attaining to it? Yes: she is blind and wasteful and indifferent; such is the lesson of evolution. But she can afford to be wasteful, for she is infinitely rich, as astronomy teaches. There are other stars and suns and systems in the universe, enough and to spare, where consciousness and life, and perhaps something better and greater, has been produced, or perhaps life and consciousness has there attained to fairer and statelier forms than on the earth, where it is just possible that the plastic forces of Nature have only made one of their poorest attempts, great as you are disposed to rate them. Moreover, Science has nowhere affirmed that all the systems of the heavenly bodies collapse at the same time; for these are infinite, and of unequal ages; they only die with years and when their energies are exhausted, as we do; while it is quite conceivable that in the depths of space, young stars and systems are being born. Thus the light of consciousness may never go out, but may be alight in innumerable worlds, even should it fail finally on one, namely, the earth. And again, even if the advanced speculation were generally accepted by scientific men, which decrees that, at the end of inconceivably remote ages, all the heavenly bodies will finally become resolved into one mass of uniform temperature, still even there life and consciousness might exist, as they might in the course of ages have become adapted to these altered conditions. So that consciousness may remain, and the night of nothingness which you dread may never take place. Consciousness may remain, or possibly something greater and better; for after all, the infinite possibilities of the universe, of which you have spoken and which Science does not deny, may allow, and almost to a certainty do allow of a much greater thing than consciousness. There was no reason in particular, no inner necessity, why consciousness should have flowered upon life; it does not do so in the case of the plants; and something else might have appeared as the flower and summit of life. Consciousness is not a necessary product of life: this Science allows; it is only an invariable effect in the animal kingdom on the earth; there may be a quite different effect elsewhere. There are many fields for Nature to try her experiments in, where matter may have had a different outcome and a much better one than consciousness. For as we know, the pessimists—now increasing in number, and reckoning men of science amongst them—lament much over this fact of consciousness, which some consider such a fine thing, but which they consider the grand error made by Nature, and the sad cause of all our woe—so much so, indeed, that a celebrated philosopher has been much exercising his mind how best this grand false step and capital blunder of Nature's may be corrected, even yet, though so late in the day. Hartmann, following Schopenhauer, as we know, labours strenuously to show us how this obstinate inherent disease in the inmost constitution of Nature, this continual breaking out into consciousness and individual life, may be finally eradicated from Nature's system. In a word, consciousness with Hartmann to-day, as with Buddha centuries ago, is the grand evil, for which Nirvâna, though differently sought for by each, is the accepted and the only cure.

Thus we see that the wise, weighing its evil against its good, are by no means agreed as to the desirability of consciousness. But however these questions be finally decided, if ever, by philosophers; whether consciousness be essentially an evil or no; whether it will finally fail altogether in the universe or no; whether there be greater and better things than consciousness elsewhere or no—on all which questions Science too has an opinion, though the present is not the place to press it;—the lesson which she categorically teaches with respect to you, the individual, is that your particular consciousness, and that of all men resembling you, bound up as each one is with its indispensable bodily basis, ceases at death. Further, though the lesson less materially concerns you, it is the teaching of Science that, at the end of a period not long in comparison with the long history of the earth, the human species, together with all that it ever produced, will disappear from the earth; and at the last, though this is less certain, and in any case will probably be immeasurably distant in comparison with the failure of our species, the earth herself will perish, by falling back upon the sun from which, in her state of nebulous vapour, she was originally separated.

Thus argues Science: but the admission that there are other worlds, with possibly higher forms of life and consciousness, possibly something better than consciousness, permits the mystic still to indulge a hope of further life. Let us grant him a hearing.

Might I not be caught up again after my departure hence, in some new and grander stream of evolution, in some other planet, sun, or star in the course of ages? Might I not find myself an atom, a conscious being, in this new stream of life, in the same entirely mysterious way as I once was on the earth? There is ample time ahead, and it is easy for the dead to wait till the favourable chance, the happy moment arises, which ushers me into life once more. There is endless time, there are infinite worlds, there are innumerable possibilities. Somewhere, then, sometime, and somehow, I shall be summoned up again; I shall awaken refreshed after my deep Lethean bath of sleep, and shall take part once again in the strange and mysterious, but withal interesting, drama of life and consciousness,—I know not how, or where, or when; but what has once happened can at least happen again, and with infinite chances may and likely will happen. The miracle and the mystery of my awakening from nothing into consciousness has undeniably once occurred; my next new birth will be only a repetition of the miracle which has once already occurred in my particular case. This is indeed so little inconceivable, that it is the fear and dread of the Buddhist that it will happen; it was to deliver the wise and virtuous man from this danger, so certain to the natural unregenerate man, that Buddha taught his one and only sure way to escape it into the blissful unconsciousness of Nirvâna.

And if we grant to Schopenhauer and Buddha that consciousness is necessarily an evil, still, after our extinction here, after having thrown off this mortal coil of individual life, this painful Nessus' shirt of earthly consciousness, which for ever frets and stings us,—may we not awaken no more into it, or into any individual consciousness, but only into the grand general consciousness where the torment and desires of individual life no more will follow us? May not our little single ray of reason remerge into the general light; our little rill flow back into the great ocean of being; our single soul become swallowed up in the mighty universal one; and may not we ourselves, an emanation of Deity, return to its parent source, as the great Averroes taught, and as Plotinus and the great mystics thought certain? Nay, does not Christianity itself, with its pessimist foundation, teach that somehow we shall leave behind this grievous weight of clay, and that with it our painful and weary earthly consciousness shall drop off; that we shall forget our past being and our terrible earthly experience; and that when we wake up after His likeness, it shall be, if not in union and absorption, at least in closer relation and more intimate communion, with Deity?

Thus argues the mystic, whose type is not extinct, as some suppose; and to him Science answers—

Something conscious, as you say in the beginning of your argument, may indeed awaken, that is, come into existence; but not you. Moreover, even if an actual transmigration of your soul into some other being somewhere else were even conceivable or possible, unless you add memory there is no possible bridge of communication or means of identifying you here on the earth with that other foreign consciousness severed from your present by none can say how much time and space. In short, if there be not the connection of memory, no possible consciousness anywhere, now or at any time, has any more relation to you than to any other conscious or unconscious being. That other would not be you : it would have no more relation to you than to any other being who may choose to claim relationship with it. It has no more relation to you than to the babe unborn, very much less indeed, for that possible being might conceivably enter into and take possession of it, which you in no wise could do.

"But if that other consciousness be not mine, if the other being be not me, it will suit all as well," obstinately pursues the mystic. So be it, says the positivist scientific thinker; but we cannot continue the argument to profit on these metaphysical lines. Your doctrine will, however, serve you little, regarding the matter from a different and a somewhat more intelligible point of view. For the list of possibilities of existence, the number and variety of conscious beings that may arise in infinite worlds, being so prodigiously beyond the range of even imagination, the chances would be decidedly against your drawing a prize in that vast lottery if all went by chance, or fate the same as chance; while of your merit, if place goes by merit, we need scarcely, in our present argument, rate yours at more than the average, which should only secure an average return—the highest merit, moreover, being only moderate. In fact, whether fortune or merit should determine your new position, the chances would be decidedly against your drawing a prize in that huge lottery, as it still would be, of possible existence. The chances are all against your coming out even so well or so high up in the list as you have done in the present life. If you are optimist, satisfied with the present course of things, the chances are many to one against the like good fortune again; while if you are pessimist, the odds, though not so heavy, still are that the change into a new consciousness would be one from bad to worse, so that, all things considered, you should thankfully accept the conclusion of Science, which allows no hope of any future life whatever.

As for sharing in the general consciousness, if any such thing there be, science professes her inability to form any conception of such a state, and prefers to abandon speculations of this description to those who like them—the mystic, the metaphysician, the religious devotee. Her final conclusion is, in brief: You die as an individual; you shall never meet this dear self, or ego, again, from which you are so loth to separate, in all the realms of space or endless periods of time. And on the whole, be thankful that it is so determined in the decrees of the universe, remembering the possibilities and undoubted hazards that, under any rational estimate of chances, you would have to encounter; and remembering, too, the dread and formidable fears and terrors that in all dogmatic religions gather around this central doctrine of a future life. These fears now fall off and disperse of themselves—fears far more terrible than the countervailing hopes were consoling; and men are now at last at liberty to turn to their proper work in the world untroubled and undismayed by the thought of a future which in no way concerns them; for which great emancipation they have to thank Science, together with that modern criticism set in motion mainly by the conclusions of Science, and still guided by her spirit and methods of proof.

§ 2. And our dear ones, are we to meet them never more? Our loved ones, for whom we would have given our blood, for whom we cheerfully suffered and made sacrifice, are we to see them no more in the field of time? Was, then, the terrible and agonized adieu by the grave's side in truth the last, the eternal farewell? If it be so, alas for earthly love! If it be so, then has Nature been malignantly mocking us when she gave us the feelings of love and affection, and made them so sweet. If it be so, we have been betrayed, and Nature, that we thought loved us, is not only deaf and blind, but has a heart of stone.

We do not ask a hereafter as a recompense for our poor virtues, nor an eternity to attain to perfection in virtue, nor yet to the full blaze of knowledge; we desire a hereafter to meet again with those we have loved, those whose presence we found on earth so fair. Virtue and knowledge are good, but the heart is left out of count in these arguments, which postulate an eternity to attain to perfection in knowledge and virtue. The heart is left out in the arguments of the philosophers, and the heart's simpler logic only asks a future for the reunion of souls. And wherefore not? Is not love and affection the most divine thing that Nature evoked in the long course of her evolutions? Is it not the greatest thing in consciousness; greater than will, greater than knowledge? Has it not been "mightier far, than magic potent over sun or star," to move the soul, to move the world? And is not the attraction of soul to soul more wonderful than that of star to star? It is our love that demands a hereafter. And Nature, so rich in her potentialities, so infinite in her resources, can she not accomplish this? So good; will she not accord us this? Nay, then, the imperious hunger of our hearts, the very might of our desires, which are a part of Nature, will force her! She must grant us this boon. She must grant the reunion, having made the union so sweet. We adjure her by all that we have enjoyed, by all that we have suffered: by our agonies at the open grave, and at the dying bed; by the might and beauty of earthly love enjoyed; yea, by the grief and pain of earthly love disappointed and driven back upon itself; and by the martyrs who have died for love of man;—we demand a hereafter of reunion, of compensation; we demand another life and stage for love.

Alas! alas!—What answer can we make to this—the eternal and terrible cry of the human heart? For we touch here at the primal and true source of the desire for another life, and of all the arguments in favour of it. We touch, too, at the real sting of death in the dread of the eternal farewell, the fear that on the further side of that forgetful shore our earthly love cannot revive or live. "Love listens and paler than ashes," as Science coldly replies to this logic of the affections:—

There is no hope, she tells us, of this future of reunion any more than of that other future communion with the good and wise. Nature *is* deaf and blind to such appeals and arguments. Our most vehement wishes are impotent to make Nature do this great and impossible thing. In fact, she could not support such a prodigious and ever-accumulating burden of life. For the animals, too, have their affections; and the dog wishes not to be severed from his master; so that the animals also must have a hereafter. But why go over again the old arguments? In a word, there would not be room in space for all the old individual lives, and these are ever on the increase. And again, Nature *is* cruel and regardless of our tears. We can clearly see that things are not arranged so as to meet our dearest wishes. Far otherwise. They are arranged so as to abundantly defeat and disappoint them. So Nature shows herself here and now; why then should she not disappoint you in your hopes of a hereafter of compensation? But be comforted; what you complain of is only a pain during this life, and moreover a diminishing pain, as Nature has provided mitigations. Hereafter you will not feel the loss of what you now so passionately ask. Further, mankind shall in time reconcile themselves to the thought that this life is the only theatre for earthly love—a conclusion that should carry with it the serious admonition, to prize more highly those that we love, from whom we must part so soon; to cherish more dearly the love that lives only on earth. But will not the conclusion tend also to harden the heart? It need not be feared; though a little hardness might not be amiss in regard to this matter. At least it will throw an additional and ineffable sadness over life? It may be so; but it also removes a standing menace from life, in killing the future fear as well as hope.

§ 3. And now that this great question has been sufficiently debated, it remains for us to review briefly the main points in the evidence, and to state what material points have been established by Science, and what she has failed to establish.

Science, we think, has made out the dependence of our mind and present consciousness on bodily conditions, so far as to justify the conclusion that the dissolution of the body carries with it the dissolution of our present consciousness and memory, which are reared on the bodily basis. At least, it raises apprehension in the highest degree that this will be the case. Again, Science—partly by what Darwin has established, partly by other evidence only recently accessible respecting the low state of the primitive man—has brought the human species into the general circle of the animal kingdom, in a sense far more deep and essential than was formerly dreamed of; and she has thereby deepened the belief, though without producing absolute conviction, that the arguments proving a possible future life for man hold likewise for the lower animals; so that if man be judged immortal they should be also, and if they be mortal so also is man. Thirdly, Science has called attention to the fact that there is something like a general law discoverable in the history of species, that they all have their term of years, though the term is usually a long one, and that probably therefore the human species itself, as well as all other existing species, will disappear, giving place to wholly different though derivative types of life. And all these things taken together, undoubtedly tend strongly to produce the conviction that death closes the career of the existing individual.

Nevertheless, we still think that Science has not shown, nor can any argument that she can possibly advance show, that we may not have another existence, or even a series of such existences, after the termination of the present one; and as this may appear an unexpected and illogical conclusion after the preceding admissions, we are bound to explain the position more clearly, as well as to try to defend it.

Science has not proved, nor can she prove, that a conscious being may not hereafter emerge somewhere, in which or through which I may awaken again into being. But it would not be really you, Science and common sense together exclaim; it could not be you without memory to make the link of connection, the bond of identity, between that other being and you, between that supposed self and your present self. No matter, we say, that other will be all as good as me, if the same feeling of individuality and self-consciousness gathers round it then and there, as here and now. And it may be me to all intents and purposes without memory. For memory is not necessary to the peculiar unique feeling of self-consciousness which I have at this moment. Memory is necessary to connect my present with my past experience, my present with my past consciousness; but it is not necessary in order to have the peculiar feeling of individuality or self-consciousness unshared by any other being, which is the essence of the fact of self. There may have been past existence without memory; there may be a future existence without memory, just as my present feeling of conscious existence is independent of memory. This last feeling may have place if all memory were suddenly annihilated, as it sometimes is under certain diseases, under abnormal psychical states, and even every morning in all of us for a moment after waking from sleep. But how, without the absurdest metaphysical theories, objects the positivist, could that other and future consciousness be you? How and in what sense can another being be you, more than any one else, without the fact of memory to make the identification? The reply, then, in a word, is—We cannot tell how; but also it is to be particularly noted that the feeling of self-consciousness, and of how I am myself now, is equally indescribable, equally beyond analysis or explanation. None can tell what makes it, how I have it, why it did not associate itself with another rather than me, why it did not become the conscious covering to another ego as its real core rather than mine,— why, in a word, to put it in the extremest form, it was not another being rather than I which was born when I was born, and which slowly awoke into consciousness instead of me; and none can pretend for a moment to affirm that the same strange mystery of awaking from unconsciousness into conscious being, which has already once happened in my case, may not happen once again. The questions clustering round the fact of my present self-consciousness are the most insoluble mysteries; but, nevertheless, they all relate to a fact realized in each and all of us; and since I am a conscious individual now, without my knowing how I am so or how I became so, why, it may be asked, may the like not have place once again? or, indeed, more than once?

But is not all this mysticism, or the old unintelligible and vicious metaphysics? Mysticism, metaphysics, it may be; but, nevertheless, it also expresses a fact that has been, that is; and it only asks us to conceive the possibility of the like occurring again. Nay, even though it should be pronounced mysticism, it is the belief of the mightiest philosophers, poets, and religious founders. For the greatest of these, though they announced and taught a future existence, still did not make it merely a continuation of our present one, a sort of second volume of our earth history, with a recollection of the first; they—at least the greatest of them—regarded a future life as certain and natural, even without memory; the insoluble question not being at all raised how we could awake to conscious life again in the absence of it. They cut the knot of this metaphysical entanglement in the Pythagorean and Buddhist doctrine of transmigration, in the Platonic doctrine of pre-existence, and in most of the great religious systems that have obtained sway over men. That we shall have many future existences before final extinction is, indeed, the great grief of the Buddhist, as that we shall have only one, be it of happiness or misery, is the belief of the Christian, though a memory of the past is not implied under either religion. The greatest poets, too, as well as philosophers and founders of religions, have had this thought of another existence; and the poets must count for much in the argument, since they possess in higher degree than others the great creative faculty of imagination which outlines the province of the possible beyond the reach of other men. They see, at least the greatest of them see, more clearly than men possessing only the logical intellect and a more limited range of intuitions, what may be possible, and how much there is room for in the nature of things. And does not the very greatest of poets, who was also supreme as a thinker, while treating this great question of a future life through the thought of Hamlet, regard a further existence as possible, without any necessary recollection of the past? Has Shakespeare not carefully considered the scientific conclusion, " To die, to sleep—no more," and while judging this a good thing and "a consummation devoutly to be wished" in face of the multiplied miseries of life which he enumerates, does he not also reject it as an insufficient determination of the question by qualifying the natural suggestion, "to die, to sleep," by the noteworthy addition, " to sleep, perchance to dream;—ay, there's the rub"?

In fact, this mighty spirit, in profound philosophic insight, as in all else incomparable, has given a summary of the whole argument in this memorable soliloquy, which has never been approached by savant or philosopher for depth and weight and point, and he has condensed the conclusions of both sides in this great debate, as well as the whole result of the argument, into a single line—

> To die, to sleep;—to sleep, perchance to dream.

Here are the alternatives (and we have not got much beyond this as yet upon the question); the first clause denoting the scientific conclusion; the second, with all that the word "dream" vaguely suggests, denoting that possibility of further life which we are here maintaining.

And not only the greatest of all poets, another only less than he, but having the one advantage over him of being a man of science and a discoverer in science, as well as poet —Goethe, the greatest of poets since Shakespeare, calm as well as emotional, a deep thinker too as well as a savant and poet, has believed in a life to follow this. It is true that he seems also to have believed in the continuation of consciousness and of the present life, because it breaks off unfinished here—an argument more than questionable. Apart from this, however, a future life recommended itself to his sober judgment as rational; while there are also evidences from other utterances of his that he did not consider a recollection of the earthly life necessary in order to realize the existence that follows it.

We have spoken of the poets; and now let us add the name of but one philosopher—that of Kant already cited. We name Kant for two reasons: first, because he was, like Goethe, a man of science, and a bold and original inquirer in science, as well as amongst the greatest of speculative thinkers. He, therefore, could look through both the scientific and philosophic glasses, and compare their respective clearness and ranges of vision. Further, scarcely amongst all the sons of men is there one that could be named, who devoted to this very question thought so deep, so strenuous, so long-sustained. And what was the report of Kant, after the meditation of years, and after regarding the question from all possible sides? It is to be read in his *Critique of Practical Reason*. I have already given the result in the preceding chapter. Let me briefly restate it. Kant believes in a future life. He confesses that he has not proved it speculatively. It can never be so proved that doubts may not be raised respecting it—doubts which are of the very essence of the question, and which it is scarcely desirable should be wholly removed. A future life is a necessary postulate of the practical reason; though whether the real ego which is to survive remembers, or cares to remember, the present life, is a point necessarily left obscure from the fact that the doctrine has not been proved from the side of the speculative reason.

§ 4. Another existence, then, is possible, likely, certain; nay, more than one such. Somewhere else after this existence closes, I may find myself again slowly awakening from a second birth, into conscious being, as once before on the earth, and in a manner wholly inexplicable even as then. But what species of conscious being—animal, angel, man once more, or something greater than any of these? and where?—in another planet, in the stars as Plato surmised, once again in our old earth, or haply out of relation to any space as Kant thought possible,—who dare pretend to say with certainty?

Further yet; as consciousness itself may rise to highest or sink to lowest content, as it may vary from the worm's to the man's, from faintest sensation to the inspirations of genius, so there may be in an infinite universe something grander and greater than any actual or conceivable consciousness. There may be species of existence, modes of being unnamable by us, which are yet infinitely superior to consciousness, more to be desired than consciousness; and this chapter of greater chances is open to us likewise. But by no means are we hinting that mere blank non-being, the mere privation of our present conscious being as shown in the stone or clod, is a greater thing than consciousness; nor that Nirvâna, the dark goal of the Buddhist's hopes— the mere stripping off of all our present modes of consciousness, sensation, desire, affection, aspiration, thought, and hope, as hindrances, not helps to happiness or peace—is superior to consciousness, or the greater thing that we may reach hereafter. We do not mean to imply that the unconscious existence of the stone, of the wave, of the cloud nor yet that the blank nonentity, the sudden precipitation into eternal darkness, and our reduction to nothing (if any such thing be possible in Nature), which the extreme materialist contemplates as the only outlook after death, is the better state than consciousness. Not any of these things, even if any of them be thinkable or possible. What, then, do we mean ? This : that the division of the sphere of existence roundly into two parts, the conscious and unconscious, is misleading; the second segment of the sphere, to wit, the unconscious, containing vastly more than the first, while also its separate divisions and modes may be wholly different from each other, though all confounded under one name—the unconscious. To divide existence into the conscious and unconscious provinces is as if we were to divide animals into men and not-men, where the second expresses a far greater sum of life than the first, though without reference to any of its differential features. So the word "unconscious," or not-conscious, strictly speaking, expresses no more than the absence of consciousness, while the sphere itself may embrace a much greater region than the conscious, while also it may have and it has modes of being greatly varied, amongst which some greater than consciousness may well have place. Thus in the unconscious sphere there are to be found the various physical forces and chemical elements; but besides these things, themselves unconscious though they reveal themselves to consciousness, there may be behind the phenomenal curtain something grander than consciousness, though indescribable, and not to be projected even in imagination upon the surface of any human consciousness.

There may be then, in the unconscious sphere, something better, greater, grander than any consciousness. There may be not one such state, but many, into one of which we may one day enter after we quit this present state. And now, what in particular may these states be? What are the states of being better than the highest conscious state, better or greater than the poet's vision of beauty, than the lover's paradise, than the enthusiast's rapture, than the sage's peace; better, again, than the unconscious bliss of Nirvâna, the pure holiday-time of simple non-existence, the utter extinction of consciousness, the *summum bonum* of Buddha and Schopenhauer? Ah! this we cannot tell. Philosophers, mystics, poets, prophets, and revealers are all as impotent as the men of science to say what may be, though they have been for ever putting their souls on the stretch to describe this great unexplored continent between consciousness and annihilation. To know and tell this would be to know and tell all. But "this eternal blazon must not be to ears of flesh and blood," nor can it be made by mortal mind. We await the only possible, the only real enlightener, Death ; or if death is only a word to express the failure of our present consciousness, we await the experience itself on the further shore.

Nevertheless, the great philosophers, poets, mystics, and revealers have all taught us something. They have shown us the possibility of such grander spheres of being, both conscious and unconscious, if they have not been able to describe the actuality by analogy, or similitude, or suggestion. They have both suggested the possibility and they have shown us the credibility of such other greater states. In particular, one conclusion of the greatest significance and importance, but left out in the scientific reckoning, has been suggested by philosophy, namely, that the removal of consciousness is not equal to annihilation, that death is not the eternal wind up ; that what follows is not the state of the flame when the oil that fed it is all consumed. In short, the suggestion of Science itself respecting matter and force, holds of consciousness and of existence generally— There is no creation or annihilation, but only a change of state. The conscious may pass into the unconscious, and into many and inconceivable varieties of the unconscious, and it may re-emerge into the conscious again, and the process may be, as sometimes we hope, and sometimes we dread, an *eternal one!*

Thus though we cannot describe higher forms of consciousness than we have actually experienced; and though we can still less tell what are the grander things than consciousness,—we can yet suggest the possibility of such to every one, as also in a certain sense the meaning of the assertion. Every one can see that with but four senses, with the sense of sight or hearing cancelled, our consciousness would not be so rich or wide as with our present five; also that if there were no such thing at all as the feeling of affection or the perception of beauty, both of which, in some people, are very faint, two of the greatest things would be removed from our inner consciousness. Thus there is a higher and a lower degree, a narrower and a wider area to consciousness even now. Still more, there may be great things and modes of being that could not enter through any of the usual avenues of the senses into consciousness at all, which would require a new sense, or several new ones, to give them to us. "It would be absurd," said Mill, "to assume that our words exhaust the possibilities of Being. There may be innumerable modes of it which are inaccessible to our faculties, and which consequently we are unable to name."*

And what we mean to imply is just this. There may be things that "eye hath not seen nor ear heard, nor hath it entered into the heart of man to conceive," as St. Paul affirmed. There may be "more things in heaven and earth than are dreamt of in our philosophy," as Shakespeare says. There may be infinite modes of being or attributes under which the one eternal substance can express itself, though to us men it has only revealed itself under the two forms of thought and extension, as Spinoza has taught. Silence is the proper, indeed the only, attitude for us in the face of these possibilities; but silence only after their existence has been pointed out and recognized; silence after we have called attention to them, and can speak no more regarding them; because to call attention to them is a

* *Examination of Sir W. Hamilton's Philosophy*, p. 14.

matter of moment to men that have hereafter to face these possibilities.

We know the existence of a world outside our conscious phenomenal world, as Kant affirms; but we know no more. Our ignorance is even greater than Kant believed; for, admitting the possibility of further existence, we cannot tell by what rule or law the succession of further existence will be determined. We cannot conclude with any degree of probability that our future places depend upon our earthly merit or demerit, both of these being on an average extremely limited, little dependent on individual will or effort, and receiving their natural rewards on earth.

§ 5. May not our future depend on our constant efforts and endeavour to conform our conduct to the moral law, to the well-known virtues of veracity, justice, benevolence, as some of the greatest of our species, philosophers and founders of religions, have taught us? We can scarcely so conclude to-day; for, though morality is evidently deep in the unfathomed Purpose and Power that rules and sustains the universe—the germs of it being implanted in our hearts and handed on by inheritance from generation to generation; and, moreover, social chaos and ruin resulting in its absence—yet apparently morality is still not the deepest thing in the universe, or even the chief thing aimed at on the earth in human society, which still subsists with a moderate amount of it, mixed with much of the contrary. Further yet; our virtues and vices, as such, are actually rewarded and punished on the earth; of average quality, they receive their average reward; and there exists no apparent reason in things why they should be rewarded and punished a second time hereafter—still less, if the monstrous notion

o

deserved any notice that they deserve an eternal reward or punishment.

There is no reason why any but exceptional virtues and vices which have failed to meet their due meed on earth, should be considered again. Except in these cases, there is no need for the supplemental correction of the earthly errors; and even in these cases, if we looked sufficiently deep, we should find that there is very little redress hereafter required, for by a subtle moral economy on the part of Nature, the eminently virtuous or vicious have already received their wages, not always the outer and material one indeed, but the inner and essential. In but few cases would the earthly inequitable decisions and arrangements require revision or redress; if we could look sufficiently deep into men's hearts to see their real pains and pleasures, the rewards and punishments that are here distributed. Wrong and injustice do exist, but the unjust are not therefore the happier even here; above all, the man of highest virtue has no cause of complaint, for Nature has paid him in a way that the others know not of—paid him, moreover, by the day and by the hour, paid him by the "piece-work" richly and liberally, in proportion to his work and in his work through the satisfied feelings flowing therefrom.

And is there nothing that we can do to better our chances in this great hereafter of possible existences? Scarcely anything, so far as reason can determine; the management of the beyond being subject to laws which transcend any pretence of reason to fathom. But though nothing positive can be stated, the doing or not doing of which would improve our future chances, yet there is a kind of premonition in our hearts that it is better and wiser to front the future, with its possible perils and felicities, with the consciousness of duty done and life well-spent; and bearing in mind this instinct of future desert or ill desert, be it rational or irrational, it is well to state that to aim at the perfection of our own being, as well as at the good of others so far as possible;—these two things, as on the whole they best promote our happiness here, so they may, though there is no certainty whatever on the matter, be of further profit to us in the future. They are at least more likely to profit than an opposite and vicious course, especially if accompanied with effort and sacrifice—a consideration which may afford some inducement to him who occupies a lower moral level to do his duty better, though the man of higher virtue will not need it. To the former the doing good actions over and above what society exacts, as of charity and mercy and pity, may be recommended as a good spiritual investment against future contingencies, which *may* be repaid with high interest, though it is also possible and rather more likely that Nature will repudiate the whole supposed debt. There seems, indeed, one case where she stands debtor—the case of sacrifice; of great sacrifice for principle, or other voluntary sacrifice, without expectation of reward, here or hereafter; and this, where nothing was demanded, may be the one case where the Purpose which rules the universe will acknowledge the obligation, though how, or where, or when, it would be hazardous to conjecture.

Our only consolation is our assurance that what takes place finally will, on the whole, be just and rational. It will be rational; for reason now rules the universe from the atom to the star, from the solar and sidereal systems to our more wonderful bodily and mental systems. It will, on the whole, be just; for though irregularities and brief pains may hereafter exist as now, so also they may be eliminated altogether as errors over which Nature has triumphed. We hope for improvement, upon the whole, for this fact of improvement in the evolution of something ever better is the deepest thing in the purpose of the universe, as even Science shows. Nature is capable of greater, juster, more rational things elsewhere, for she is constantly reaching after these things here, and with this assurance we may rest.

It may, however, be said that the further existence here shadowed forth is hardly worth the having, being indefinite, uncertain, unsubstantial, and little consoling at the best. And this may be true to an extent; still, it is not to the point. The question is not what we should like in the future, but what may possibly lie before us, what is the range of possibilities, and amongst these if there be any ground of reason, any likelihood that one thing rather than another should befall us. It may be said, too, that the doctrine is the old one of transmigration of Buddha and Pythagoras. Yes; in some respects, but not in all; for the transmigration here suggested may not only be into another consciousness, but also into something unconscious—a state to be carefully distinguished, however, from the utter non-being and imaginary annihilation of the materialist. But, on the whole, the doctrine is as little palatable as consoling, it will be said. Nevertheless, it contains a truth omitted alike in the dogmatism of science and in the dogmatism of theology. The existence here suggested is possible, likely, certain, while the annihilation of science is not possible; and the more express and definite pictures of theology will never be realized, there being seemingly no provision made for them in the economy of things. As to the prospect before us being unpalatable, it must be repeated that unpleasant existence may be possible hereafter as now; but there are also chances of something better than the present, and our hopes lie in this direction. Rationality and justice will rule there as here, and likely in higher degree; nay, even goodness, here evidently at work though shrouded, and evidently progressing though hindered, may be manifested in more unstinted measure; and fortified with these reflections, we may still front the future which none can avoid, with less fears than our fathers, and if not, on the other hand, with their firm faith and sanguine hope, yet not destitute either of faith or of hope.

This at least appears certain—we shall never escape out of the circle of existence into annihilation. We shall never get away either from consciousness higher or lower than our present, or from something quite other than consciousness, but quite as important and significant, and which yet is as far as the opposite pole from annihilation. We may have full and ample taste of both conscious and unconscious existence, in ways and modes that we dream not of, nor can describe, the present life being far from the conclusion of our "strange, eventful history."

§ 6. To recapitulate: What we here affirm is, that another and a conscious existence is possible, and more than one such. A higher conscious existence is possible, and also a lower; and amongst the many possible, the continuation of the present would seem the most likely of all, were it not for the difficulty of connecting the future drama and continuation with the present prologue—when the bridge of memory is broken down. Unconscious existence is also possible, as of the stone or the plant, and also, what is of much greater importance, unconscious existence of a great and grand order, which we cannot attempt to describe, but the notion of which all can see the drift of who have the poetic or pantheistic conception of a great universal spirit, and even all who think of God, the Infinite Spirit, as wholly unlike the finite spirit. Annihilation should also be included amongst the list of our possibilities, were it not that the word is a name which contains really only the minimum of meaning, or rather contains no meaning, except the cessation, the removal of existence in one form. For we have no evidence, but all the contrary, that there is any such thing. Science herself rather whispers that there is no creation, nor destruction, but only change. This is what she implies in her postulate of the indestructibility of matter, and in her proof of the conservation of energy. Further, even of the kind of existence of the stone, the wind, or the wave, of inorganic nature in general, we know nothing. To know, we should be, as the poet in his invocation to the West Wind—" Be thou, spirit fierce, my spirit "—desires to be. There may be a particular spirit even here, which we cannot perceive or fathom, even as we believe, without doubt, that there is one universal, mighty, all-pervading spirit, under these and all things, " a motion and a spirit that impels all thinking things, all objects of all thought, and rolls through all things."

And we are by no means certain that the best exponents of scientific doctrine would be disposed to contest these conclusions. Scarcely would Herbert Spencer, with his doctrine of the unknowable, and his various express declarations regarding the many and various possible forms of manifestation of the ultimate and transcendent power, which has only thrown out man as one of these manifestations, but who, with his marvels, will pass away, to be followed by other and unimaginable forms of existence. Nor could Haeckel, who affirms that the soul question is in a wholly different position from what it occupied twenty years ago; who thinks that "all matter is in a certain sense alive;" and who quotes Bruno approvingly to the effect that "a spirit exists in all things, and no body is so small but contains a part of the divine substance within itself, by which it is animated." These admissions allow room for a future existence different from annihilation, as they even allow for further conscious life; the only questions of difference remaining being whether the present "I" could ever partake in such further existence, and in what sense it could be said to be me, and how such existence now concerns me,—metaphysical questions, the difficulty of satisfactorily answering which is, indeed, too evident; but as very similar difficulties can also be raised about our present existence, we recommend them to be either avoided or briefly resolved, by simply affirming that an inexplicable thing which has once happened may happen again, without our being called upon to explain it further. What happens daily, what is for ever happening around us—the awakening into conscious life, the slow evolution from unconsciousness into conscious being—may happen again; nay, what happens to myself every morning when I awake out of deep sleep—death's counterfeit—may happen to me after death. I know not how; I am not bound to explain; nor can, in the one case more than the other.

What the men of science—physicists, physiologists, naturalists—seem really to imply and to intend to say, is that we cannot have a future life after death, because our mind and memory depend on the body, and are necessarily dissolved with it, while to have and to feel a future existence, we should at least carry our memory with us, to make possible the knowledge and identification of ourselves by ourselves. Now, for my part, I am disposed to accept the premise that our present memory ceases with the body, but for reasons already stated, by no means do I regard the whole argument as valid, or accept the conclusion drawn from it, that therefore we cannot have another life. This is the only difference between me and the men of science, which may, however, as already hinted, be really less than it seems.

BOOK II.

THE GOSPEL, AND THE SOCIAL CREED OF SCIENCE.

CHAPTER I.

PESSIMISM AND POSITIVE SCIENCE.

§ 1. THE new system of pessimism is a very remarkable phenomenon of these latter days. Appearing in an age of vaunted progress and great material prosperity, pessimism, as the shadowy handwriting on the wall at the banquet of the Babylonian monarch, pronounces our modern civilization as weighed in the balance and found wanting. Nay, our philosophical pessimism strikes deeper; it denounces conscious existence itself, however highly and variously developed as necessarily evil, as a fundamentally vicious thing, an all but irreparable error into which the ultimate principle of existence, unguided by reason, necessarily strayed.

Unlike the other current systems, pessimism takes its stand within, upon the fact of consciousness, which, far from having been an accidental appearance in the course of the evolution of the universe as the Evolutionist and Darwinian asserts, or a chance but unique product of the physical energies in the present bodily machine as the extreme materialist affirms, was and still is an essentially necessary outcome of the ever striving and dissatisfied will of the universe to live, and to attain to conscious being, if only to find (through the assistance of philosophers) the vanity of it.

Consciousness was a necessary result, a mistake that must have been made soon or late, here or elsewhere, but which, having been once made and found incurably bad, can only be finally set right by a retracing of the steps made by the unconscious will, by a return to unconsciousness. There is no other remedy; consciousness being demonstrably an evil in its nature, a ceaseless striving for something which it has not, and a constant dissatisfaction with what it already has. There is no remedy to be expected from its further development, which will only drive deeper its sting, and give us a keener sense of our poverty, vanity, and misery. In fact, the evils of life increase in direct proportion to the widening and deepening of our conscious life, and the most gifted, the men of the deepest thoughts and feelings, are the most unhappy of all. Such are the essential features of the modern pessimism.[*]

As an estimate of the worth of life, the pessimism of Schopenhauer and Hartmann is no new pronunciation. It is at least as old as the days of Job and of Solomon, the first of whom enlarges upon the misery, the second upon the vanity, and both upon the worthlessness of life. It is not even new as a metaphysical theory; for its essential conclusions, reached, moreover, by the same methods of metaphysical and psychological principles confirmed by an appeal to men's experience of life, were taught by Buddha more than twenty-three hundred years ago. In fact, just as the essence of modern materialism may be recognized in the atomism of Democritus, so the main features of modern pessimism appear in Buddha's theory of existence,

[*] For an account of the systems of Schopenhauer and Hartmann, see Sully's *Pessimism*, ch. iv. and v., in which volume also the whole subject of the worth of life is fully and ably discussed.

projected some half-century before; so that if history does not repeat itself, philosophy, or the state of the human mind which gives birth to philosophy, apparently does.

The last-named great spirit it was who first systematically taught that man, from his inmost mental make and constitution, from his insatiable wants and lusts and omnivorous desires, no less than from the external troubles and fatalities of life, must be miserable, until, having entered once for all upon the only path to peace, he has attacked the disease of life at the root; until he has seen through its illusions, and cured himself of its desires; until he has extinguished within himself the consuming fires of lust and hate and the all-too-eager desire for life. Nor can the wise man, the sage, attain to a consummated peace, the only earthly happiness, till he has detached his desires completely from every earthly object round which their tendrils are thrown; until, finally, by supreme effort of concentrated meditation and virtue, to which only the perfected saint and sage is adequate, he has destroyed finally, all desire for material or immaterial existence, all desire for life on earth, all desire for further life hereafter. Then only it is, having reached this last and most glorious summit of earthly piety and virtue, that the heavy burden of life's miseries and sorrows falls off, that the perpetual pain of existence ceases to fret, and the ever-vexed and perturbed consciousness becomes calm and peaceful as the surface of the sleeping lake in summer evening. For then at length has been already reached on earth the peaceful and holy state of Nirvâna, the blissful prelude and foretaste of that grander Nirvâna, that state of supreme unconscious peace, of soft, sweet, infinite, and eternal rest, to be enjoyed by the perfect hereafter. As for the bad and imperfect, they must plunge again into the storms and vortices of existence, as the punishment for their demerits here, until, by entering hereafter on the path of escape pointed out by the great deliverer, they also soon or late (and it may be never) escape from the pains and penalties of conscious being into the happy and silent shores of Nirvâna.

The pessimism of our modern teachers, then, the "occidental Buddhism," as it has been justly styled, of Schopenhauer and Hartmann is not new; and it is even remarkable how much of the system of its modern founder, including the proffered remedy for life's ills of quietism, or "the denial of the will to live," is contained in the metaphysical and moral teaching of Buddha.* But it is certainly new to find such a pessimist system emerging in the nineteenth century, and offered by its modern founder as the last result of philosophy, logically filiated to the Kantian metaphysics, and offered again by his chief disciple, Hartmann, as the only philosophy which accords at once with the highest inductions of science as well as with sound metaphysical principles. And it is a new and very noteworthy phenomenon to find this despairing philosophy appearing and finding a sympathetic response in the hearts of men of the advanced and cultured and conquering races of Western Europe, and just at the moment when the triumphs of modern progress were being chanted in full chorus and were ringing loudest in all men's ears. Just when the jubilant chorus was loudest, the note of desolation and despair has broken in as a discord, and rings sufficiently loud and clear to make the optimists of progress pause and ponder. Contemporaneously with the

---

* For an account of the Buddhist system, see *The Legend of Gaudama, the Buddha of the Burmese*, by Bigandet, pp. 430-480; also *Buddhism* by T. W. Rhys Davids, in the series of "Non-Christian Religious Systems," published by the Society for Promoting Christian Knowledge.

great discoveries of science, with the march of invention, with the wonders of steam and electricity, in an age of boasted general advance and improvement, this philosophy of despair has appeared. A strange portent surely. What may it mean that in these days of telegraph and railways, of universal suffrage and cheap press, of constant discoveries in science and inventions in the useful arts, in an age of diffused knowledge, diffused material comfort, extended political power to the people, in an age of general enlightenment and progress in all directions, there should suddenly appear and find acceptance, amongst the cultured and fortunate classes first of all, a philosophy affirming the nullity of all these things, and the worthlessness of existence, however supplemented by progress? Does the phenomenon portend that modern civilization, hollow and despairing at its heart, of which such philosophy is a symptom, is about to perish as former civilizations have perished, to sink as religion has already sunk? Is it the symptom of a state of things gravely amiss, and deep-seated, not in our spiritual state, but in our social constitution, with its terrible contrasts of want and luxury, which points to social revolution as its only cure? Or, finally, is it merely an exceptional product in philosophy, phantasmal and ephemeral, an offspring of the abysmal individual melancholy of a man of genius, who has made it attractive to a large circle of readers, just as the despairing poetry of our century has been found attractive; a philosophy which, on the whole, had better have been cast in the poetic than the philosophic form, and which will dissipate itself anon without producing other than a poetic result, a momentary and not unpleasant agitation in the emotion of the reader, which has no effect on conduct? All these three questions may be seriously asked concerning the pessimist philosophy, the transplanted Buddhism, which has at length appeared and found disciples in Western Europe. The view last intimated seems, on the whole, the nearest the truth;[*] though there are some who think that the spread of pessimism is rather a sign that the internal constitution of society is wrong and requires readjustment.

That a systematic pessimist creed should have appeared ages ago amongst the monotonous myriads of miserable beings that swarmed South-Eastern Asia, and that such a creed should be hailed as the word of deliverance and salvation, is sufficiently intelligible. "Man is a weed in these regions," as De Quincey has said; existence is lightly valued at the best—is an evil rather than a good in the general estimation; the doctrines of pessimism and Nirvâna go hand-in-hand, and are well suited to the nature of the people of these countries. The immemorial tyranny of caste; the special oppression of conscience by the priestly class; the necessarily deadly struggle for existence amongst the teeming millions; the misery of life, added to the utter mystery and inexplicability of it all;—these things are amply sufficient to account for the first appearance and the general acceptance of the system of Buddha ages ago in Hindustan, where it was born, as the like circumstances account for its reception in the surrounding countries after it had been rooted out of India. The soil was everywhere ready for the seed of Buddha's teaching. Pessimism is the natural creed of a people and a society where the many mutually crush each other by their numbers, where they are crushed again by the ruling classes, and where, tormented by superstitions, they have permitted the priests

[*] Sully's *Pessimism*, pp. 152, 153.

to obtain a spiritual despotism. In such a social and spiritual state, the prophet of Nirvâna came and was hailed as saviour. But that a like creed should appear in the advanced and wealthy nations of Western Europe, and should find disciples, not amongst the poor, but the superior and cultured classes, seems at first sight a somewhat strange and unaccountable thing.

Nevertheless, its appearance is not so inexplicable as at first one might suppose. Some of the conditions which favoured the reception of Buddha's teaching,—the pressure of population and the inequality of social condition,— exist in modern Europe. But added to these there are special causes peculiar to our age and civilization. The prevailing disbelief in the old theological dogmas, the deepening doubt, extending to ever wider circles until now it has reached the masses, of any compensating happiness hereafter for all the miseries and injustices suffered here; these things, joined to an increased intensity in the struggle for existence, to which our more flaccid fibres and more sensitive nerves are less equal, suffice to account for a certain failure of heart and hope, a diminished joy and zest in existence, and a desponding feeling as if the Power that rules the world had in our day dishonoured His acceptances, and become bankrupt as regards His promises to pay in a future life,—all which things are of the essence of the pessimist mood of mind, and offer a fitly prepared soil for a pessimist philosophy professing to be deeply and scientifically grounded.

It is not, then, wholly strange that a degree of despair should have set in in the midst of our vaunted age of progress. But it would, we think, be strange if the mood became very general, if it were anything more serious than a black and passing cloud. For, after all, assuredly, in spite of all our failure of faith, existence is not less a good, the banquet of life is not less royally spread or decked than in the most halcyon days of the happiest former civilizations. Assuredly neither the Greek of the time of Pericles, nor the Roman in the days of Augustus, nor the Arabian in the golden prime of Al-Raschid, had as much reason, on the whole, as we to-day to enjoy existence. Neither Greek, nor Roman, nor Arab, in the palmiest days of their civilizations, possessed the multiplied comforts and luxuries, the expanded sciences and literatures, the increased treasures of art, the more developed and refined social life, which are accessible to-day to greater numbers than under any former civilization. Nor was their art so highly developed; nor had they our modern feeling for the endless beauty in external nature—that great new sense with which our modern poets and painters have endowed us. And yet we cannot enjoy; we have lost our appetite at the feast of life, which the Greek, with a less rich and varied repast, enjoyed so much, though he had no more hope of future felicity than our present unbelieving generation.

§ 2. In spite of the misery around, of the sorrow within, of the future hope shrouded or wholly withdrawn—should it even amount to that—we feel that pessimism is not the true gospel for men to-day. It is not true that life is necessarily an evil, which is only disguised by irrational illusions. Life may be an intolerable evil for some unfortunate ones; it is not so for all, and it was not always an evil even for the most unfortunate. The direct contrary of the pessimist proposition may be held; life for most men is not an evil; up to the day of death, if asked, they would so reply; and there is no going beyond the individual's testimony to his own case. His testimony to his own experience of the worth of life is more to be relied upon than any system of philosophy, which at best applies to average cases. It is useless to say that he is under an illusion. The agreeable illusion is part of the pleasure he feels; he thinks his life, on the whole, enjoyable; he would live it over again; and he would gladly accept another hereafter, only just as good as the present. And so far from consciousness being necessarily an evil, are there not times in the life of all when the content and essence of consciousness is itself perfect felicity; moments when we have seemed to hold happiness in our hands, which we would scarce have exchanged for that of the angel; hours of felicity so full that we have asked ourselves could we desire more or higher bliss? Have not most of us, at some time of our lives, felt what Othello, in a moment of overjoyed consciousness, expresses:

> My soul hath her content so absolute,
> That not another comfort like to this
> Succeeds in unknown fate?[*]

But the possibility of even a moment of such happiness destroys the pessimist argument, that life must be an evil, because consciousness is always a want, and therefore a pain.

Such is the pessimist syllogism: all Want is pain; the essence of consciousness is a want; therefore conscious life is an evil. But consciousness, as we have already shown, is not merely a want; it is frequently also a having, a possession, a satisfied content, and sometimes a perfected

---

[*] *Othello*, Act II. Scene i. See also in same scene, where he speaks further to the same point:

> I cannot speak enough of this content,
> It stops me here; it is too much of joy.

felicity. The artist's consciousness of a beautiful sunset, of a smiling summer sea with light summer clouds above it, of the strange and sublime vision of Nature from an Alpine summit,—these are not wants, but satisfactions, the opposite of wants. The glad contemplation of the beauty visible over the face of Nature, and of a subtler fugitive beauty caught by the artist amongst the complex conditions of human life; the tranquil joys of the intellect face to face with or only in pursuit of truth; the pleasure in the society of superior minds; the different pleasure from the presence of those we love;—all these are instances of satisfied, not dissatisfied consciousness; their true meaning is not a privation but a possession, not pain but pleasure, and sometimes without any alloy. Nor is it true that it belongs only to youth to enjoy life. There are appropriate satisfactions for our maturer years, even for age; though it must be allowed that the ratio between our joys and griefs becomes, on the whole, a diminishing one with years. Still, there are compensations. Neither our pains nor our pleasures are so keenly felt. We reach a state of tranquil equilibrium in maturer years, in which an intelligent comprehension of life becomes possible. There lies an elevated table-land in the middle of life, before we begin to descend the downward slope, from which we command a wider intellectual horizon. At this period the perception of truth is clearer and stronger, while it is reinforced by the experience of life; the perception and relish of beauty in Art or Nature, high and satisfying pleasures, long remain undiminished; and the desire to serve our species, if we have ever had any such desire, becomes greater. So that even after the joys and raptures of youth have all gone by, there may be much enjoyment of a higher, though a more tranquil sort.

Life, in short, is adapted to happiness as well as to misery. Nature is striving her utmost to produce happiness, as well as to produce beauty. And how near to a splendid success she has been! At moments, we feel convinced that Nature is aiming at human happiness; and we know it from our own experience. We feel sometimes that, but for some slight hitch or hindrance somewhere interposed by the malevolent powers, but for something trivial not in the essence but the accidents of things, a grand general success might have been made! Nay more, that Nature will yet succeed in her aims at human happiness, if only men themselves will learn to aid and second, by all the ways that Science and Wisdom point out, the efforts that she is constantly and kindly making in their behalf. Having derived so much satisfaction from life, and so much good from society with all its imperfections, we argue that much more is possible yet, and that this problem of happiness, so far as we have any right to expect it, may yet be solved satisfactorily for man. But again comes the desponding mood; and in these alternations between exaggerated optimism and exaggerated pessimism, man in these days lives; while it is only by duly checking the one against the other, that a sober, balanced judgment which may guide rational expectation and practice is possible.

The pessimism of the philosophers in any case is not a true gospel. It does not contain the true word of life for man to-day in Europe; and even if it were wholly true, it would be the kind of truth which it does not profit to insist upon. Unless with the diagnosis of the disease there is also the accompanying prescription supplied as by Buddha, there is no good end served by preaching pessimism.

Quietism, asceticism, denial of the will to live, as recommended by Schopenhauer, will not suit our Western populations in the midst of the pressure and struggle of existence. Possibly, indeed, a tincture of this quiescence might be of service as an alterative medicine to the system, in these days of feverish competition and too keen pursuit of wealth; but quietism would not at all suit as our constant habit and way of life. We want rather a fuller life, more wisely conducted; for it is to be particularly remembered, in discussing this question of pessimism, that many of the ills of life are of our own making, many more the making of others, both of which might have been avoided if the lesson of Bishop Butler and of positive science were more deeply borne in upon our minds, that we are under Natural Government, where we should rule our actions by a knowledge of the regular sequence of cause and consequence. And this consideration may serve to introduce that system and view of life which professes to regard the world wholly from this the scientific point of view.

§ 3. From the point of view of Positive Science, there exist in the universe only phenomena, and a regular order in these which it is the business of the scientific investigator to discover, and which, when ascertained and concatenated, constitute Science, the only knowledge, real, true, and fruitful. At least, if there be existences in the universe other than phenomena, actual or possible, we shall never know aught about them beyond the bare fact of their existence; and if there be other knowledge than that of the facts and laws of phenomena, it is barren and useless.

That there exists only phenomena for the human understanding, the author of the *Critique of Pure Reason*, himself greatest amongst the metaphysicians, has satisfactorily and finally demonstrated. There exists for men only phenomena, and Science gives us the only reliable and systematized knowledge of these, which knowledge is merely the invariable relations, or the unchanging successions and the constant co-existences of the same facts or phenomena. These are all that man can know, all that Science can discover; but happily such knowledge is all that we require, and all that we should ask. It suffices for an intelligent understanding of the universe, for the mastery of Nature, for a wise and rational regulation of life and conduct. What more would man require? Truth for man is only science—a knowledge of the facts and laws ascertained by science, or by historical investigation, working by the methods and animated and guided by the spirit of science. Philosophy itself is only science, at least, if men insist upon a philosophy other than the general conclusions of science in the mental and moral departments of inquiry; if a distinction must be drawn between science and philosophy, then philosophy can only be the systematic connection of the highest conceptions and generalizations supplied by science—causation, evolution, the law of gravity, of the persistence of energy, of natural selection, and the application of these to explain the facts and lower laws of things. Philosophy, or metaphysics, as Aristotle conceived it, comes thus after physics, and exhibits the skeleton system of laws, which holds the cosmos together, and which governs life and mind, with the lower laws affiliated to the higher, and these again to a few or one highest, which Science has reached or hopes yet to reach.

But all philosophy which does not rest on a basis of science and fact, all philosophy which pretends to penetrate behind phenomena, and to make even a single affirmation respecting what it affects to discover in that *terra incognita* of things in themselves, or which continues to indulge in feats of logical legerdemain, with the abstract notions of existence and non-existence, will be recognized as the empty pretence and delusion which it really is. More particularly metaphysics, or ontology, which has always pretended to a knowledge of the real being and essence of things other than their phenomenal manifestations, and which has aspired to lift the phenomenal veil and to solve the final mystery of existence, will be wholly discredited. It is a spurious department of knowledge, which has never dealt with aught beyond fictitious entities, phantasmal creations, or empty verbal nothings; and it has only so long imposed upon men because of the genius of some who devoted themselves to its prosecution, having first imposed upon themselves. It aspired to get beyond or behind phenomenal appearances, to the world of true and real being; in reality, it got no further than the vain analysis of empty abstract notions, and the fictions currently agreed upon by the metaphysicians;—unless, when the private phantasms and monstrous mirages of the individual mind were added so as to form a new system. It advanced no further than these, which were after all phenomena, though of a peculiar sort, as representing nothing beyond their own chimerical selves. Happily, however, metaphysics is now very generally falling into the disrepute and discredit which so long ago overtook the pretended science of astrology.

The above is the most general point of view of the positive scientific thinker. It is the common point of view of science, of what is called the experience-philosophy, as well as of the positivism of Comte. But the positive thinker must not be identified solely with the disciple of

Comte, for the point of view and frame of mind is common to many who by no means accept the positivism of Comte as a scientific and full philosophy. The positive spirit is, in fact, as old as the days of Bacon, who is the true father of it in modern times, as well as of the inductive method of discovering general truths, which recognizes and applies it. And the same positive spirit has, ever since the time of Bacon, not merely governed the whole course of physical scientific discovery, but has also manifested itself with increasing force in all other departments of inquiry, and it is now dominant in biological science, in mental, moral, social, and political science, in the whole field of criticism and historical research, and even in much of the current philosophical speculation. In all these departments of knowledge, men seek either for the fact, as in history and criticism, or for the law of recurrence or coexistence amongst the facts, as in science. Even in moral and social speculations, the positive attitude to the problems presented, existed long before the time of Comte, who is erroneously believed by some to be the initiator of it. It is the positive spirit which governs the moral and political speculations of Hobbes's *Leviathan*, it is the spirit in great measure of Locke's great *Essay on the Human Understanding*, the completely pervading spirit of Adam Smith's *Wealth of Nations*, as of Hume's famous *Treatise of Human Nature*. In fact, so generally has the practical positive spirit always shown itself in English speculation, that Continental critics, like M. Taine, make it a reproach to the English mind, affirming that it has some peculiar bent from Nature and some special sympathy with the positive spirit, which prevents it getting beyond the visible and tangible facts of sense, and rising to lofty speculation. But whether this last be so or not, and whether the charge is to be regarded as a ground of reproach, or in the light of an honour, since the spirit is now becoming universal,—a fact it is that, from the time of Bacon to our own, all the great works of the English intellect outside the sphere of poetry, and notably in philosophy and morals, have been remarkably distinguished by the positive spirit, and governed by its methods of inquiry and proof.

Positivism, as here regarded, is, in its philosophical references, rather an attitude of mind to all philosophical problems, and a method of treating such of them as are legitimate and soluble, than a system of philosophy itself. It is true that Comte has offered his positivism to the world in the latter character,—as a philosophy with an appended doctrine. But the pretensions of Comte's Positive Philosophy have not been generally credited in these respects, especially after being further supplemented by his religious fancies. By positivism, then, we do not specially refer to Comte's characterization of it, any further than as it recognizes, and anew emphasizes, the general positive spirit and methods which existed before his time, and which at present obtains amongst thinkers on all subjects except theology and metaphysics, and sometimes even on these.

The positive point of view, which is no other than the ground of proved experience, is professedly that of the modern evolutionist and materialist, of Darwin and Spencer, of Haeckel and Huxley; although the materialist, in his ambition to give an explanation of the world from matter only, finds it extremely difficult to adhere to the positivist injunction to keep clear of the metaphysical vortices, which, in truth, are always perilously near all assertions respecting the ultimate principle of the universe. But, however difficult it be to maintain it, especially when hypotheses are necessarily employed, and however great the temptation at times to abandon it, the positive point of view is that of evolution and materialism. It is that of Darwin in his *Origin of Species*, whose great law of Natural Selection, inductively gathered, and deductively applied to the explanation of vast classes of facts, and many inferior empirical laws in the organic world, is as splendid a result of the positive method in the domain of biology, as the Newtonian law of gravitation in the sphere of physical science. And the whole immense philosophy of evolution, in the hands of Herbert Spencer, is nothing more than an attempt to solve, by positive, natural, scientific, and phenomenal causes, the old problems of the creation of the universe and all living things within it, man included, together with the origin of language, thought, morality, religion, and all else which distinguishes man—problems which had so often been previously attempted by the theologian and metaphysician, by occult, fictitious, supernatural, or unintelligible causes.

§ 4. The rise of this positive spirit and way of viewing the universe, three centuries ago, was in great measure due to a reaction from the barren and wearisome scholastic metaphysics, in alliance with a futile physics which rested on metaphysical hypotheses instead of experiment; and the general prevalence of this spirit at the present day is owing to the grand scientific discoveries and brilliant results in the sphere of practical invention which have followed in the wake of its adoption. To these last chiefly, but also, it must be allowed, to a widespread conviction that metaphysics is still as empty as in the days of scholasticism, that the abstractions of Hegelian metaphysics and the elaborate futilities of Duns Scotus and Aquinas are still much on a par. The notion is more and more commonly accepted by the cultured, that, even for an explanation of the mysterious universe in which we are, and for answer to all the legitimate and intelligible questions that the mind of man can raise, we must look to science and not to metaphysics. Science alone speaks the words of truth and reality, and metaphysics, as ever, where she pretends to enlighten us and explain things, deals only with empty abstractions converted into realities, or with fancies, delusions, and chimeras. She raises insoluble questions, and pretends to have given an answer; she raises unreal and unmeaning ones, with whose strange knots and perplexities the mind that has foolishly allowed them to enter contends laboriously and painfully, as sometimes in dreams we struggle with strange and fantastic problems, only to wonder and smile in the daylight, after awakening, that such absurd questions should have perplexed and tormented us. The metaphysical questions are either insoluble and should not be raised, or unreal and fantastical and need not be; in either case we may dismiss them for the future. Science will answer the real questions.

I do not consider this to be the whole truth of the matter; nor the distinction made between science and metaphysics the true one; for after all metaphysics should be only another name for sound philosophy. But the preceding is the view of Comte and his followers. It is also pretty much the view of Mill and Bain, who have handled philosophical questions in the positive spirit, and of men who, like Professor Huxley, deride at once Comte and the "pure metaphysicians." According to the late G. H. Lewes, himself a positivist, but who fairly reflects the views common to all positive scientific thinkers, the spirit of man in prepositive ages had been goaded and driven by an inquiring evil spirit within, into the deep waters of ontological speculation, where it speedily and surely got sucked into the circular currents and bottomless vortices of empty metaphysical controversies respecting Being, Existence, Becoming, First Cause, Real Substance, and the like. It was urged viciously into a region of insoluble enigmas and transcendental riddles, where the brain grows dizzy with "thoughts beyond the reaches of our souls," which are pressed upon it; into a region where light or knowledge never comes or has come since men first began to speculate; into a land of chimeras dire, where the mind wandered perplexed and lost, discussing ceaselessly, as Milton's fallen angels on the "hill retired," in the infernal abodes, the whole dismal circle of metaphysical enigmas—"providence, foreknowledge, will and fate, fixed fate, free-will, foreknowledge absolute," with others similar; and still, as ever, the mind of men, as the mind of the evil spirits, could find "no end, in wandering mazes lost." At length Positive Science came, with her true methods of interrogating Nature, and showed man a means of escape from the fatal fascinations of metaphysics. The whole vicious circle of metaphysical problems might be evaded, and real profitable questions might be substituted for them, sufficiently difficult to attract man's energies, and yet not insoluble. Or if the old questions of the origin and final goal of the universe and man, of free-will and immortality, must still engage the mind of man; if the metaphysical virus is still so far left in the blood through heredity, that it will still raise the old questions, let them be attempted from the scientific side, by the scientific and experimental methods of inquiry and proof, with deductive reasoning resting on a sound basis of inductively ascertained facts, which will give a certain or probable conclusion according to the weight of the evidence, and the degree and kind of verification possible. And let all the conceptions which we bring to bear in the discussion be filled only with the facts of experience, and be emptied of their old fictions, question-begging hypotheses, and unreal, unknown elements. Let the notions of matter and substance, creation and cause, providence and purpose, be freed from their unknown and hypothetical contents, which are incapable of verification, and be filled only with the facts taught by experience or science, which facts these symbols alone represent, and for which alone they should stand. Were this duly done, then indeed we might receive a correspondingly positive and scientific answer to our old metaphysical inquiries.

However this may succeed, it has become gradually clear to man, partly from the failure of the great metaphysicians, who have, twice within the past two hundred years, attempted in vain to take the problem of the universe by storm, and partly from the express teaching of two of the greatest amongst them, Kant and Hume, that the human mind could not advance beyond phenomena; that it knew nothing even of its own wonderful self beyond its phenomenal modes and affections; and that whatever problem might remain for philosophy, whether in determining the conditions and boundaries of the knowing faculties, or in weaving into systematic unity the final conceptions and laws handed in by Science, still, that the business of Science herself was to trace and discover a systematic order in the several departments of phenomena presented by Nature, external or human. Further, men have begun to perceive more clearly that a knowledge of phenomena and their constant conjunctions, as it is all that we can know, so it is all that we really require to know; and that such knowledge will go much further than was at first suspected, even towards the answering, not merely of the old metaphysical questions of free-will, providence, and the like, in a scientific manner, but even in giving answer to the question acknowledged since the time of Kant to be the chief philosophical question, namely, How we come to have knowledge or experience, or "What makes experience possible." This question is answered in our days by positive science, and from the general point of view of experience, by psychology, physiology, and the demonstrated fact of inherited mental aptitudes, by which it is shown that all knowledge in the individual is unfolded from a germinal point, just as his body is; that each individual is born with the potentiality of developing all the inherited ideas of the race; and that, in the race itself, or rather in the total series of animals of which man is the last and highest, all knowledge gradually unfolded itself from a similar zero point, by insensible gradations. Thus Herbert Spencer and Darwin explain from experience what was regarded by the intuitional school as the *a priori* and mysterious element in knowledge, not to be accounted for from any experience. Our *a priori* notions are brought under the facts and laws of heredity and evolution, and thus the question of knowledge itself, so far as answerable by the human mind, is answered from the positive scientific point of view. Knowledge has unfolded itself gradually in the total organic world, as we know it now does in each individual. But the question how the first faint glimmer of any knowledge first broke in a world previously unconscious, is as unanswerable as the question how life first appeared. All that we can say is, that from its commencement it was conditioned by the material organization of the brain and nerves, as life was bound up with peculiar aggregations of matter; but we cannot tell why a brain was necessary or how life came from matter. These are the metaphysical and insoluble questions. Thus finally a knowledge of the sequences and conjunctions of phenomena which constitute science is sufficient to answer all legitimate questions. Such knowledge serves at once to explain the universe, to guide our life, to give man the mastery over Nature, to rule the forces without and within. It will explain the world, ourselves, society; enable us to assign the natural origin, to show the natural course of evolution, to predict the probable final destiny of each; and such an explanation—which, unlike the past metaphysical ones, is both intelligible to the human mind, and likely to lead to profitable practical result—ought surely to suffice for men.

§ 5. But whether the positive point of view and positive scientific methods are or are not adequate to the solution of all questions of philosophy, they are fully adequate to all the demands of practice. Positive knowledge, purified from all metaphysical questions, is all that is required for the conduct of the individual life by the individual, or of the collective national life by the statesman or legislator. That there exists only phenomena, and a settled order amongst them which is ascertainable, and which is the best and only safe guide in practice, is all that the moralist, the statesman, the reformer, the philanthropist need postulate. For all these have only to adapt phenomenal means to ends, subject to the ascertained order of the phenomena, without other question asked than the suitability of the means to the end, and where, consequently, metaphysical questions, even if they have reality in themselves, do not enter. In all departments of practice we have but to know the established order of sequence and coexistence amongst facts, and to act accordingly. This is the case too with the practical inventor, with the physician who deals with our bodily disorders, as well as with the political reformer who attempts to cure the social maladies. The physician requires only to know the laws of the human body, the causes of diseases and their remedies, without raising the question of what is "vitality" in itself, or what is the ultimate cause of life; the inventor of the steam-engine required only, in addition to his own inventive genius, a knowledge of the laws of heat, of motion, of the propulsive power of steam, without once being required to raise the inquiry whether heat, and steam, and motion were anything in themselves other than their phenomenal appearances, or whether a hidden reality or entity lay under or behind them, what was the real nature of heat, or how it could possibly transmute itself into motion,—questions which, however absorbing and interesting to the metaphysician, would be entirely irrelevant from the point of view of the inventor who conceived, or of the engineer who constructed, the machine. In all cases, however the metaphysical questions be answered, or whether they be answered at all, concerns not the man of practice. In all the practical arts, in all the sciences that relate to practice, for the prudent conduct of life, for the moral conduct of life, as well as for all purposes of scientific, that is, of real and possible, explanation of Nature, man requires nothing more than the knowledge of phenomena and their invariable successions and coexistences; while for the effectual discovery of these laws of phenomena amidst the complexity and obscurity of their involved circumstances, he requires only that positive inductive method of interrogating Nature first conceived and pointed out by Bacon, which has since been so successfully applied in practice by physicists, chemists, naturalists, physiologists, and economists; and whose whole method of procedure has been so completely systematized and described in all its parts, and subordinate aids, induction, deduction, hypotheses, observation, experiment, statistics, by positive thinkers of the past and present generation, in particular by Comte, Whewell, Mill, and Bain. This is the method of inquiry which has borne so much fruit in the past three centuries in the explanation of Nature, man, and society, and in the subjection of the powers of Nature to human wants. This inductive method of search after Nature's laws has already given us our whole body of scientific truth, and the resulting mastery over Nature. It is this same method further extended, though still limited to the finding and explaining of facts and laws, that will at length give us a moral science and rules of life suitable to man's real nature and circumstances in the world, and a science of society which will explain the conditions of social well-being. According to some, we shall even get from the resulting laws and conceptions a new philosophy and a new religion; but if positive science cannot serve us thus far, it will render the other and more pressingly needed service.

CHAPTER II.

THE MESSAGE AND PROMISES TO MANKIND.

§ 1. SCIENCE is the true revelation to men—the only revelation that men have ever received or can receive. For Nature reveals only the secrets which her patient worshippers, after a careful interrogation and close observation, have had the skill to extract from her else close and impassible breast. She has only revealed the "open secret" of her laws to her devoted inquirers, who have carefully watched the ways of her present behaviour, and have detected the marks of her past behaviour; reserving a final secret at her heart which none can fathom or discover. This secret is incommunicable by her; nor could it be understood by mortal ears if it were otherwise. The fancied whispers of inspirations by the prophets and founders of religions were but the private imaginings of individuals, which the ardour and vehemence of their own souls, conjointly with the spiritual wants and fears of their fellows, intensely desirous of a revelation, permitted to pass for such in rude, uncritical, and credulous ages. Men wanted a revelation, a voice from the void; and the revealer, himself a representative man, more intensely feeling the want than the others, after long and lonely religious contemplation, believed that to him was communicated the secret, and he came forward to supply the want. But he had not got the secret. Nor did the philosophers succeed better. The cloud-constructed systems of the great metaphysicians who attempted, by a different route and fashion, by the might of their own reason, to take by storm the secret that they knew had not been voluntarily revealed, came no nearer to disclosing the actual truth of things or the final reality and mystery at the bottom of them. The religions and absolute philosophies alike report only the reveries or imperfect imaginings of the individual, which were mistaken by one for the voice of Revelation, by the other for the last truth of Reason and Nature.

The revelation of science is, indeed, much less precise and circumstantial than that of the religious founders; but it more accords with facts, with the historical fact as witnessed to by marks which geology reads, and with the present actual facts and laws which, during the human historical period, we believe to have been never different. The chain of established scientific truths and laws contains a less sublime scheme and conception of the universe than the grand systems of Plato, or Leibnitz, or Hegel; but it is at least more simple and level to our intelligence, it is much closer to the actuality of things, and it always admits of verification. The scientific conception of the universe can be compared with the actual facts; it is merely gathered and generalized from these facts; while the scientific story of Nature's development challenges disproof or refutation, by confrontation with inexplicable facts and by every applicable inductive or deductive test. Science may be open to correction in detail, but she believes she holds the substantial truth. In the case of the philosophical systems, they have either no counterpart, being constructed wholly from the imagination, or if there be any original corresponding to the philosophers' scheme, it admits of no comparison with the copy. The truth of Nature is the system-maker's reading of her, deduced from abstract principles conceived in his own breast, and shaped together by his own mental constructive power. But that the systems do not read either the truth or reality of Nature is proved by their contradictions with each other, as well as by their own internal inconsistencies.

§ 2. Science will bring not only material but spiritual comforts and alleviation. It will bring both truth and fruit: truth, in itself; fruit, from its indefinite adaptability to the material wants and wishes of men, as well as from its further application to the conduct of life. Science in itself is the true, in its application is the good. The truths of science will save you; in the sequel they will save the world; they alone can do so. They will save your soul, in the only sense in which it can be saved—by pointing out to it the right way of life; by giving to it a fuller, freer, better life on the earth, the only certain theatre of its existence and activity; by giving to it light, by supplying it with sustaining and strengthening truths; in a word, by showing it the universal empire of law, which embraces both it and the cosmos, the knowledge of which is the sum of truth, and to accommodate ourselves to which is the sum of wisdom and virtue. And this truth will not only save you, it will set you free, as it is ever the work of truth to do. It will set you free by delivering you from the vain fears and terrors and superstitions which so long held the soul of man in degrading bondage, adding their formidable terrors to the miseries of life. It will further set you free within the bounds of natural law, by enabling you to accomplish your desired ends the surer the more you know the unvarying course of things, to which on the one hand your aims must be accommodated, but which on the other can be indefinitely turned to serve you.

Our perturbed spirits shall at length find rest under the reign of ascertained truth and universal, unvarying law. Our minds shall also be at peace with respect to the final insoluble mystery of the universe, into which not even the angels can penetrate. We shall give up the attempts to solve it, accepting it as a final fact, and being content with a knowledge of the general laws of phenomena. This knowledge of the order of the world, of what we can know and of what we must be content to be ignorant of, will bring back to us our banished peace of mind. The sweet serenity of spirit, the most precious jewel of our souls, will return to us again. We shall take heart of grace, and, knowing the liberal terms that Nature allows to the wise, knowing at least more clearly than men ever knew before the conditions under which we live,—fixed and immutable in some directions, alterable in others, and by ourselves for our advantage, —we shall once again, as men born under former happy civilizations, put on a cheerful courage, and find enjoyment in existence. We shall no more go round bewailing our evil conditions, asking who will show us any good? Our new-born pessimism shall disappear, direful and phantasmal as our old superstitions. The spirit of man shall get rest after its long and searching probation, after all this feverish agitation and disquietude, prolonged for three centuries, respecting the nature, the origin, and the final destination of the soul.

Resignation, the last, the greatest, and most difficult of the virtues, will follow under the new dispensation of natural law holding all things, the world, and man, and society in its embrace. Resignation to the unalterable evils of life which the old Stoic strenuously tried to inculcate upon himself, which the religion of Islam prescribes as its central precept, which Christianity supplicates from heaven, becomes almost for the first time a possible and natural frame of mind to man; the lesson of science being borne in upon his mind from all sides and by countless instances, that the course of nature, the laws of the universe, and the laws of life, from which certain evils must result, are fixed and unalterable. It is natural, when we know that the order of the world is carried on under laws which will not change for our wishes or our prayers, to be resigned to the special evils which the general laws bring with them. It is natural to try to be resigned to the inevitable in any case, and it is wise; but when we learn that some of the inevitable ills are the result of general laws which bring a greater sum of good; that others of our ills are not inevitable, but reducible in amount through the beneficial help of these very invariable laws and the unchanging nature of things and properties of matter; and that finally both the greater good, and the continual diminution of evil within limits, are only obtainable on the twofold condition of the invariability of the laws joined to our knowledge of them;—then the spirit of resignation to the order of things, which is demanded from us on account of the residuum of evil, becomes tempered with gratitude on account of the larger good.

When we reflect that the particular evils from which we suffer and from which no deliverance can be obtained, are natural effects of the general order, parts of the total chain of cause and consequence which binds the cosmos together; and that to ask for an exception in the operation of natural law, for a single remission of the result in our special favour, would be tantamount to asking for the abolition of law and for the dissolution of the universe;—this thought and lesson when deeply impressed upon us, tends to beget in us the spirit of resigned if not of cheerful acceptance of these evils which can be demonstrated to be unavoidable; while the additional experience that rebellion against natural law only increases our evils by bringing besides its own special punishment, makes us take still further to heart the lesson of science and experience. Still more, when we remember that the invariability of physical and natural law, which sometimes presses so severely upon us as to call for all our patience, is precisely that feature which not only makes possible all the good that we enjoy, but which also gives us our mastery over Nature, with all the positive good which thence results, as well as partial deliverance from evils which are *not* inevitable,—then our resignation becomes the easier and more natural, our gratitude the greater. The religious sentiment of resignation to the evil, of gratitude for the good, and of complete final dependence upon a law-governed cosmos is thus naturally produced in us.

We think no more of asking Nature to spare us from special evils, which are a part of her general beneficent order, when exemption could only be obtained on conditions which would be subversive of this order, and which, even if possible or conceivable, it would be impious as well as absurd to ask, as rendering impossible a greater good to others and even to ourselves.

§ 3. But are we not thus shut fast in prison behind the bars of these necessary laws? Are we not bound in the fetters of these unbroken chains of causation which Science everywhere discloses in the world of mind as in matter, in the succession of thoughts and volitions, as well as in the succession of physical facts and events? Are we not on all sides, and everywhere we turn, met by the iron links of necessity, massive or fine, in these unvarying connections and inseparable conjunctions of facts which constitute the universe on the scientific showing of it? In a word, is not the full accomplishment of science, and the complete establishment of the reign of law in matter, in mind, in the human body, in human societies, only the completion of our subjection to necessity and fate? Not so, replies the positive thinker; less now than ever does necessity press upon men, and it is to the universal reign of law, and to science which has found and demonstrated it, that we owe our deliverance. For though the universe is indeed, in a sense, a huge machine, though the order of the world is invariable and ascertained, though fire invariably ignites gunpowder, though lead sinks in water, though all animals die, and the dead do not rise again; though all this be true, yet we find that the laws of Nature are not our tyrannical masters, and the empire of necessity does not oppress us. On the contrary, we find that even while we act under laws, we can bend their action indefinitely to our will and pleasure and advantage. And this is practical freedom, the only real freedom, the freedom to pursue what we desire. We can set the laws to act together or in opposition to each other. We can set two or more causes in action together, and make them to unite, or alter, or cancel their special effects. We can increase, vary, modify, neutralize the operation of laws, but only by the action of other laws. We can summon one law to our aid to deliver us from the evil effect of another law. We can get one cause to counteract another cause, water to extinguish a conflagration, quinine to cure an ague or fever. In like manner we may link together several instances of laws with their effects into a series in a machine, as the steam-engine, which is but the conjuncture and constraint of the laws of heat, of motion, of the expansive force of steam and its propelling power upon a given movable mass; all which laws, in addition to others, are fulfilled in and by the machine, and are made by it to work submissively and untiringly towards one desired end.

But to master and constrain Nature we must know her, and we must obey her. We must have an accurate knowledge of the law, a right estimate of the behaviour of the forces that we use; for the same force that will serve us submissively if we understand it, the same law that will work our will if we go with it, will destroy us without mercy in the opposite case. The first preliminary condition of Nature's service is knowledge—that we should study and know her, that we should learn the sequences that Science has slowly gathered through the centuries; and where her laws admit of definite mathematical measurement, that we should not mistake in the application of our formulæ or in the calculated strength of materials, as otherwise our bridge will not bear the strain upon it of possible forces, but breaks down; our vessel, with its centre of gravity placed too high, capsizes in a sudden gale; our lighthouse, with its foundation sapped by the action of the waves, is blown down in a storm. The condition next after knowledge that Nature exacts is obedience. We must first know, we must next obey; but these two conditions once fulfilled, there is nothing that she may not grant us; nothing that we may not hope for, even marvels that cannot now be dreamed of by us any more than the marvels of steam and electricity by our ancestors a few generations back. Already we have tamed and made all the great agencies and forces of Nature our potent, though as yet only partial, vassals. Heat, light, electricity, water, wind, and steam, already perform for us all manner of service; in the future they will do still more marvellous things. By more exact and concentrated observation, by the subtle and well-pointed interrogation of Nature's more hidden ways of operation, at last comes the great discovery for which these prepare the way, which had already existed in the hazier form of hypothesis; and the discoveries of the laws invariably lead, by help of a different class of minds, to the great practical invention which further presses the inexhaustible forces of Nature into the service of man. By observation and experiment prompted by hypothesis, the discoverers first learn the general laws of phenomena, then the more special, both together constituting the science; and the science illuminates the path of endless practical inventions. It is to this double labour of the men of science and the practical inventors, of the Newtons and Watts, that we owe all our mastery over the once formidable forces of Nature; in particular, we owe it to the extraordinary discoveries and inventions of the past half-century, which, further, besides multiplying our comforts and emancipating men's muscles from strenuous toil, have greatly revolutionized our social and industrial life.

Let men only learn Nature's ways of behaviour—first her ordinary, and then her more secret and exceptional but still general processes—and all things are possible, and may be attained from her. She will relax her rigidity; she will grant everything to knowledge. To ignorance and rebellion only is she merciless and cruel; and to both equally so.

Knowledge is the true prayer, the only one to which Nature hearkens and responds, as the pursuit of knowledge is her true and accepted worship. By knowledge alone man has been delivered from the forces and scourges and fatalities of Nature, blind and mighty and destroying —fire and flood, lightning and tempest, plague and famine, shipwreck and untimely death. To appease the wrath of these awful and destructive powers of Nature, the primitive man supposing them deities or demons, in trembling fear built temples, and offered prayer and sacrifice of everything that could be conceived to appease offended deities, in vain; while modern man, by a knowledge of Nature's laws, not only averts her anger, but converts her most formidable forces into his powerful servants. Thus by knowledge only, he has performed the miracle of taming the blind and inanimate forces of Nature, much more difficult to subdue than the animals or savage beasts, and utterly insensible to supplication, or prayer, or sacrifice. Let us only know her conditions, and accept them, and Nature will be propitious indeed. Where she had else been our scourge and destroyer, she will give us all things liberally to enjoy. And who are they who have enabled us to placate Nature, the priests of this true worship who have made atonement, the mediators between ordinary men and Nature who have rendered her propitious? The priests have been the discoverers and inventors in the sciences and the arts; the temples Nature herself; and the inner shrines where the worship has been carried on, have been the laboratory and the observatory, the study of the natural philosopher and inventor, and the workshop of the engineer.

The mastery of Nature has not been the sole result

of physical science. This has, indeed, followed from scientific knowledge and discovery, and material advantages and comforts, great and important, have again followed from it. We have further got an explanation of Nature, for which the human mind craves as much as for material results. We have learned the settled order of the world: that nothing can disturb it outside the circle of natural causes; that nothing ever will disturb it which is not the result of natural causes; and that such disturbing causes, which are rather of the nature of growths, are always of prodigiously slow development. By the progress of physical and natural science conjointly, we have at length been delivered from the terrors of superstition and ignorance, and the tyranny of dogmatic creeds, which took advantage of them.

§ 4. And even in the general practical sphere, Science has done more than merely minister to man's material comforts and happiness. After discovering the laws and obtaining the dominion over the forces of external nature, Science has come to man himself, to human nature; and here, too, she has ascertained the laws, physiological and psychological, as manifested in his mind and frame; and from this knowledge, supplemented by the practical science of medicine—itself a slow growth of traditional experience and knowledge—we may hope in future to regulate the expenditure of our physical and mental energies with a wiser economy; we may even hope, by the improved resources of the medical art, to come to terms with, if we may not wholly subdue, the maleficent forces within, which show themselves in diseases or disordered function of body or mind; and it even appears certain that we might save ourselves half the diseases, and a large fraction of the unhappiness and minor miseries of life by common attention to the known and demonstrated laws of health.

In the natural order of inquiry, and according to the order of difficulty and complexity, Science has first addressed herself to the study of the physical world; next to the organic world, or the world of life; and lastly to the phenomena of the social world.* At the summit of the series of living beings, Science encounters man, the most complex and finished product of life, furnishing the subject of the two co-related sciences of physiology and psychology. In man Science finds two systems, a bodily and a mental one, totally dissimilar and yet wonderfully fitted together, and working into each other, as an existent fact; a wonderful and indissoluble union, forming the marvellous whole—the man himself, with a bodily organism capable of movements the most express and admirable, and with a mind capable of producing the most wonderful thoughts; in "action like an angel, in apprehension like a God." The physiologist discovers in the living human body a system far more truly wonderful than any solar or sidereal system moved only by physical forces—a system in which the parts are variously and exquisitely adapted to each other and to the whole, with mutual actions and sympathies, subtly transmitted between parts adjacent and parts remote, and between the total bodily and total mental systems themselves, all conspiring to the common final ends of life, movement,

---

* As a matter of fact, the three orders of inquiry have been carried on contemporaneously, both under the Greek and modern civilizations. The above is, no doubt, the order of complexity; but whether it is the order of difficulty, as Comte and Spencer and Mill affirm, may be made a question. Political economy and sociology, so far as they are sciences, do not seem more difficult than the physical sciences in the deductive stage, which draw on all the resources of the mathematical sciences as well as on experiment.

and thought. Here, too, Science finds laws, both of bodily function and of mental faculty, of structure and growth, of mutual action of parts, and of secret nervous communication. From the cunning disposition of the elementary atoms and cells, to the finished physiological functions and anatomical relations of the full-grown organism; from the first faint dawn of infant or embryonic sensation, to the crowning marvel of consciousness and inspired thought;—all the phenomena in the human being are subject to law; and many of these, of much consequence to bodily and mental health, and for the regulation of life, physiologists have already mastered for us. When the various functions duly perform their work, when the whole mechanism, bodily and mental, works smoothly and harmoniously, there is annexed to this state the general sense of health, and a feeling of joy and satisfaction in existence; but when any of them fails, when any part of the bodily machinery is out of order, when a certain organ performs its function badly, when the normal relation between important organs is disturbed, or their mutual action perverse,—the earth becomes for us "a sterile promontory," and all happiness is attacked at the root. True, some organs may discharge their functions ill, without impairing our spirits, but in these cases we are often lulled into a false security. The general rule, however, is that disordered function, however slight, affects our spirits; when more serious, it produces disease; and in both cases diminishes happiness or satisfaction in existence. Moreover, our bodily system is a machine so delicate that it is subject to all kinds of disturbing and disordering causes short of those which stop its further action by breaking it up completely. It is subject, in addition, to all "the skyey influences," to evil influences from our fortunes, our fellows, our ill-adapted or adverse circumstances, our passions, as well as to mysterious possibilities of disturbance or sudden failure inherited from our ancestors, and lying sleeping possibly for years in the ultimate atoms and cells of the frame. All this Modern Science, physiology and embryology, has taught us; but she has done more than point out the evil,—she has come to our assistance and partial delivery. By the light which the science of physiology has given to medicine, by the aid which chemistry, electricity, and botany have supplied, as well as by the many discoveries of the powerful remedial effects of certain drugs and agencies, the modern physician is enabled to attack declared diseases with much more knowledge and skill. He is able, moreover, to contend much more successfully with the disturbing causes within; while we ourselves, by a knowledge of the general principles of physiology and by ordinary attention to the known laws of health, may in great measure escape those diseases and ailments which people so often bring upon themselves, and may preserve ourselves in good bodily health.

§ 5. But the mind diseased, can any medicinal art minister to it? The "rooted sorrow," can Science pluck it from the memory? Can physic or the positive conclusions of philosophy—

> Raze out the written troubles of the brain,
> And with some sweet oblivious antidote,
> Cleanse the stuffed bosom of that perilous stuff
> Which weighs upon the heart?

And the answer of the positive scientific thinker is, Yes, to a degree; science and the philosophy founded on science do enable us to deal with and to diminish this class of ills. Science can really minister to the mind diseased, as well as teach us to escape the causes of such. She can veritably mitigate the deeper soul-sicknesses, as she can effectually cure the more ordinary but less malignant forms of the same general type of disorder. For mental physiology and medical science now well understand that mental disorders, both of the serious and superficial sort, are really bodily disorders; that the mind diseased is but the brain and nervous system diseased; and between them they have discovered a curative treatment as well as a mental hygiene. There are both material and moral medicines prescribed, which act directly upon and compose the disordered molecular action, at the root of all serious mental disturbance. And there is a moral as well as a physical therapeutic and regimen for our more serious and deep-seated soul-sickness, our melancholies, world-weariness, despondencies, abysmal depressions, and paroxysmal despairs, as well as for the lighter and more evanescent moral ailments of the same general nature, though less virulent in degree, which are the common human heritage. Even when there is functional cerebral disorder, amounting to mental aberration, there is now a possibility of complete cure, or at least of mitigation which was not possible in the old days of ignorance and barbarous treatment.

And can Science, the mere ascertained sequence and conjunction of phenomena—can even physiology and psychology enable us to banish from the breast the evil passions, the poisons in our cup of peace—remorse and hatred and fear—or aid us to dissipate in our fearful imaginations gloomy apprehensions and the monstrous magnified shadows of the coming evil? Yes, to some very considerable extent they can; and the incurable residuum, a knowledge of the universal order, will teach you to bear with patience, if not with fortitude.

Can Science deliver us from the endless cares and the

disturbing perplexities of conduct, the trials, difficulties, and dangers, the disappointments, and sometimes the total defeats, with which we meet in life? No, Science cannot deliver you from these, nor should you ask it. Science cannot cure this class of griefs, which is of the inmost essence of life itself; but she can teach you to minimize them, to see them in their true nature, to reduce them to their proper size and reality. Further yet, she can enable you to see a soul of good in these things evil, to find a jewel in adversity itself; and even to extract a balance of advantage from the general probation of life of which you complain. Indeed, you know little what you really want, and what would be really for your good, when you ask the removal of all trial and trouble from life; and the total removal of difficulty and danger would be far from the heaven of happiness you dream it would be. It would cause you *ennui* and weariness and nausea of life, but not the peace you long for; the weariness of a life without aim and effort and struggle, and without the nourishment and renovation of nerve, the genial outcome of spirits, and the real peace in the brain and breast which good aims and sustained effort ever bring with them, even when they do not lead to full fruition. Even Schopenhauer, the modern pessimist prophet, admits that the dead calm of full fruition and accomplished desires would be as bad for men as the present torment of life from the restless craving of unfulfilled wants and desires; his own idea of peace and felicity consisting not in the fulfilment of our numerous desires, but in the "denial of the will to live," and consequent extinction of them. And he is right, so far as he contends that the dead calm of fulfilment would be a worse and more abysmal fate than our present evil condition. This state, where no effort is required, and all trouble is removed, the state where every wish receives fulfilment without action or effort, might suit the angels, but it would not suit men as at present constituted. We are made with faculties both for contemplation and action, but chiefly for the latter. We are made for competition, struggle, combat with our fellows, with nature, with fate, even with the problems and difficulties which thought and conduct themselves present to us. In short, trial and difficulty and danger are for ever inseparable from the life of man, as from the life of every living creature on earth, and without it we find it a little difficult even to conceive the happiness of the gods, reduced, as Aristotle argues, to contemplation merely. The notion of life and trial are with us at least so inseparably linked together, that we cannot conceive of the first without the second. And then the evils necessary for our state of probation are the necessary conditions of all that we call progress, and all that we call virtue, which things bring happiness such as we can appreciate. The evils are the condition of all perfection or approach to it in every direction, in every course of excellence and aspiration. Our nature is adapted and shaped beforehand with special reference to life's ills. We inherit the spirit of struggle and combat. And what man would really have his life free from the dangers which give a zest; from the difficulties which stimulate and do not daunt the brave; from the trial of merit which disciplines and strengthens our fortitude, or our powers of achievement; nay, even from the salutary temporary defeat, which is often the best preparation for, and the prelude to, the future victory?

But, however we choose to regard them, it is at least certain that these immemorial and universal evils in some form and in some degree must for ever continue. The excessive degree of probation which kills us before shaping us to our surroundings, or which hardens the heart without improving the virtue,—this, we may indulge the hope, will with time be mitigated; it is being mitigated; but whilst men remain men, and until they shall have far more closely approximated to angelic nature, they cannot be, and it is not desirable that they should be, freed from the trial, difficulty, and danger incident to human life.

There are, indeed, other real ills which bring no counterbalancing benefit in their train; ills in abundance, for which no knowledge or art has provided effective remedial drugs or even mental palliations. There are the stings of conscience, the corrosions of long-continued remorse and sorrow, the sickness of heart for the hopes long deferred, the despair of heart for the hopes for ever defeated and overthrown. There is the fierce and prolonged probation, which paralyzes or slays, which assaults us before and behind and from all sides, and which, sufficiently long continued, will harden the heart to pity and dull it to good; a probation which, instead of improving our virtue, rather corrupts and envenoms it, turning it into its opposite; which, in dark moments, may make even the virtuous man doubt the reality of virtue, and the kindly man dislike his species. There are these and other evils—the wreck of health, ruin of fortune, loss of friends by death or estrangement, for which no physical or moral medicine has yet been provided in the pharmacopœia of science, and for which scarcely any soothing anodyne has yet been discovered. But if science has failed, did theology or philosophy ever do much to cure or assuage these classes of human griefs and pangs? Theology offered a remedy which, admittedly, only operated occasionally through the medium of complex moral and spiritual miracles; philosophy, with greater show of reason, according to the system we consulted, advised us to fortify our spirits so as to bear the ills, or to make light of them, or to fly from their causes. Nevertheless, the pains remained in all cases: men continued to suffer, in spite of religious or philosophical consolations. We now know better; that some bitter evils are incidental to the universal human lot; that they are a part of human destiny, like death itself, which cannot be shunned. We know, too, that they follow from natural causes, and that, therefore, no moral miracle can possibly be wrought to deliver us from them; and if there is to be the least mitigation, it must, we know, be wrought by natural means, and in an intelligible manner. But happily we also know something more than formerly respecting the sequence of our mental states and their physical concomitants, the evil as well as the good; and we can do something at least, through the united forces of physiology and psychology, to mitigate the mental pains which we cannot cure. We are taught that if the evil and depressing passions, "the vultures of the mind," have destructive effects upon our nerves and health, as they surely have, we must resist and control or shun the causes which produce the disastrous effects. We are thus compelled, under severe natural penalties, to regulate our life more wisely. We are driven to a greater self-mastery, a stronger and wiser self-denial, it may be even to a greater renunciation of objects dear and desirable; and we shall certainly be required to cultivate a stricter conscience, and one more void of offence to all. In this way, by natural, which also include moral means, we may really reduce our worst sorrows, troubles and trials to within a narrower and endurable compass; and when we have in this way done our utmost, it is then our duty, and it exhibits the right spirit, to accept, if not contentedly—which might be demanding too much from men—at least unmurmuringly, silently, and stoically, the irreducible burden of grief that we must bear. We thus return to stoicism; we must cultivate the spirit of resignation, which a knowledge of the fixed general order of Nature in the physical sphere has already prepared us for, but resignation only with respect to that portion of our mental, moral, and physical pangs and maladies for which we are assured there is no alleviation. For we are not called upon to lie down quiescently under ills which we can really, in however small degree, reduce by our wisdom and resolute endeavours. The virtue of resignation must not be confounded with apathetic indifference, or with Mussulman fatalism, or even with the quietism—the denial of the will to live—of the pessimist; these are only vicious frames of mind resembling it; resignation is the high virtue which is only asked from us with respect to those numerous unalterable ills which, like death, must be accepted, though to cultivate it, and attain to it, in these cases where it is really demanded from us, is the summit of human virtue, showing piety, patience, and fortitude in one.

§ 6. In spite, however, of all mitigation of our probation from science, or philosophy, or medicine, does not the feverish and increasing intensity of the competitive struggle for life, resulting from our crowded and ever-increasing population, tend to swell the list of sufferers from mental and nervous maladies, owing to the greater demand made on the energies of the brain, the modern weapon of combat, at least with the educated classes, in the battle for existence?

Do not brain and nerves give way or fail more frequently than in former times, when men seemed compact of firmer fibres with stronger nerves? To some extent probably, though the extent may be easily exaggerated; since such cases are now, through statistics, brought more prominently before our notice than formerly, and since our trebled population, since the beginning of the century, would necessarily show a trebled number of such cases even if there were no relative increase. But even if there be not only a greater absolute number, but a greater relative proportion of such, there are more than compensating considerations.

The greater demand on organs may have a double effect: It may both produce fitness of faculties, and also, if they are below average excellence, it may produce further unfitness; especially if, as in our modern life, the work is itself becoming more complex and exacting. But in a far greater number of instances, the more stringent demands and severer competition of our more complex social life merely make manifest and patent inherent unfitness, without in any respect causing or increasing it. The severer conditions serve the purposes of probation, by discovering and disciplining excellence where it already exists, while at the same time revealing inherent incapacity. This is the general rule; the cases where competition produces failure and unfitness, the exception. Competition, indeed, is not to blame in general; it is the chance and uncertainty which accompanies the competitive *régime*—an accident which is no part of its essence—that mostly produces the mental failure, or reduced nervous vitality, which, even more than lack of brain, results in the various avenues of competition in the loss of the battle of life. Happily, however, this chance element, through the operation of various counteracting agencies constantly on the increase which tend to produce a solidarity in men's fortunes, is being constantly reduced within narrower limits. But while the chance element is being minimized, the competition itself, in some shape and in certain directions, must remain a permanent fact in human existence. It is even a most important factor in furthering the utilitarian end of the greatest ultimate good of men. It may indeed and it must be mitigated, in certain directions; but it could never be wholly dispensed with without producing stagnation or retrogression. In fact, it is impossible to conceive it wholly abolished, being, as it is, the deepest, most universal law of life when many units live in a state of social aggregation. Amongst communities of ants some competition exists; even in a socialistic community it could not be done away with. There would still be competition, if not for property, yet for things which could not be divided, and which all could not have; if not for divisible and material, yet for immaterial things—power, fame, excellence; or if not for self, there would be competition to do the most good for all or for others. Competition, in short, is the necessary and eternal means adopted by Nature, wiser than we, to perfect all the species of animals, and the human species conspicuously; and competition, in its nobler and more justifiable forms, is the generous desire to surpass, the source of all that is great in human endeavour, and of all that is excellent in human achievement. It is the quick spur to merit and virtue, quite as much as the external prize of wealth or fame, and men can never dispense with it, as the best men will never be without it. In its lower form, however, in the shape in which it so often manifests itself—of the selfish desire to amass together the greatest possible amount of wealth, or of the material means to happiness, it deserves no such high commendation as we have bestowed upon it; though even in this form it is on the whole beneficial, and its excess is far preferable to its absence. In the present state of civilized communities, competition on the whole, including its coarser forms, works beneficially, and works also towards the production of the superior future society. It selects the brain and nerves best adapted to the changed conditions of modern social and industrial life, of which the chief characteristic is the freer scope allowed to individual efforts, and in which the prizes are now more than formerly to individual energy and ability. By the prolonged process of natural selection, which essentially implies competition, as alone giving nature's selection free play, those men will infallibly be found and elected to continue the race who have not only brains and bodily organs fitter for the work involving keener competition, but who will also find a special pleasure in the keenness of the struggle.* They will enjoy the contest, as men in ruder ages "drank delight of battle with their peers," in their coarser trials to find the fit for the different and simpler conditions of life.

It is true, indeed, that natural selection, having in view only the perfection of the type and species, often presses heavily and mercilessly upon the individual. With a grand goal in view, Nature, in steering towards it, seems utterly regardless of the means employed to reach it. Blind and careless, even cruel and merciless, she shows herself to the existing units that are not aids and instruments to her further aims. Her path is constantly over the prostrate bodies of the present slain,—indifferent,—looking only to her goal— the happier better species hereafter. And this is her only

* See Spencer's *Principles of Biology*, vol. ii. p. 503.

justification. But in later times and in our own day there has arisen the protest of human nature against the cruelty of objective impersonal Nature. In the case of men themselves, Nature as human nature, begins to relent in her severity. There has come a mitigation in the sterner aspects of the fierce competitive struggle, as also in the consequences to the conquered, now less disastrous than in former less humane times. There is quarter to the vanquished in the social battle of life, as there is in modern civilized warfare; there is even aid to the wounded in both cases from an increase in our sympathy and humanity.

There is, moreover, a greater recognition of the gulf of disastrous chance into which the worthy and the intellectually capable may be precipitated as well as the worthless and unfit; and this reflection makes men inclined to deal more considerately with the cases of failure that a change of circumstances or a turn in fortune's wheel might have made their own. This sphere of chance may not really be greater in modern life, but it is more seen and more felt; and our system of individualism, of which the socialists complain, necessarily brings a certain amount of it with it. But with the evil has come the mitigation.

Further, there is the felt community of interests amongst the members of different classes, and callings, of associations and companies with common aims and objects, which abates competition to the extent of the common interest inside such groups and societies, leaving it to exist only between the various groups themselves, or in lessened degree between the individuals composing them. All this, however, does not prevent the application of the law of natural selection, nor do away with the need of competition in its other and salutary forms. The considerations above pointed out mitigate the harsher features of competition, but they do not show that we could dispense with competition—the one sure and constant means employed by Nature to improve society, and to achieve intellectual, moral, and physical excellence in the race. By this sorting and eliminating process constantly at work, if its natural course is not deliberately frustrated by men themselves, in the permission and encouragement of the inferior or worst specimens—the criminals, the imbeciles, the vicious, the diseased by inheritance—to multiply their kind instead of the better specimens, a race with superior brains, healthy frames, and moral dispositions fully adapted to their environment, will inevitably in time be evolved ; a race from which the weak and worthless and wicked will have been slowly but surely eliminated, and in which, thanks to the beneficent laws of heredity, they can no more re-appear to deteriorate the high type attained.*

* See Spencer's *Study of Sociology*, pp. 340-349.

CHAPTER III.

TO THE POOR. SCIENCE AND SOCIALISM.

§ 1. YOUR gospel is good, exclaims the modern socialist. Science, we allow, has done much for man's collective, and something for his individual, benefit. She has multiplied man's material comforts and enjoyments, increased the productive powers of labour, triumphed over the destroying forces of Nature, mitigated the diseases of the individual body; and for all this she deserves the thanks of mankind. But the diseases of the social body, chronic and destroying: the crime, and want, and poverty the fruitful parent of further crime, and vice, and misery; the social sores and ulcerating wounds of the modern body politic; the drunkenness; the degraded, disease-fraught frames; the still more degraded minds; the massed misery and shame of our great cities; the pauperism and prostitution;—all this dismal, broadening river of human want and wretchedness and shamelessness, scarcely if at all diminished by our vaunted civilization or religion, even in its relative amount, while it has vastly increased in absolute amount, while moreover, the sufferers, having tasted the tree of knowledge, have become more keenly alive to the fact of their nakedness and misery, and while the race itself has at last awoke to a keen consciousness of these shameful and intolerable things;

—all the evil of this social hell, of far greater dimensions than the social elysium which modern society also contains in its midst,—can Science do nothing to check, or to cure, or to mitigate it?

Can Science help us to stem this tide of social human misery, the greater part of it, including the crime and vice, being directly traceable to poverty alone, or to the blunted feelings, the perverted moral perceptions and despair, produced by poverty, while the fact itself of poverty, is, as the socialists contend, the necessary result of our present social and industrial system, our present consecrated *régime* of competition and individualism, and of the social injustice which lies at the root of it? Can Science help us to check or control the causes which produce all this misery? Can she aid to diminish the gulf, ever deepening and dangerous, between rich and poor; the monstrous and growing contrast between misery and luxury; between the gilded splendour and perfume, the pomp and pride, the varnished vices and forgiven sins of the elect of the social heaven on one side, and on the other the dismal dwellings and pinching privation, the squalor and stench, the disease and drunkenness, the unforgiven sins and shames of the unfortunates of the social Inferno, which stretches wide and hopeless outside the gates of the social paradise? Can Science, we ask, help us here? And if she cannot, of what avail are her other services and gifts to men, which are intercepted and monopolized by these same wealthy who already have, to the further detriment of those who have not? If this gospel of Science is not for all mankind, if it is not " the gospel to the poor," as Christianity, though perverted from its Founder's purpose, was meant to be,—of what use is the message, and to what purpose all the vain noise and blowing of trumpets? If Science cannot aid to mitigate the evident miseries of the many, if she can only offer us the continued operation of natural selection as a panacea for our admitted social griefs, whence all the jubilations, and why should men of science indulge in optimistic boasts? If the poverty of the majority forbids even the most elementary conditions of happiness, the first necessaries of life, were it not honester for Science and Evolution to acknowledge the case of the pessimist as proved, and keep a little quiet, leaving to men not yet prepared to accept the pessimist solution nor yet the satisfied conclusion of the rich that " the poor must be always in the land," some other way than by scientific counsel of working out their own earthly salvation?

The practical problem for Science in the sphere of society is, according to the socialist, to find a means of curing or mitigating poverty, and the miseries, alone deserving compassion, that flow from it. Can she find a remedy other than the slow one of natural selection, which is, in fact, neither cure nor consolation for the present generation of sufferers, which at best seems little more than a consecration, in the name of Science, of the evils complained of, or an assurance to the victims who are not selected that their sacrifice is for the future good of society. We do not demand of Science, says the socialist, that she should perform the miracle of remedying evils which are a necessary part of the universal human heritage and destiny, as sorrow, sickness, disappointment, or death, but only that she should aid us to remove or lessen want and poverty, with the long and disastrous train of evils that thence proceeds,—which things we maintain are curable. We admit that even if Science could or would show us undoubtedly the true scientific causes of these, it would be something, even though her remedies were useless. Now, the socialist maintains that the great social evils are due to our present social system, that they could be cured by the necessary changes in it, and are demonstrably incurable under our present system. Science, on the other hand, seems to affirm that the causes are resident in human nature, in the reproductive instinct which ever tends to produce a redundant population; and she offers us two most unsatisfactory remedies. The first is her new and universal medicine of "natural selection," and the survival of him who can best equalize his nature to his environment—a formula which, applied to human societies, virtually recommends that the present state of things should continue; that the purifying and eliminating process which has done so well in the past should still go on or be applied more stringently if greater results are required; that in short, natural selection—which only selects those who can adapt themselves to their surroundings, subject to chance and change, and which slays, or slowly saps the strength, or pauperizes so many of the rest—is to go on for ever, and all will come right generations hence by this marvellous curative process. The second scientific remedy is the old and thrice-famed one of Malthus, so strongly recommended by Mill—the "prudential restraint," which, however, contrary as it is to the teaching of Herbert Spencer, whose optimistic eyes, discerning good ever in things evil, sees future possible civilizations in the pressure of redundant population, is also at variance with the doctrine of our contemporary pessimist philosopher, Hartmann, who, while, to the optimist, he plays the part of Ahriman to Ormuz, at the same time discerns in the instinct in question the deepest, most obstinate, and most universal, albeit irrational, instinct of nature, the all-powerful will of the species to live.

The cause of our chief social evils—persists the socialist—is the constitution of society, our present social system,—a system partly of consecrated hereditary privilege, which is, however, happily everywhere dying; but mainly and more perniciously, our present industrial system, of individual competition, of employer and employed, of capital and labour,—a system not dying, but everywhere in feverish active life all around; whose first principle is each one for himself; in which all struggle furiously to push their way to the front, to "get on," as the expressive phrase is, which means to get and to grasp the greatest possible sum of the good things going, that constant and concentrated effort, skill, and cunning, conducted within the bounds of the civil but by no means the moral law, may secure; a system certainly not favourable to the further development of the social, or kindly, or disinterested virtues, being scarcely compatible with the primary virtues of truth, or justice, or honesty, but, on the contrary, directly tending to develop the intensest forms of selfishness; a system, moreover, which works badly for mankind, or for nations, or for classes in the gross, being demonstrably inconsistent with the "greatest happiness of the greatest number," it being mathematically certain that in the competitive race the greater number will be wholly distanced, that a considerable number, from chance, or circumstance, or strain in the contest, will break hopelessly down, while the happiness of the few who win the prize is a small set-off against the misery of the many who fail,—a lottery system, of few prizes and many blanks; in which the best do not win, where the fortunes of the few are made by the failures of the many;—

a system, moreover, in which the few successful must, after all, however grudgingly, subscribe to the support of the same dismal and forlorn army of the failures, and paupers, and criminals, which it has in great measure produced.

And yet this *régime* of feverish competition, with all its evils and disastrous chances for the lower classes, who perish like flies beneath its fluctuations and panics, and with all its odious and vulgar accompaniments, the pushing, struggling, and trampling on the fallen, as they show themselves in the better classes; this wretched and evil system of individualism, worse than the feudalism which it followed, where the vassal at least shared the bread as well as the fortune of his lord, and where pauperism did not exist;—this system is, it seems, to be consecrated in the name of Science, and pronounced an eternal and unalterable fact and law of social existence. Competition, the ordeal of battle, the survival of the strong, is the universal law of all life, evolution-science affirms. Competition regulates the flow of capital, determines an average equality of profits, influences wages and rents, finds the fit within the several professions and callings, is the spur to all invention and excellence, and, according to the orthodox political economy as well as evolution, competition is an eternal fact of human nature, the most necessary factor of social and national progress.

But this very competitive and much-lauded *régime* which certain writers on economic and sociological subjects would stereotype as necessary and eternal law, is an essentially modern as well as an evidently modifiable thing; a stage in the course of evolution, if the evolutionist wishes; a passing phase of our civilization, which began, as recent research discloses, in a form of communism, which has passed through a series of continuous changes to unlimited in-

s

dividualism, and which no less clearly in certain directions manifests a tendency to pass again into communism—the final goal of civilization, if society be not previously dissolved. The primitive form of society, according to the historians of evolution, was communistic;* but without pressing this point of history in the remote past, our present system of unlimited competition is a wholly modern thing, and, moveover, corrigible or wholly removable if found hurtful to the total social body. The socialist maintains that the system of competition, the essence of our present industrial and social system, is hurtful and vicious, the fount and source of all our social evils; so much so indeed, that, being given its bare notion and type, all the dark catalogue of social evils and shames, pauperism, drunkenness, prostitution, could be deduced from it by the thinker in his study, nay, by any man of intelligence, with strict logical and almost mathematical rigour, so close and clear is the dependence of the one on the other—of our present evils on our present system. The thinker might deduce our griefs from our present conception of society and its constitution, without taking the trouble of subjecting his conclusions to the terrible verification which our criminal statistics, as well as the lanes and alleys of our great cities, so abundantly furnish.

But our new Evolution-Science, after examining the social maladies with the tranquillity becoming to science, offers for cure and comfort her formula of "the survival of the fittest" in the long struggle of existence protracted for generations. Our evolution doctors, with professional gravity and calmness, write out their prescriptions for

* See, on this point, Spencer's *Principles of Sociology*; Lubbock's *Origin of Civilization*; Maine's *Village-Communities*.

society's weal of "natural selection and the survival of the fittest." They give us, moreover, the old time-honoured, well-intentioned professional advice, signifying little. We must not be drunken nor imprudent; we must get sound scientific knowledge, above all, of the doctrines of evolution; we must not rebel against the laws of nature, or of life, or of the social organism. To which the economist adds that the poor must not have large families; while the evolutionist further moves that the species should not be recruited from its inferior specimens—its criminals, idlers, and imbeciles. As to general regimen, we must let Nature have her course; above all, let natural selection, which is Nature's way, have full and free play. Progress, improvement in the health of society under these conditions, will be sure to follow, though it will be slow. It must, in fact, be slow in order to be sure. There is no hope in revolutions, but only in evolution, and the latter is slow, very slow, we are plainly told. The drastic heroic treatment by revolution is dangerous to the life of the body politic; if it does not kill, it may permanently debilitate or destroy the constitution. Even legislators can do little to benefit or improve men, certainly no speedy good result need be looked for from their action. Even if legislation contemplates a particular good to be realized, and aims persistently at it, by the perversion and complication of things, or by the irony of fate, a quite different result and one wholly unexpected comes out. So teaches and advises evolution, and the prophet and expounder of evolution doctrine, Herbert Spencer. We thank Science and her teachers; but happily also, we remember and may remind the evolutionists of another of their doctrines — that there has always been and that there still is another form in which the struggle for existence shows itself, and one, moreover, in which the survivors would not be the same, nor the fittest in the same sense, as in the other form of the struggle approved of by the evolutionist; that, in fact, the old ordeal of actual battle, and the survival of the conqueror, is not yet wholly antiquated or out of fashion with men, and before the majority consent to perish slowly one by one under the eternal pressure of poverty and the operation of natural selection, they may prefer to make appeal to the ancient, but still lawful and still practised trial of the strong, if an earlier amelioration of their condition be pronounced impossible. The issue would at least be more quickly decided; the end would be worth the cost, worth at least the hazarding the very moderate minimum of happiness which the majority enjoy at present, and which small amount, moreover, is all that optimist science and evolution are able to promise them for generations to come, with which to sustain their patience.

But we are seasonably advised that we must not rise in rebellion against Science and natural laws. No, certainly. Where it is a question of unvarying physical or natural laws, of settled sequences that will have place whatever men may do, it would be foolish to try to defeat them. But let it be well noted, we do not regard all your so-called sociological and economic laws as of this description. For all these lately discovered laws of society are made by the actions and behaviour of men; they are only possible by the consent and volitions of men; and these are determined, as Science knows and teaches, by motives, which, in the case of masses of men, turn mainly on considerations of self-interest. After the laws have been pointed out by Science and recognized by men, it still depends on men's agreement whether they are to continue or no. It depends on the assent and consent of men whether any ascertained social law, any observed relation of men to each other, any particular definition of property, even any particular structure of society, is to continue to exist or no. There may be good reasons to think that the consent of men, which permits the laws, will not be revoked; still men retain the right and the power to revoke their consent, if their interest requires it. Men can abrogate sociological laws as well as statute laws, if they find them inconvenient, if they press heavily upon them, if they interfere with the greatest happiness of the greatest number. There is no fatality about them, as about physical laws. Undoubtedly, sociological laws can be changed; and they will be changed wherever they run counter to the law of self-preservation—the first and most imperious of Nature's laws, as Darwin and Spencer rightly maintain it to be. Moreover, some of the supposed laws would soon disappear under the influence of a powerful new sentiment, such as has given birth and life to religious and social revolutions once and again.

Thus, then, the laws of society and Science, with which we are threatened, are not physical laws, that we should accept their fatal necessity with resignation and bowed heads. They are not universal facts to be accepted and made the best of. They are alterable, all of them inconsistent with men's general wishes—all of them which hurt, all which are not obviously implied in the mere notion of men living together at all. These last are not, indeed, alterable, because they are profitable, because men alive to their interest will not alter them. When men, naturally gregarious animals, come together, they must, indeed, live under some moral laws, devised under a sense of the general interest; and they must soon discover and put in practice some economic expedients for making labour more effective, such as the division of employments, and sometimes the co-operation of efforts, which are also obviously prompted by a sense of interest; and some kind of regulative agency will appear as alleged. But the various kinds of laws manifested—moral, economic, sociological—all spring from a sense of general interest, and are to be tried by that test when they seem to depart from it. This, in brief, is the essence of the matter and of the science of society, so much talked about in later times; and whatever laws the science of sociology may discover, this remains a permanent and overriding generalization, that the supposed invariable behaviour of associated men will only continue invariable so long as men are generally contented so to behave. Any predictions made on the assumption of invariable human nature, in the sense of invariable physical nature, can only be depended upon so long as men are so contented. But they may become discontented with economic and sociological as well as with civil laws, that they think are not for their good; and whenever they are oppressed or hurt they will be certain to become so, and also apt to apply the best remedy they can find. This is as general a law of human nature, as much a biological or sociological law, if you will, as any that could well be laid down.

The mistake of the writers on the science of society is to regard existing social and sociological laws, the existing constitution of society, as either unchangeable or not to be changed except extremely slowly. True, there could not well be a science on any other assumption, though there might be a history, a description of the phases and stages through which societies have passed; and therefore the still greater mistake of these writers is, perhaps, the notion that there is any science of sociology at all, when the past career of nations and course of civilization is so capricious, and the future course of social as of general evolution admittedly so little predictable. History seems to be the proper name for such a study, whose chief business is a description of what has been and of what now is. At least, if sociology be styled a science, it is certain that it cannot look far into the future, however it may explain the past; and still more certain that it need not be appealed to in order to bind men's hands in the shaping their own fortunes, by the spectre of necessity in the shape of scientific law.

For the subjects of the supposed science, being men and not physical or chemical substances, are not the same from generation to generation. Nay, men may change even within the limits of a generation, under the strengthening and vivifying force of a new faith. They are modifiable by themselves, or by circumstances, when living in isolation, and they are eminently modifiable when associated together in masses.

Where Science might fairly find a useful exercise for her deductive powers would be in the logical derivation of our present social disorders—pauperism, crime, immorality—from our present conception of life as a competitive race, from our present constitution of society, from our present imperfect definition of property, from our present consecrated system of individualism, from our present conventional morality not differing essentially from its opposite in so many cases. Given this general state of things, and our worst social maladies are given which flow as surely and necessarily from it as the properties of a triangle from the definitions and axioms of geometry. Deductive Science, we say, might find a profitable field for her labours in the logical affiliation of our social evils to our social system; but she would greatly hazard her credit for prophesying, if she ventures to predict that the many who see the present evils, and who also more or less suffer from them, will sit down patiently under them and wait for natural selection to deliver them, when they see a more direct and speedy way to their abolition. In short, the majority cannot wait for the social millenium prophesied to come, generations hence, by Herbert Spencer; and they have no faith that natural selection, if unnaturally hindered, as now, will ever select the best in the future, but far more likely the miscellaneous elect, as at present—the cunning, the physically strong and unscrupulous, the skilful schemer within the bounds of law, the immoral, the unpitying, the worthless, the impotent every way rather than the worthy. Such being the case, argues the socialist, are we to wait with folded arms because, generations after we are gone, natural selection, that is, a name for the results of endless chance, or rather, in the case of human societies at present, casts of the dice loaded with fraud and injustice, may perhaps—though it is only a perhaps—bring all things to rights? We do not think so. For us, if we miss the chance which this life offers of getting justice, no second is ever allowed. For this also Science has taught us. And we do not think that either as rational or moral beings we are called upon to wait, but rather to try to hasten the coming of social justice and righteousness, and the removal of social evils. We feel that now is the time to realize whatever is possible. And let Science understand that we know that we are the real final social forces. To us it belongs to mould the shape of society—a thing not done by chance, or by passive waiting, but by the active co-operation of men's energies and volitions. Nor is there any reason why we should wait till the science of sociology has made up its mind as to what are the necessary laws that we must or should be guided by. We might wait long, indeed, for scientific unanimity here; rather it is for us men to make the new laws for sociology to study, and the new social phenomena for this still infant science to meditate upon; and to make them, moreover, clear and decided.

§ 2. Thus argues the socialist of our days, not without a certain amount of truth and reason in his denunciation of society, but also not without passion, and with an undue sense of what is possible, or what changes are speedily practicable in human societies. It is scarcely correct to affirm, as some socialists do, that economic science is enlisted on the side of our present industrial and social system. Political economy, as Professor Cairnes * affirms, is, or should be, indifferent, as between rival theories of social constitution, its business being to determine the effect of any accepted system or the probable effect of any proposed new system on the production and distribution of wealth. And, in fact, there are eminent economists with a decided leaning to socialist views, as the late Herr Duhring, Lange the well-known author of the *History of Materialism*, and even our own greatest authority on economic questions since Ricardo, the late Mr. Mill. Political economy is neutral in the controversy, or rather, is appealed to by both sides; but the doctrine of evolution

* *Definition and Logical Method of Political Economy.*

and the new science of sociology, as conceived and expounded by Herbert Spencer, is decidedly opposed to and casts a damper on the socialist's aims and aspirations. The sociologist, therefore, the disciple of Herbert Spencer, we shall call upon to answer the argument of the socialist; and the answer is to the following effect:—

Men cannot make any great and sudden improvement in the condition of their society, as the socialist supposes. They cannot easily change its structure at all, but good changes are far more difficult of accomplishment than mischievous ones. The latter they can make if they choose, if they are foolish enough, but the former they cannot. It would be extremely difficult to materially alter the structure of modern society, so complex and connected in all its parts, with its many and mutually dependent functions, all pre-supposing each other, all acting upon each other, as in the physical organism; with established economic, as well as political, civil, religious organizations, all the slow evolution of ages, and answering to experienced social wants and necessities. You could not materially and at the same time suddenly alter even the economic constitution of society, the thing chiefly aimed at by socialism, because the production and distribution of wealth depends on causes not to be easily altered: the first on laws of physical and of human nature conjointly;—and the second on facts or sentiments of human nature;—the one class of facts or laws being unalterable quite, and the other but slowly so. You cannot in the latter case quickly change hereditary notions and sentiments respecting property, or the right of each to the ownership and disposal of whatever his own energy, ability, and industry may bring. You cannot arbitrarily compel men to regard each other as equal, where Nature has set her ineffaceable stamp of inequality; or force men to regard each other with feelings of love and brotherhood, where the feelings do not exist in the heart. You cannot do these things, and men cannot make the above changes; but without them no sudden regeneration of society is possible, and no scheme of socialism that has yet been suggested is workable.

Before you can change society materially for the better, you must first alter and improve its constituent units; and this, as all the laws of life and all the experience of history teach, is a thing not to be done easily or speedily. Men's natures, regarding them in the aggregate, cannot be quickly changed. One generation cannot be raised much above the one immediately preceding it, because it inherits the same general nature, the same sentiments, ideas, prejudices, and imperfections as its predecessor. Even were society ripe and ready for a new social or religious departure, as at the rise of the Christian or Mohammedan religions, the Reformation, or the French Revolution, yet such revolutions, slowly prepared for and slowly accomplished as they really are, are yet never brought about by intellectual conviction of the evils of the existing systems of things. There is further required a widespread discontent and a general enthusiasm, aroused and sustained by one or a few leading spirits, and men now lack alike the motive and guiding force. But even if there were a sufficient amount of diffused discontent and social misery everywhere prevalent, to be fanned by the socialist propaganda into a fierce destroying flame all over Europe, from Russia with her nihilists, to Spain with her socialists; and even if, in the general conflagration, the existing social order should be dissolved,—still all this would not in the sequel deeply or essentially alter the social structure of any modern civilized community. It could only produce temporary change or temporary chaos; because, after the wave of fanaticism and destroying fury had spent its strength, supposing only men had not in the interim annihilated each other, they would return to their old average, normal, human natures; the governmental and other regulative agencies, and an industrial system essentially the same in character as the old, would re-emerge, and most things would settle into their old grooves and forms; even the old social maladies, to cure which was the aim of all this destruction, would reproduce themselves in equal or probably increased amount, though possibly affecting different persons and sections of society. After temporary anarchy, things would revert of necessity to the pre-revolutionary state, because average human nature, from which they sprang and of which they were the will and expression, remains the same. You have not touched the real root of the evils complained of, by these supposed revolutions. The French nation did not essentially change its social structure by the various revolutions from 1789 to 1871, because the French character remained essentially the same, thus reproducing continually the same or similar evils.*

But, interrupts the socialist, though the French people did not perhaps alter what you call their social structure, did they not succeed in altering their material fortunes? Did they not alter permanently the relation of classes to each other, almost annihilating the power of the nobility, and redistributing their property amongst the nation? In short, the French got the strength in the revolutionary fever to change, and change permanently for the better, the

* See Spencer's *Study of Sociology*, ch. vii. p. 121.

fortunes of the majority of the people; they effected a revolution in society, if not in the political and social structure according to your metaphor; and such a change, only more thoroughly accomplished and accompanied by safeguards to prevent as much as possible a return to the old system, is precisely the general aim and goal of the socialist's endeavours. A man, we grant, cannot change the structure of his body, nor yet of his mind, but he may at critical moments in his life so act as to change for the better his whole future, and what a man can thus do for himself by taking the tide at the flood that leads on to fortune, a society or a nation may do for itself by a revolution. It may improve its happiness and fortune without altering its structure. So much, at least, may be said in reply to Herbert Spencer.

Nevertheless, replies the sociologist, the disciple of Spencer, you would not thus, by enforced social equality produced by revolution, stamp out poverty,—far less the other social maladies that have always afflicted society like inherited diseases, which in great measure they really are. You would not thus eradicate them; because you have not touched the source, but only the symptoms of social diseases; you have not reached the perennial and poisoned spring from which proceed all other social evils, poverty included, namely, our average, weak and imperfect, foolishly selfish, and corrupt human nature. The deep cause of all our woe lies here, lies in that imperfect thing called human nature, which only the sanguine enthusiast or foolish philanthropist dreams can be quickly and largely changed. That it is not to be easily changed, is the decided teaching of evolution; and yet without a very considerable improvement in it, no corresponding improvement in society is possible, as without a permanent and radical regeneration in average human nature, no great social regeneration is possible. Without alterations in individual men, no alterations in social arrangements and institutions, no legislative enactments, or forced equality, promise much in the way of good result; for, waiving the consideration that it would be extremely difficult to make the alterations, yet even if they were decreed by the authority of the State, still, men's natures remaining the same, after a temporary experience of chaos, productive of much evil of all sorts, they would return in great measure to the old lines, the worse, if the wiser, for their experience of anarchy, with all its horrors actual and in apprehension.

Even under the best conceivable socialistic *régime*, so long as our present human nature remains what it is, our worst social maladies would really remain; crime, immorality, intemperance, insanity, diseased minds and frames would still exist, possibly less concentrated than at present and more diffused, possibly assuming other forms, but inevitably present in equal total amount. They would necessarily still exist, because they are the inevitable products of the old unchanged human heart, from which proceed the evil thoughts that lead to crime and vice, and of the unchanged inherited physical constitutions, from which our bodily and mental maladies spring. As for material poverty (to speak nothing of worse kinds, intellectual and moral, which not unlikely would be born in the socialistic Utopia), unless the most stringent restraints were put upon the increase of population, it would soon manifest itself in a universal instead of a partial privation; while even from the beginning, unless our selfish human nature was wholly changed, so that men would be keenly spurred to live and labour for others, the total result of production would be very much less than at present, with a corresponding narrower dividend for each. It is as near as possible to demonstration, with our existing human nature unchanged, and charged with envy, antipathies, selfishness, rivalry, desire to dominate over others; with many good qualities unsuited for such a state, as with many evil ones the exact opposite of those unwarrantably postulated by the socialist; with the impossibility of giving ability either its proper field or due incentive and reward for superior productive efforts, that socialism for generations hence would even be adverse to the most effective material production; and consequently that poverty and want would be greater than now, only more uniformly divided. It is all too likely, moreover, that in such a society the higher wants of art, philosophy, literature, would scarcely be born, or would be stamped out as foolish or perverted sentimental cravings, though science, in so far as it ministers by applications of steam or electricity to man's productive powers, might be possibly encouraged; and it is clear that such a degenerated society, even if it were materially successful, which is more than doubtful, would still afford but sorry accommodation for cultured or elevated human beings.

Thus even if no mitigation of social maladies were possible, it would still be better to bear the ills we have than fly to others of which we know nothing save their great magnitude and variety; better for society to suffer with resignation all its present griefs than resort to the desperate remedy offered by the socialist, which would indeed be for it little less than voluntary suicide.

If, indeed, there were any hope that a radical and permanent change for the better could be effected by social revolution, without a previous radical change in the natures of the social units; if, by spending the blood of one generation, all future generations could be redeemed from social misery and want, then, indeed, considering the very moderate amount of happiness which existence promises to the many, it might not be rash and desperate counsel to advise them to try the hazardous adventure of revolution; the result, for which the present generation would have to pay, might be worth the price, at least to future generations; but, as shown, there is no hope whatever that any such consequence would result from the certain social convulsion and chaos. Thus from the point of view of science and evolution—

> All things invite
> To peaceful counsels, and the settled state
> Of order, how in safety best we may
> Compose our present evils, with regard
> Of what we are and were, dismissing quite
> All thoughts of war.

And with respect to the poverty of the masses, pursues the disciple of Mr. Spencer, the real fact is that it is produced, not by social arrangements or the imperfect constitution of society, but in great measure by the individuals themselves; by themselves directly and largely, by their parents partly, or by the general imperfections of human nature, if you choose, but not by society, nor could it be removed by any new constitution of society of human device.

The socialist reasons viciously when he contends that poverty and crime necessarily follow with mathematical rigour from our present social system. The true view of the matter is quite different. It is not—our social system being given, our social evils necessarily follow;

but, being given our present average human nature, with its course of historical evolution behind it, then *both* our present social system, and also our present social evils, are necessary products of it and of its history. Our social structure and concurrent social evils are common effects of the same set of causes; the one is not the cause of the other. Criminals are thus not "society's failures," for society did not make the inherited evil disposition to crime. Society is not responsible for the mass of pauperism. Existing society, at least, is largely guiltless of both. Our widespread pauperism and crime, in a word, are directly the results of our evil or imperfect human nature and human passions; and these last being given, the former could in the mass be predicted from them. In the total amount they could be scientifically predicted from the constancy of the causes, if our yearly statistics did not save us the trouble, and there is hence unhappily but little hope afforded of any great or speedy reduction in the gross total. Yet this doctrine of scientific prediction does not carry with it any fatalistic conclusion as regards the efforts of individuals; for though statistics show a uniformity in the number of capital crimes, no individual is bound to commit a murder to make up the list that Science anticipates, and no one is compelled to contribute his quota to the expected quantity of pauperism in a given year. The reverse is, we know, the truth; men are morally bound not to swell these evil lists; and the doctrine of predictable scientific averages neither frees any from their individual responsibility, nor forbids statesmen and others in influential positions from trying, by all rational means, even though they can effect little, to minimize social ills.

But in particular, with respect to poverty and its

causes, each one has the matter, as it affects himself, largely in his own hands, and upon this Mill, no less than Herbert Spencer, insists. We know, from the teaching of political economy, without any doubt, that the main if not sole cause of it in any modern nation in which there is a general disposition to labour, is the excessive numbers of the labourers, necessarily diminishing the rewards of each; this, joined to vices for which they are responsible, and to disease or weakness for which they are not, is the cause of poverty, and we know the only possible remedies which Nature has left us—either limitation of the numbers, increase in the resources of production including the character of the producer, or emigration. What is, however, most to be desired, and what must be insisted upon, is that each one should, in a fully peopled country, be made to know, first the economic and social conditions under which he lives, and then that he should be made to feel that the care of his own case rests with himself, and that he shall be rewarded or punished by just and natural consequences, as he acts in the one way or the opposite, without hindrance from others in seeking his own legitimate good, without demoralizing help from others to shield him from the consequences of his own imprudence. Only by the severe but necessary discipline of reason and self-control applied to each by himself, and by letting the worthless, the imprudent, and the incorrigible suffer the natural penalties of their own actions, can our society prosper. This is the only final way. Moreover, it is the only just way, and in the end the most merciful and humane way, as any other course would produce a greater quantity of suffering. Finally, it is also the way of Nature—wiser than we. It is her way, her lesson everywhere taught, whether a foolish philanthropy or impracticable and Utopian socialism will accept it or no.

It is the obstinate facts of human nature, and the fixed conditions of the human environment, that on all sides stop the way to the socialist, and make his programme impracticable and impossible. If men were only higher rational and moral beings, as we can easily conceive them to be, and as they tend slowly to become, all poverty and crime, and most of the vices and diseases that now deform and desolate society and individual life, could be extirpated in two or three generations; but unhappily here lies precisely the difficulty; for men as a rule are not, even in our boasted civilized communities, very high rational or moral beings, nor are they capable of being quickly made so. Their nature, as already repeated, is not capable of being quickly and permanently changed for the better, as all the science of biology, all the experience of history, added to our own personal experience, abundantly demonstrates; from whence it follows that we must be content to progress slowly in the extirpation of poverty and the other social evils, and mainly by each one endeavouring to provide for and improve himself, and next those who are legitimately dependent upon his exertions. For these various reasons, it is not an experiment in socialism, but rather a fuller and fairer development of the present system of individualism and property that is required—of that system which, as Mr. Mill has truly remarked, "has never yet had a fair trial in any country" (*Political Economy*, bk. ii., ch. i., " On Property ").

As for competition, its evils tend to abate, and it is already ceasing where it is desirable that it should cease, viz. between those classes, professions, and trades, where there is a community of interest; but no society can dispense altogether with competition, which indeed is the condition and spur of all excellence.* True, it exists still in evil forms also; but on the whole at present it produces far more good than evil. On the whole, there are good reasons to think and to hope that our progress in the future will be at an increased rate, because men themselves are more consciously aiming at reforms, improvements, and beneficial changes than in former ages, and because their leaders and representative men, statesmen, reformers, thinkers, are sounding and exploring all possible avenues of progress; but still, with all these grounds of a hopeful future outlook, the kingdom of heaven which a regenerated human nature would bring, being itself not merely the promise but the substance of such, is not at hand. It will not come during this generation, nor the next. It will not come quickly. The miracle of a speedily regenerated society has been more than once promised by sanguine prophets and social reformers in these latter days, but the miracle has not yet occurred, being, indeed, many times more difficult of accomplishment than even the religious miracle of the instantaneous and radical conversion of the single human soul. It is very true that men are loth to abandon long-cherished illusory hopes, and this dear delusion of a happy society, this ever-vanishing vision of a "perfect state" as possible with imperfect men, and about to come, is one of their oldest, most constantly recurrent, and still passionately cherished delusions. It is the last delusive hope which the toiling multitude, and many generous spirits far wiser than they, the last which men generally, ever hopeful though ever disappointed, are prepared to give up. Yet

* Mill's *Political Economy*, bk. iv. ch. vii. sec. 7.

the hope is no other than a delusion, and it is the chief lesson of the new scientific faith, that none such are good to entertain; that to endeavour to find and know the truth, the actual naked truth, will profit far better; that much of men's grief and misery on the earth has been due to this old ostrich habit of trying to fold themselves round with pleasing but treacherous fictions, instead of knowing and facing actual bracing facts; for the fiction is invariably exploded in process of time, and then men find they have been fed on bankrupt promises, while they have been led disastrously away from their true and right course, which had else been made clear and acceptable to them. Fictions have their place and function in the realms of poetry, but not in the sphere of practice, where action must be taken. There only the fact can profit us to go by; there failure to apprehend rightly the actual facts and actual conditions which Nature, in her regular behaviour from age to age, has left for man's knowledge, and appointed for his guidance, is ever attended and must be attended with fatal and disastrous consequences. To ascertain the facts and conditions is the special work of Science; to impress the lesson resulting is the duty of the philosopher and moralist who builds upon science.

The kingdom of heaven, then, for which men have long prayed, the civitas Dei, the perfect state, will only come when it has already existed in men's hearts and shown itself in their conduct, but that will not be in our day, nor in our children's, although they will be appreciably nearer to it. Nevertheless, the happy time, which will come at last, though late, and by the slow operation of the same perfecting processes which have raised man from the brute to the savage, and from the savage to the civilized man, will not be delayed by this true teaching. It will be delayed only if men, as heretofore, persistently pursue the opposite course, long ago censured by Bacon, of embracing fictions, "flattering hopes, false valuations, imaginations as one would, and the like," instead of the "naked and open daylight" of truth; of living upon illusions which burst, instead of knowing the literal terms which Nature allows, and facing and accepting the actual facts which she puts before us; the former being the bad habit to which our poor species has ever been addicted, in all directions, and not merely with respect to the future of society, but the future of the individual.

§ 3. In the preceding part of this chapter we have shadowed forth the outlines of a great and far-reaching controversy, the most important in the history of our species; but which, though probably as old as human society itself, and certainly as old as the Republic of Plato in which it is discussed, or as Christianity which began with a communistic form of society, has yet only within the past half-century come to be felt as a controversy involving real and living issues of a momentous character, and not Utopias only remotely bordering upon the possible, or vicious theories, which, reduced to practice, would disintegrate and dissolve every existing or conceivable society.

Though only in abstract, we have tried to present the essential lines of the socialist's argument, and his general indictment against society, together with the reply of the defender of existing society, from the new standpoint of evolution, and from the less comprehensive point of view of economic science. But while acknowledging an amount of truth in the arguments of the socialist on the one side, and of the sociologist and economist on the other, we do not find the position of either wholly satisfactory. While we subscribe fully to some of the socialist's indictments of existing society, thinking it almost as bad as could be in some respects, we still demur, with the sociologist, to the socialist's contemplated remedies. We object to those advanced, and still more, perhaps, to those not advanced and scarcely even half-defined to himself, but which are, nevertheless, evidently harboured in the breast of the socialist, and sometimes vaguely shadowed forth. We submit that to prove society imperfect is not the point; for this is granted on all sides, though to different extents. It would be granted by even the greatest social optimist, the extremest political conservative, that society is not perfect. The real question relates to the practicable cure of admitted evils, and involves a comparative estimate of the efficacy of different modes of treatment, and also, in the opinion of the conservative, the question whether some cures would not be worse than the disease itself; and the great objection to the socialist's mode of treatment is that it would kill the patient if society could be induced to take the medicine, while nothing short of force would induce it to do so. It would dissolve society if administered. Well, some may say, the objection is not insurmountable. Better that a bad society should die, and make way for a better, since the death of a society does not imply that of the individuals composing it, nor yet of civilization and culture. But there is a greater objection. There is no logic or persuasion, short of that of force, which could induce society to take the socialist's medicine. Even if poured violently down her throat, society would nauseate it and cast it up again, so long as human nature remains constituted as it is. Even if the socialists got the control of the governmental machinery, and made a general confiscation, a new definition of property, and new legislation, limiting to the utmost conceivable extent the power of individuals either in the acquisition or disposal of property;—still, human nature remaining generally the same as before (even in the socialists), and not being alterable either by vote of the majority or the compulsion of cannon, the self-seeking impulses and dispositions inevitably remaining, and the affection for wife and child remaining—which things are the real springs of the desire for property—the laws abolishing individual property could not be carried out; and after temporary social chaos, invading all order, extending to all departments of life, of whose nature and extent and effects no revolution yet realized gives us any conception, exhausted society would joyfully hail any self-styled saviour promising deliverance from the unendurable delirium and horror of social anarchy. Things after their temporary wrench would resort to their old grooves, society being the sadder and the wiser, but scarcely the better, from the costly and not bloodless experience. In a word, the best-laid schemes of the socialist must founder on the old rock of human nature, which, alike on its worst as on its best sides, in its innate selfishness as in its deep affections, presents at present, if not for ever, an insurmountable obstacle to the socialist's programme.

Thus far we are with the defender of society, from the standpoint of evolution, against a social revolution to end in communism. On the other hand, we believe in opposition to the doctrine of Herbert Spencer, that the nature of man is modifiable more quickly than he supposes, at least at particular epochs, in certain directions, and for a considerable time,—even though it suffer a relapse. It may be transformed for a time by a great faith and enthusiasm, though it fall away again from the state of grace. It is modifiable at certain epochs if the right spirits appear to modify it; and under the modification, if widely spread, as at the rise of Christianity and Mahometanism, men are capable of the most extraordinary things, at other times impossible, being possessed of many times their ordinary strength and heart. The nature of men may be so modified without being radically changed at such times, that it may suffice to produce the most remarkable change in their future fortunes and in that of the race to follow them. Thus the nature of the Arab was so modified by the tenets of Mahomet, that he became ruler from Bagdad to Cordova; the nature of the French people became so modified by the precursors and actors in their great Revolution, that they combated combined Europe for a generation, and effected an agrarian and political, if not a social, revolution, unexampled in the history of European nations. Such changes in masses of men which make important changes in societies, though not radical changes in either case, have occurred, and are possible again.

These times of renewing and regeneration of human nature seem to occur at intervals, according to some law which Science has not yet fathomed so far as to be able to state all the conditions, or to predict the time of recurrence of the seasons of grace. But they have their causes; and they recur. And moreover, upon such a period of renovation, there are signs that we may be now entering; nay, perhaps we have already entered upon it for some time without being fully aware of the fact.

It is true that religious faith of the dogmatic sort is undoubtedly "dry" at the present time. But our social faith, our faith in an improvable society, and one soon to be improved, is by no means so. On the contrary, the social hope seems to wax and strengthen as the religious wanes. And it is possible that if the masses of men generally take to heart the new scientific teaching, which in effect makes the future life of little or no practical account, and the present life everything, thus reversing the comparative value placed upon them by religion; if they should come to the conclusion that now or never is the time to realize, if not happiness, at least greater social justice and social equality, so far as the latter is compatible with Nature's inequalities; and if, moreover, they can get men of genius and honesty and energy to espouse their cause—a thing not in itself impossible, and unlikely only because of the rarity of the combination, but of which we have had a few examples already in the present and the past generations—then, without a total revolution in the nature of men or things, social and political results of a remarkable kind and of great importance might be brought about in a comparatively brief space of time, the doctrine of slow social evolution notwithstanding. Without any change in the social structure, which, with Herbert Spencer, we think undesirable, though we do not, with him, think it impossible, a great improvement in the general condition of the mass of mankind might be realized in a *moderate space* of time. Without confiscation of property, without any necessity for attempting to evolve a new social order out of the antecedent social chaos, which the socialist revolution would first usher in, and which, by advanced Continental anarchists and nihilists, is contemplated with so much serenity, not to say satisfaction of spirit, there might still be, well on the safe side of chaos, and far short of socialism, or even in a direction opposite to it, a greatly accelerated rate of social progress, and,—to go no higher,—a great improvement in men's material fortune. And there might be all this accompanied by the greatest of all guarantees of order, namely, the wider diffusion, through the body and soul of society, both of clearer perceptions and a more general practice of the great social virtue of justice, the only final condition of stable equilibrium in society. The general diffusion of clear ideas of justice, and the embodiment of justice in laws and institutions, would itself alone constitute this greatest improvement.

But for the realization of this, it is not socialism that is required. What we really want is, in fact, a better development of the present system, imperfectly described as one of individualism and competition. If it were really one of individualism, with the reward for real individual effort and ability, things would be somewhat just. We want individualism better developed, rather than socialism for which human nature is unsuited. But we want individualism accompanied by justice, the sense and perception of which seems as yet to exist in very imperfect degree and to be almost blind in certain directions, whether amongst individuals or classes. We want individualism, but with the individuals starting in the race on something resembling fair and equal terms, with the prizes of life awarded in reality and not in name to talent, ability, and energy well directed. We require competition, too, because competition, implying emulation, is the spur to improvement and excellence in every direction both as regards the higher productive efforts of the mind, as well as material productions, and because where the competitive spirit is lacking, men and nations slacken in their efforts and begin to stagnate. But we want competition applied to all, with a fair field open to all, and with no favour shown to any of the competitors—competition accompanied by just conditions, and with a sense of justice in the competitors themselves, so that, if we cannot redress Nature's injustice and inequalities, we may not add to them. We want, in fact, rather more than less competition, because at present the best prizes are given to those who have been wholly exempted from the competitive trial, which is unjust; and again because the nations of the world are now brought into closer and keener competition with each other, and only the nation in which this competitive spirit is widely diffused can permanently hold her own and prosper. Thus it is not individualism and competition which really hurt men, as the socialists maintain; it is the evil things, their direct opposite, which at present prevail, and which hinder their full and fair development.

It might be urged with some show of plausibility that superior faculty and energy should *not* be rewarded in proportion to their amount—a proposition which is certainly held, if not expressly asserted, by many besides certain socialists and trade unionists: by hereditary and privileged imbecility, by the rich who have not laboured, by the dull and incapable of all ranks and callings. The principle is even partially assented to by such a just and capable thinker as the late Mr. Mill, who, in criticising certain forms of communism, thinks that the highest justice would not reward superior ability in proportion to its superiority, as that would be "giving to him that hath," thereby increasing Nature's injustice in making men unequal. But to this and to the above views it may be fairly replied that the first injustice being of Nature's own making, what follows naturally afterwards is not unjust. What cannot in the nature of things be prevented, save by interposing artificial obstacles more evidently unjust, is not to be regarded as an inequitable system; at least it is one which, if allowed full play, would greatly profit men in general for a considerable time to come.

Even if it were unjust that superior faculty, being to some extent its own reward, should be further rewarded by a correspondingly large share of money or material things, still it must be remembered that in the fields of industry at least, talent and energy will not work for less; if they are not adequately rewarded, if they do not ensure a return in proportion to their excellence, they will not be exercised, and in such a state of things all would suffer. The wealth of the nation, which is finally distributed far and wide to all, has for its mainspring the somewhat selfish but most beneficial energy of men aiming at their own benefit, striving to become rich, and this source would be in a great measure dried up if energy, industry, and talent could not upon an average calculate upon something like a corresponding return. But for the satisfaction of the above-named objectors, who think that talent should not be rewarded, there are surely cases sufficient where Nature herself has made the kind of compensation required—cases of her giving ability of the highest kind and of the greatest importance to men, without giving anything more in the shape of money reward, cases of talent and genius and energy, which hardly brought to their possessors even bread. Here, if Nature has erred in making men unequal, she has redressed her error, and made compensation; though we can scarcely think she has always acted justly even here, in letting the scales incline so heavily in the other direction, against her own favourites, whom she selected in the first instance.

On the whole, if not absolutely conformable to the principles of the highest conceivable justice, it seems the fairest principle that can be applied on the earth, for a considerable time yet to come, that men should get the highest price they can by all fair and honourable means for the commodity produced or the service rendered, in the open market of the world. And what is desirable, if it were possible, would be that the price should bear some fair proportion to the ability and energy of the producer, joined to the utility of the product or service. It is true that on these principles the great poet or philosopher, a Spinoza, or a Milton, whose commodity, truth or beauty, may not be much in demand at the time in the market, may starve. But the spiritual producer usually knows beforehand the somewhat severe conditions imposed by Nature in this respect, and if he is wise, like the two above named, he makes his calculations and acts accordingly. Besides the chief payment of the man of genius is made in other coin than money—in fame, in spiritual influence, in the pleasure flowing from his work—and as of these he generally receives an amount in proportion to his work, on the whole, the principle of rewarding faculty according to its extent is carried out even here.

§ 4. In denying the possibility of realizing the socialist's ideal for a long time to come, we say or imply nothing against the practicability of workmen in certain cases of association becoming their own capitalists, and sharing the profits as well as the wages of their labour amongst themselves. There can be no objection to this mode of eliminating the individual capitalist and employer, other than what relates to the likelihood of failure. For our own part, we heartily wish all such attempts the success which they have in several instances merited on other grounds than their being good commercial ventures. Such attempts are useful and instructive, even where they fail, as showing us the cases of production where the principle of co-operative labour is inapplicable, as also the probable cause of the failure of its application; but they are still more instructive, and should be distinct subjects for congratulating not only the associations themselves but society at large, as aiding in the solution of the most difficult social problem, whenever they prove commercial successes, as has been the case in several instances in France and Germany, and in one or two cases in England. All such social and economic experiments are to be wished continued and greater success, and of all promising experiments of a similar character, it is to be desired, as Mill remarks in his *Political Economy*, that, if possible, the means were procurable, and that every facility be allowed for making the experiment. The difficulty, however, is that such associations must either save their capital from the earnings of their members, or they must borrow it,—neither being easy for workmen to do. For this reason alone the progress of co-operative labour must be slow; but there are more formidable obstacles. There are deeper reasons, founded on the nature of man and things, why the instances of successful united production must be limited for a long time to come, if not for ever. For the cases to which the principle of co-operative labour applies are limited. There would be many more, indeed, if men's natures were changed and improved, if love for others and mutual confidence—the qualities requisite for success—were really as common as the advocates of co-operation assume them to be. Ever we come to the same check—imperfect human nature, which has not much progressed in this direction since Christianity first preached to men the love of one another; the same old, unimproved human nature, which still bars the way alike of general progress and of co-operative production.

For a business can no more be carried on successfully without a single directing and controlling head, than a bridge can be built, a campaign conducted, a ship sailed, or an epic poem created. There must be in co-operative production, as in all other kinds of production, a single brain interested and responsible, which guides and governs the whole, over and above the instrumental hands which perform the mechanical processes and manual dexterities. There must be a head to guide and govern the whole course of labour from start to finish, to appoint to each one his suitable part in the division of labour, to buy and sell and watch the market, to know when to contract or extend operations. There must be such a president and directing intelligence, or the whole concern will speedily collapse in the presence of the competing production possessed of this advantage. For here, as everywhere, the law of Darwin holds, that a slight but continued advantage decides the battle in favour of its possessor, determines the fittest to survive. A single head must, therefore, either be evolved from the body of the workers in the association, or it must be imported from without and paid for. The former case Mr. Frederick Harrison, a competent judge and a friend of the workmen, thinks, on the ground of their previous habits and training, would be the more unlikely; but supposing such a one to be found—one likely to make the adventure a success, with the necessary knowledge, intelligence, and executive ability, amongst the members of the association; he will, with human nature as generally constituted, and assuming only the normal ratio of benevolence or class-regard to selfishness, become dissatisfied to remain unless he can get the market price within the association which his energy and administrative talent would command in the general field of competition. He will be dissatisfied, in short, to remain merely the manager, and if he be paid in proportion to his share in the success of the undertaking, and if, as we must assume, his savings be invested in it while he continues in the association, he becomes in the end virtually the capitalist, with the other members as inferior partners, which would be in effect an abandonment of the principle of associated labour—a result which would not, indeed, be a return to the old system of labour and capital in constant conflict, but a compromise between that system and co-operation.

On the other hand, if the association import a competent salaried manager from the outside, which, with the best authorities, as Mill and Thornton, we assume would be the rule (the case last considered being very exceptional), then the interest of the head of the concern in its success would probably not be as keen and absorbing as that of the individual capitalist, and this single circumstance alone would in most cases decide the battle adversely to co-operative production. The interest of the manager would be less keen than that of the master, while the intelligence would on an average be equal, and this fact would make all the difference between a decided success, and a constant struggle to exist ending in the winding up and the consequent dissolution of the association of workmen. The whole argument may thus be summed up at the present time. Some

U

kinds of labour, whether directly productive or subsidiary to production, are obviously unsuited for co-operation; while in many cases where it really would apply if human nature were somewhat better than it is, and if the feelings of class regard and brotherhood and love, which are postulated, were really present in sufficient force and permanence, yet the facts being otherwise, the further difficulty or impossibility of getting the able and honest and zealous head, wholly devoted to the interest of the body of workers, would be certain to ensure commercial failure more or less decided, soon or late.

Human nature, however, may improve faster in future; and class human nature, where there is identity of interest, might be expected to develop the qualities necessary for its own existence and progress. And there have been fraternities of monks living and labouring together successfully and in common. Why might there not be like fraternities of working men? The thing is possible, but the sentiments which would keep such societies together must be more than commercial, even to make a commercial success. There must be as strong regard for the community as in ants; there must be industry, too, and there must be not only a strong class feeling, but also fraternal feeling for the individuals,—this and the possibility of making the head of the concern share these feelings. Both Mr. Mill and Mr. Thornton regard co-operation as the final solution of the problem of labour, and the goal of the workmen in the future. It will certainly be more generally tried; but I think that the day of its universal adoption is far more distant than either of these friends of labour believed, partly because they wished it. At least, if we assume that the rate of development of the necessary qualities—love and mutual trust—in the workmen, and at the same time the rate of extinction of the interfering qualities—selfishness, and dislike, and jar, and hatred—in man in general, is to be only as rapid as in the past, then the future Utopia of labour is a good deal further off than sanguine friends suppose.

§ 5. There is, indeed, one conceivable and remotely possible contingency which, if it ever became realized, would have a great effect on the future of labour and of all social progress. If the highest intellect and virtue in society, deeply stirred by pity and by a higher sense of justice, ever come to take up the cause of the poor; if, as we see some tendency in that direction, the aristocracy of thought and letters and art, possessing as they do the ear and appealing to the heart of the public, should place themselves at the head of a new social crusade; more than all, if one man of eminent genius, a single commanding and reforming spirit, should appear, filled with enthusiasm and devotion to the work, who should be the Luther of the social reformation, then indeed the naturally slow course of evolution might be accelerated into revolutionary speed. But though the highest minds of the present and of the past generation have meditated much on the great social problems, and have been all friends of the poor; though Fourier, Mazzini, Victor Hugo, Louis Blanc, and Mill have all pleaded powerfully in their behalf; and though contemporary intellect is on the whole not unfriendly to any projected form of socialism which, like co-operative labour, promises anything good and practicable,—there has not yet appeared, nor does it seem likely that there will shortly appear, the Luther of the new social reformation, the St. Bernard of the new holy war in behalf of the workmen. Still, the appearance of such a spirit or of more than one, is within the range of possibility—a hope which the poorer classes may indulge in, and a possibility which the rich and ruling classes might profitably reflect on; the continuance of the need of such reforming spirits being the one cause likely to call them up at last in the fulness of time.

But in the mean time, while the toiling millions need not wholly abandon hope of some general improvement in their condition, even within the limits of a single generation, the advice of both Mill and Spencer is good, more especially as coming from the former, who proved himself the sincere friend of labour—the advice to trust most of all to their own exertions, and in a world which grants to them at present only harsh conditions, to endeavour, by prudence and foresight, by knowledge and attention to the monitions of science, by patience, self-denial, and resignation to the inevitable wherever necessary, to work out to the best of their own ability their individual and social salvation.

At the same time, a word of admonition, if not of advice, might even be profitable to rulers, statesmen, and legislators in these days. The socialist and nihilist movement all over Europe, from Russia to Spain, the simultaneous attempts on the lives of most of the Continental sovereigns, as the recognized key-stone of the social fabric, are surely symptoms of some deep-rooted disease, of something seriously wrong in our present social system, which is well worthy the attentive consideration of statesmen as well as of thinkers; and something for the cure of which neither more stringent repression nor aggressive foreign wars, the favourite treatment hitherto adopted, will suffice in future. The root cause of the socialist movement is in reality the poverty of the many in our modern rich communities, joined to a rankling sense of injustice, neither of which, difficult as they may be and are of cure, are to be removed by internal repression or foreign aggression ; but, if by anything, by internal reform in institutions, and by the removal of social injustices which still everywhere exist, notwithstanding the reforming spirit that has been active for a long time in their partial removal. For justice may be reached on the earth, even though fraternity and equality be only ideal aims.

BOOK III.
THE FUTURE OF RELIGION AND MORALS.

CHAPTER I.

ON THE MATERIALISM OF ATOMS AND FORCES.

§ 1. SCIENCE is often, in our days, characterized as atheistic. What is the justice of the charge? It depends on what we mean by science and what by atheism. If we mean by science, as in strictness we should, a knowledge of the laws of phenomena, their regular sequences and conjunctions, the discovery of which is the business of science, then science is not and cannot be atheistic, no matter what meaning we attach to "atheism." But if we mean by science, what those who bring forward the charge mostly mean, namely, some of the philosophies professedly based on the conclusions of science, as materialism, positivism, evolution, then it depends on what these several philosophies conclude respecting the First Principle and Ultimate Reality of things, and very particularly it depends on the definition of atheism or of God which we ourselves shall agree to accept.

Now, there are three philosophies current which profess to be based on the verified conclusions of science, the three above named—positivism, materialism, and evolution (or Darwinism, substantially the same as evolution). Are these atheistic? Let us consider them severally. Does positivism deny the existence of a Deity? No. It merely ignores the question. It does not raise the question, because it is a metaphysical one, and to positivism all metaphysical inquiries are vain and insoluble. It neither affirms nor denies the existence of God, because, if God exists, it must be in the sphere outside phenomena, and the scientific human mind is only competent to deal with phenomenal existences, and is only concerned with these. It is true that, by ignoring the question, positivism becomes practically atheism, though there is no real reason why it should be so, beyond the fact that it has banned all metaphysical questions. The positivist belief, that the hierarchical classification of the sciences may serve for a philosophy, and that the quintessence of experience, as proved and tested and generalized by science, should guide our life and constitute our conception of the universe, is not really exclusive of the question whether God exists or no—a question which has been answered in the affirmative by positive thinkers like Locke and Bacon, long before the time of Comte. The question—Is there a cause of experience, of phenomena other than the phenomenal facts themselves? is indeed metaphysical, but it is also one which the human mind perpetually insists on raising, whether it can answer it or no; and positivism is only practical atheism, so far as it ignores this question, involving the question of the existence of God; while, so far as it denies that there is anything behind experience, or more than isolated phenomena self-produced, it is speculative and genuine atheism. In brief, then, when the positive spirit fills the man of science, when his philosophy goes no further than the conclusions of science, when he tries following the prescription of Comte to seal up the metaphysical eye, his philosophy is to all intents and purposes atheistic, though the question of the existence of a First Cause has never been raised. For not to raise the question of God's existence at all is, in any system of philosophy, equivalent to a denial of it, and this, which is involved in its proscription of metaphysics, is the defect in all the forms of positivism, as in all philosophies which build solely on the facts of experience as the only existence.

§ 2. Materialism, in one of its two modern forms at least, may justly be regarded as atheism. The supposition that matter, conceived as consisting essentially and fundamentally of atoms and molecules, could, through the proper placing and packing of these atoms, produce the order, beauty, life, and thought of the universe, without some principle of arrangement, combination, or guidance, lodged in matter or diffused amongst the individuals, something different from the matter, and at least faintly analogous to reason and intelligence,—is so hopeless and stupid an attempt at explanation, precipitating so many difficult questions and solving none, that it may fairly be described as absurd as well as atheistic. For, if we dispense in our explanation with everything but the homogeneous atoms, there is no possibility of concert between neighbouring ones any more than there is between those on the earth and the remotest star; and yet some internal concert between the atoms there must have been, if there was no marshalling external principle, in order to produce, we will not say such a whole as this great law-governed universe, but even a single substance or a single molecule. Even if we import chemical affinity into the atoms, and then life, as Haeckel does, or even mind, as Leibnitz did and some modern atomists seem inclined to do, yet the question would even then remain, how the atoms of our original solar system, individually intelligent and active and living, had such an understanding with each other and with those of remoter systems as to form into separate worlds, and to break off into such immense and accurately ordered marches, without some controlling principle of intelligence, not contained in the individual atoms, to direct their movement. Nor does modern chemistry or the doctrine of natural selection applied to the molecules really make the revived atomism of Democritus more credible or intelligible in our day than Cicero found it in his. For, besides that the action of chemical affinity at first, and of natural selection afterwards, in producing and continuing life, is a point in dispute, or, more strictly speaking, is not yet proved, still, even were it otherwise, the mind would never rest satisfied with the explanation that matter alone produced life and thought, not even if it were granted that all matter was, as Haeckel affirms, in a certain sense alive. The cause assigned is not adequate to the total series of unlike and marvellous effects. The reply of Cicero still holds good: It is more credible that the letters composing the *Iliad* should have come into their proper places by chance, than the atoms should have produced the cosmos without a marshalling agency. To assign a conscious mind and purpose resembling the human may be and is an imperfect explanation; but it is, we are assured, by much the lesser error of the two. It is more philosophical to assign the highest than the lowest known cause as the first principle of things, even though we know that the highest is inadequate.

Nor will the modern and more refined materialism, which starts from the notion of force instead of matter, and which builds itself mainly on the new doctrine of the conservation of energy, be found in the end more satisfactory to our minds or more philosophical. For, even granting the proof of this law in all its generality, though it is yet, as Lange, in his *History of Materialism*, admits, only an ideal aim of science; even admitting that force is never found dissociated from matter, and that all the various forms of force—heat, mechanical, radiant, chemical, electrical, nervous energy, could really produce and reproduce each other without loss through the whole cycle of changes, according to determinate rates of exchange;—even granting all this, still it is only phenomenal force, or energy, that is thus exchanged; for it is only phenomenal heat, electricity, etc. (that is, these energies as they impress our senses), that we ever encounter or ever can encounter. We never meet with real, efficient, ontologic force or matter, and unless the materialist is prepared to go the length of Hume, and deny that there is anything in the universe, either material or mental, but phenomena, the doctrine of the conservation and transmutation of energy will little avail him as a basis for his materialism. For if he admits, as some materialists incautiously do, that there is something real behind our phenomenal matter and energy, something different from the sensations which alone, according to the idealists, make matter and energy for us, then this something can no more be described as matter than as mind. For matter and mind are only known to us by certain feelings and sensations which are given in our consciousness, and this unknown something is not thus given. That there exist only phenomena, as with Hume, is the only position that a materialist who wishes to be a monist can hold. This, however, is not the position of Kant or Herbert Spencer, the two thinkers of greatest authority at present in the scientific world, both of whom believe in this real something behind and different from phenomena, and both of whom repudiate materialism.

On the other hand, if the materialist stands consistently

by his monism, and holds fast to phenomenal matter and energy as the one reality which has produced thought as well as all else, we may grant to him that consciousness and thought are products of one form of energy, namely, of cerebral activity; but a product only in Hume's and Mill's sense, which is also the strict scientific sense of the word, that is, a consequent having molecular cerebral action for its invariable antecedent. Thought cannot be said to be produced by molecular movement in any other than this its only scientific sense, that is to say, it is not really produced at all by it. There is nothing more than a constant connection of two wholly dissimilar things. Unless matter or energy is literally transmuted into thought; unless thought is finer matter or energy—an affirmation which the hardiest materialists have scarcely dared to make—materialism could not establish itself as a monistic system. Finally, even if thought, imagination, ratiocination, could be experimentally exhibited to us as an energy which manifests itself like electricity or heat, still this material objective thing would be different from the subjective thought and consciousness which would be necessary to cognize and examine it, as the material organ of vision remains different from the sensation of sight.

It has, however, been granted by some materialists that thought, though a product of physical energy, is not itself properly to be reckoned amongst the list of energies; but this is in effect to surrender the materialist's position, that there exist only in the universe matter and energy; for if thought is not included amongst these, it is an independent existence, an irreducible entity, and we return once more to the old dualism of matter and mind.

Thought has been erased by the materialist from the

list of energies, for two main reasons: First, because, if thought alone could act directly upon or move mechanically a single atom of matter, it might have been the first principle of movement at the beginning of things, as it might still be the final sustaining and moving power in the universe. But there is a second and a stronger reason. Our modern materialists, in their anxiety to reduce all in man to physical and in particular to mechanical laws, are compelled to ignore all that is not a physical, and in the last analysis a mechanical or moving, energy. For energy of motion is the final one to which heat, electricity, chemical affinity, nerve force, and all others, if there be others, must be reduced; matter in motion being the final explanation of the world. Whatever cannot be so reduced is not a physical energy, and thought clearly cannot be reduced. It cannot be reduced, but it may be ignored as immaterial, as an accidental surplus product of the real physical energies; and thus we reach the conception of the man-machine, the final outcome of this view of things.

The doctrine that man is an automaton, a most perfectly constructed machine, would logically follow from the denial of all other than physical energies. He does not move himself, he has no power of self-direction, no control over his actions, for all is determined by the internal physical energies, and in particular by the latest mysterious movement of the cerebral atoms, supplemented by the executive muscular and nervous energy requisite to carry out the mysterious mandates corresponding to a particular position of the cerebral atoms.

Man is a machine that can move about; his movements are the resultant of internal mechanical forces, as the motion of a locomotive engine is of the expansive force of steam generated in the boiler. He does not move himself, he is not even moved hither and thither by the force of conscious motives, as the necessitarians hitherto believed; he is not moved by the love of power, or wealth, or fame; he is moved in each instance simply as certain mechanical forces shall settle it amongst themselves. · He goes as they direct, fancying all the time that he is free, or at least that he is following a motive, a part of what he calls himself.

This doctrine would certainly destroy freedom of will and freedom of action, in a sense far more deep than was ever dreamed of by any necessitarian, who merely affirmed, like Mill, that our volitions followed motives—conscious motives, related finally to our pleasures and pains. In the desire to reduce everything to physico-chemical causes, and in particular to universalize the law of the conservation and transmutation of energy, this is the hopeless pass to which our physicists bring the science of man and philosophy in these days. Thought, consciousness, is not a physical energy, therefore, to be logical, it is nothing or next to nothing, for the universe is made up of matter and physical energy. At best, consciousness is nothing very particular, an accident that turned up amongst the other transmuted things, not a lawful physical product, but, as Professor Tyndall has termed it, a " bye-product," no way essential to the purely physical processes going on in the brain. Thought is not even a cause, it is at most a spectator looking idly on; a state of consciousness is only, according to Professor Huxley, a sort of symbol of the dark mysterious movements of the atoms taking place behind, but which, though its true cause, it no more resembles than the registration of the hour on the face of the clock resembles the inner movement of the machinery which really causes it.

Consciousness is thus, according to the automatonists, an accident; but at least we may add it was a fortunate accident, a very happy hit, however the forces blindly at work turned it up. For, according to all, including the materialists themselves, according to 'Huxley, to Haeckel, according to the author of the *History of Materialism*, this accidental product is the sole source of all our knowledge, the sole means of our reading and interpreting the universe and of finding its laws, including the law of the conservation of these very energies themselves; and in the long run, these very energies are only known as modes of this consciousness, which, though nothing as a physical energy, yet knows, and in a certain important sense, as the idealist maintains, creates and conserves all things. In fact, the author of the *History of Materialism* admits as much where he says, "We are justified in assuming physical conditions for everything, even the mechanism of thought; but we are equally justified in considering not only the external world, but the organs also with which we perceive it, as mere images of that which actually exists." In fact, consciousness, which is not force, or energy, and consequently not matter nor capable of acting on matter, stands declared as a wholly distinct thing from matter, divided from it by an impassable gulf; and we thus return to the old dualism of Descartes, while the materialist is aiming at monism. But if, as this passage from Lange allows, the external world and the organs with which we perceive it, including, of course, all forms of energy, be "mere images of that which actually exists," then we have here shadowed forth two systems, both different from materialism. For these images are each and all pictured on the canvas of consciousness, and are never produced elsewhere, and so far as the images are said to make up our universe, as they certainly compose all that we directly know of it, we have an assertion of idealism. To this system, indeed, both Lange and Professor Huxley agree; but also—and this is a most material point—if all be the "*mere images of that which actually exists*," a third system, very different from both materialism and idealism, is indicated—the system of realism, as old as Plato, and held by Kant and Herbert Spencer, who both believe that there are real things or a real something behind the phenomena that compose the material of our knowledge, though they do not make the old Platonic mistake of supposing the phenomena to be copies or images of it, but merely effects, or modes, or expressions of it.

But after all, is not consciousness, or thought, an energy of a certain sort? Bare consciousness, the mere passive knowledge of our mental states, may not be energy, though it is the unique product of it; still, the severe effort of thought in which cerebral energy is drawn upon and consumed should, we think, when produced, be reckoned as energy, at least as stored-up or potential energy. It is admittedly the product of energy; then, unless there is a waste, contrary to the law of conservation, this product should count as energy. It has, to use the scientific language, energy of position, or potential energy; and, in fact, it may sometimes exert a most potent energy. But it is not energy of the sort that physics is concerned with, says the materialist. Thought cannot move a single cerebral atom, thinks Lange, not so much as the millionth part of a millimetre out of the path marked for it by the laws of dynamics, without rendering all the formula of the universe inapplicable. But still, the thought which has burned up my cerebral energy to produce it, may, when produced, react on the cerebral atoms of other minds, if not on those of my own. The objective thought expressed in the law of natural selection, in the drama of *Faust* or of *Hamlet*, or even in the law of the transformation and conservation of energy itself, has produced a great commotion in the cerebral atoms of many the first time that they were put into nerve-communication with it. But it was not the thought, it was the atoms themselves which produced the agitation on receiving an external material stimulant, replies the materialist. At least, we reply, the stimulant was due to the thought, which was the occasion, the producing cause of it. When an orator produces excitement in his audience, does not thought move the atoms from their quiescent state and customary paths? Or is it only the cerebral atoms of the orator acting on those of his audience? But this, at least, we cannot suppose in the case instanced of our being moved by the reading of *Hamlet*. Here the original producing atoms have long been scattered, and yet the spiritual energy which, in association with the material atoms, once gave birth to this marvellous product is still here in this book, arrested, crystallized, and most potent to stir our brain and thrill our nerves. For, as Milton has pertinently observed, "books are not dead things, but do contain as in a phial the potent efficacy of the spirit that bred them."

Again, may not joyful news exalt the state of the atoms, sad thoughts depress them, steady thought and brain labour quiet and compose them? May not even the "written troubles of the brain," revived and read by the light and power of memory, strongly move the very molecules themselves which, nevertheless, must be employed, as we grant, to produce the painful impression? No, the materialist retorts, these written troubles are merely persistent painful positions of the atoms; their revival by memory is merely a fresh agitation of them, the pressure upon an old sore. But what makes the pressure? Not the atoms themselves, but the fact of memory on its conscious side. When our past troubles and sorrows are revived in consciousness, our brooding over them, that is, our conscious thought of them, still reacts upon the atoms, and thus thought, thus consciousness, is still an efficient power or energy.

But, says the thorough-going materialist, to cut the matter short, thought, emotion, cannot act on the atoms of the brain, because, in fact, thought is only made possible by the atoms, and is no more than a conscious symbol of a particular position of them. It is always an effect of some arrangement of them; and when you affirm that thought, or volition, or emotion acts upon them, what really takes place is action amongst the atoms themselves, of which action, thought, or volition, is but a symbol, or expression, or result. When you say that painful memories meditated upon affect them, the brooding over the painful memories is itself only a painful position of particular brain particles, a persistent and unnatural pressure on them.

We reply, all this may be true, and yet thoughts from without and even from within may and do move men, and consequently must move the molecules of the brain. They must be the first causes of the brain agitation which is not self-produced. Ideas from without move men mightily; and they move the world; consequently they must move the brain atoms into the new position which may serve to express them. In like manner, volitions act upon the cerebral corpuscles. A strong determination is borne in upon us from the outside from counsel, example, experience, and this also compels the atoms into the requisite physical places. But it makes the atoms obedient servants instead of being blind and arbitrary masters—an important difference. It delivers the will from mechanical necessity and random chance, and gives it a practical freedom by allowing conscious motives to determine our volitions and govern our actions, instead of the last chance or self-determined position of unintelligent atoms. In a word, thought acts on the atoms as well as these on it. Thought remains an energy which can act not merely on our own cerebral atoms, but, what is more directly to our purpose, on the thoughts and acts and feelings of others. The law of the conserva-, tion of physical energy is not perhaps defeated; but it is inapplicable here. It is inapplicable, or it must receive a new extension. For physical energy is not all energy; there is spiritual energy also, however little the extreme materialist may be disposed to accept the fact. There is spiritual energy, which is conserved like the physical, but which, unlike it, is ever on the increase. The thoughts of great minds live after them, and, by producing ever new thought, are a constant and inexhaustible source of ever new energy.

> Their echoes roll from soul to soul,
> And grow for ever and for ever.

The only question remaining is whether this unique and indestructible and increasing energy can be explained completely and solely as a product of the due position of cerebral particles—a question to which all thinkers, except the most extreme materialists, will, we think, still give as decided a negative in our days as in the days of Descartes and Kant.

§ 3. Let us now assume, what all men believe, what

Kant and Spencer have tried to establish on philosophical grounds, what even materialists such as Lange and Huxley are driven to admit, that there is something more in the world than phenomena actual or possible, that there is a something behind or under or immanent in all phenomena, even under the cerebral atoms. This something it is not necessary that we should be able to describe; and indeed it is sufficiently evident, as all positivists assure us, as well as Kant, that, admitting its existence, neither our senses nor our understanding can ever penetrate behind phenomena to tell us anything further respecting it. But the mere existence of this transcendent something is quite enough to destroy all materialism, and indeed, unless this noumenal existence be regarded as mind, all idealism as well. This something behind can neither be matter nor yet force, for these, as we see and feel them, are entirely phenomenal. Nor can it be anything even remotely resembling matter or force. It cannot be, as some suppose, an original of which these are copies, which is a wholly groundless and unprovable assumption. We cannot even prove it to be mind resembling our mind. All that we can say of it is, that it is an existence, a substance, of which mind and matter are, as Spinoza held, modes, or symbols, or manifestations.

But if this Something be once granted, it is quite sufficient to destroy all materialism, and, unless it be in some sort mental, as Berkeley held, all idealism as well. It would even destroy the eclectic system of material-idealism, defended by Professor Huxley.* For clearly this Something is an element not to be ignored, if we desire to derive the universe from a single principle, be it matter or mind. For might it not be the moving principle of all things, the root

* *Life of Hume*, p. 82.

and source and support of thought, of matter, of energy, as mere emanations from it and manifestations of it? Perhaps it is at this moment the first principle and real quickener of my thought, deeper than the molecular movements in the cerebral atoms which Huxley regards as the ultimate cause of consciousness,[*] but which are themselves moved and animated by this first principle. In a word, may it not be the moving principle of thought, that which prompts us to these high and searching inquiries respecting itself at this moment, as it equally was the moving principle of the homogeneous nebular gas millions of ages ago? And, indeed, we must all believe it so to be. It is one and the same eternal substance which was then, and now is, at the bottom of all things—a substance, one, eternal, infinite, and unfathomable beyond its phenomenal manifestations; the secret sustainer and necessary ground at once of the universe and of the human reason, and whose withdrawal for a moment, if we dare make so wild a supposition, would cause the frame of the universe to disjoint, would produce the wild welter and hurly-burly of the atoms both in the brain and in the cosmos, and would make all things revert to the chaos and ancient night from which the old mythologies derived them. Indeed, the bare notion so shakes the reason in trying to imagine it, as to prove that the final support of the human reason and of the solid material universe are one and the same—the Infinite Substance of Spinoza, the God in whom all mankind believe, and of whom the theologians have ever been vainly endeavouring to present us with sensible images.

A state of chaos, whatever may have been the crude beliefs of men, there never was in the cosmos, nor ever can be.

[*] *Life of Hume*, p. 79.

The existence of God as the eternal support of the universe, as the inmost nerve and essence of thought, is our guarantee to the contrary. And this belief is confirmed by Science. Far as her ken stretches backward in time through millions of centuries, she discovers law; deep as she penetrates now into space, she finds the same. But, replies the materialist, these laws are only the necessary behaviour of matter; and matter, filling space, the seat and source of its own energies and governed by its own necessary laws, is God. There is nothing but matter, coarse or fine, together with the energies which play about it, filling up space; nothing but matter, composed ultimately of similar atoms, from the solid spheres to the azure abyss in which they swim; itself merely a fine ether, a subtler and more attenuated matter. Democritus was right. There exists nothing but atoms and the void; save only that the void is ether, a rarer matter. And in reply to this, we can only ask the materialist, How can this be maintained to-day, when it is acknowledged that all we know of matter is only phenomenal, only what our five imperfect senses tell us; when, further, the most important fact about matter is now seen to be, not the matter itself, whose atoms seem vanishing quantities, but the various Protean energies that play about it, and when these various energies, transmutable as they are into each other, are themselves only known phenomenally, as interpreted by a higher spiritual energy, which last, however mysteriously conditioned by these lower physical energies, can in no respect be regarded as a product of them, since of productivity science knows nothing beyond the bare fact of succession?

And, in fact, notwithstanding assertions to the contrary,

it may be doubted if this is not the position held by the author of the *History of Creation*, as we have seen it is that of Lange in his *History of Materialism*. For Professor Haeckel has prefixed to the title-page of his work the great lines from Wordsworth's *Tintern Abbey* in which the belief in God, which we defend, has received its most splendid poetic, if not philosophic, statement, the lines where the poet tells us of—

> A Presence that disturbs us with the joy
> Of elevated thoughts; a sense sublime
> Of something far more deeply interfused,
> Whose dwelling is the light of setting suns,
> And the round ocean, and the living air,
> And the blue sky, and in the mind of man;
> A motion and a spirit, that impels
> All thinking things, all objects of all thoughts,
> And rolls through all things.

If this passage does not recognize something more in heaven and earth than is dreamt of in the materialistic philosophy, we are greatly astray in our interpretation of it. And how Haeckel would reconcile this assertion of "something far more deeply interfused" with his own oft-asserted *monism* and materialism, it would be hazardous to say. Perhaps he would attempt to do so by denying that he is a materialist, as in one place he does. But how, then, is he a monist, as he so often asserts? And how does he deduce the universe, including life and thought, from physico-chemical laws? Certain it is that this something recognized, in the passage quoted, as underlying both matter and mind, is also something very different from matter, in whatever form encountered, or from the forces of matter, however they be transformed or combined.

Professor Huxley's materialism is more consistent and

more outspoken. In his last utterances upon the subject, he states it clearly; while at the same time he gives us our choice between the materialistic and the idealistic solutions. "For any demonstration that can be given to the contrary effect," he says, "the collection of perceptions which make up our consciousness may be an orderly phantasmagoria generated by the ego, unfolding its successive scenes on the background of nothingness; as a firework, which is but cunningly arranged combustibles, grows from a spark into a coruscation, and from a coruscation into figures and words and cascades of devouring fire, and then vanishes into the darkness of night."

"On the other hand," he continues, "it must no less readily be allowed that, for anything that can be proved to the contrary, there may be a real something which is the cause of all our impressions; that sensations, though not likenesses, are symbols of that something; and that the part of that something which we call the nervous system, is an apparatus for supplying us with a sort of algebra of fact, based on these symbols: a brain may be the machinery by which the material universe becomes conscious of itself." *

Now, so far as one holds the first of these two alternative positions here offered to us, he is an absolute egoist and idealist, as Fichte was. The world is phenomena and nothing else, constructed by the ego, which is the single and solitary existence on the vast vacuity of nothingness.† But so far as one holds the second

---

* *Life of Hume*, pp. 81, 82.

† This, however, is not quite the view of Hume, as Professor Huxley must know; for Hume surpassed Fichte in not only destroying matter, but in dissolving the ego itself. He denied that there was an underlying spiritual substance, or ego, any more than a material substance and he

view, and believes in a "real something which is the cause of our impressions," he is clearly not an idealist, but a materialist—if this real something be matter, as at first it appears to be. However, we are told that, even if this view be accepted, we should be "still unable to refute the arguments of pure idealism. The more completely the materialistic position is admitted, the easier it is to show that the idealistic position is unassailable, if the idealist confines himself within the limits of possible knowledge." Here we have the choice between idealism and materialism presented to us. But, as Professor Huxley elsewhere admits that "our knowledge of matter is restricted to those feelings of which we assume it to be the cause,"* it would not be difficult to show that in reality he is at one with Kant and Spencer and those who admit a something behind, different from what we call matter and what we call mind. As he speaks of "the unknown cause of sensation," which Descartes calls the "je ne sais quoi dans les objets," and Kant the "noumenon," or "*Ding-an-sich*,"† it is clear that here is a something different

took away all unity, reality, identity, and substance from the ego, by resolving it, or what we call "self," into a series of internal phenomena, "a bundle of perceptions," to use his own remarkable phrase. With Hume, there is only phenomena in the universe, self-produced, or wholly unknown as to their causes, since we have no conception of causation or productivity beyond the fact of observed succession. With Fichte, the ego exists as a creative agency; with Hume, it does not exist at all as any single or real thing; not even as the light of consciousness or thought, nor yet as will. In strictness, Hume is not even an idealist. In his view there exists only phenomena, which come and go without any reason. We should not even ask the reason. We believe, indeed, that they will appear again, that the sun will rise to-morrow; this is an instinctive belief, engendered by custom; but for all that, this universe of shifting phenomena might, for aught we know, collapse to-morrow, without leaving a wrack behind, not even an impression or an idea, the only things he believed in. Hume is, in fact, a nihilist in philosophy, and almost the only one.

* *Life of Hume*, p. 81. † Ibid., p. 85.

from what we call matter, and that he is neither a materialist nor an idealist, but a believer in an unknown reality, the cause of all our sensations.

In spite, then, of the doctrine of evolution, and of the conservation of energy, there is still a vacant space left for Deity; not, indeed, for one endowed with the customary anthropomorphic attributes, but for one all the more transcendent for that very reason. Before the cosmic vapour broke from its quiescent and homogeneous state, there was an existence different from it; under it there was something superior to it and animating it. It is not asserted that matter was not coeternal with the principle that first moved it, and of which it was but the phenomenal expression. This may or not have been the case; but if, as is true, we cannot think the absence of matter, much less dare we suppose the absence of its immanent moving principle, which declared itself in the cosmos, in life, and at length in human thought as Hegel maintains. In a word, behind the materialist's army of hydrogen atoms, prepared to create worlds, we are still compelled, even on the materialist's own showing, to posit a marshalling and directing agency, to postulate a principle of movement which we cannot mentally picture to the imagination, but which we must yet think as existing.

CHAPTER II.

ON THE EVOLUTION MATERIALISM AND THEOLOGY.

§ 1. THE real sting and danger of Darwinism in its theological reference does not lie in the pessimist views that it sometimes suggests even to evolutionists like Haeckel; for we see that both its distinguished founder and the thinker who has worked it into a new system of philosophy, discern, with some reason, a spirit of good in the evil things that evolution and natural selection bring before us. The origin and permission of pain and evil was, indeed, always an insoluble enigma for theology, on the supposition of a Being of infinite goodness as well as power and wisdom; for why did He not prevent it? And the hardy optimism of Leibnitz, which attempted to solve the difficulty by boldly asserting that evil was not really evil but only a privation, a negation of good, or at all events a condition of greater good, is, to say the least, as compatible with the scientific story of the rise and progress of man as with the theological story of his fall and only partial recovery. The danger of Darwinism lies in another direction, namely, in showing us a natural explanation of all the evil, real or apparent, from necessary causes that could not conceivably be otherwise; and again, in raising up before our vision the old and threatening apparition of chance, as a co-ordinate shaping agent, with a blind and mechanical necessity in the evolution of all things, the evil as well as the good. For, given the nature of all individual living beings, as essentially and necessarily self-conserving; given the necessarily geometrical rate of reproduction, and the blind strength of the reproductive instincts; given the necessarily limited supply of food; given the large chapter of contingencies that must for ever beset every species of animals, and still more every individual;—given all these, and Darwin shows us clearly that the struggle for existence necessarily begins; the struggle for life, which in so many cases means death to other beings, begins; and good and evil are necessarily introduced to the world together, to begin an eternal strife. Even moral evil, which appears only in man, is necessary as well as moral good; neither can appear till some society exists, after which both are necessary and predictable from the nature of the social units and their incidental circumstances. In the whole Darwinian picture of the universe and its process of evolution, necessity and natural selection rule as by native right, while " next to them high arbiter Chance governs all."

Yet more. Though the evolution doctrine, in the hands of Herbert Spencer, is not materialism, and declines to be identified with materialism—which is characterized as a futile hypothesis—nevertheless evolution has furnished new arguments and suggestions of which the materialist has eagerly availed himself in order to dispense with the notion of mind and purpose in the explanation of the origin and present existence of the universe. The revised materialism of Buchner and Moleschott in Germany, a quarter of a century ago, had mainly based itself on physiological conclusions and on the new law of the conservation of energy, in attempting to show that mind in man, like every other force, or energy, in Nature, was an inseparable concomitant of matter; in particular that thought was a product of cerebral action, which in its turn was merely energy transformed,—in the last resort the energy of heat due to the food consumed. Matter and force are inseparable, and this force, after various transmutations, being stored up in the brain and nerves, found a vent in thought and feeling, as in other organs of the body it animated and performed other functions. There was no entity called the soul anywhere apparent or discoverable by any test; there was but an elaborate brain organization, whose special function it was to think, as it was the function of the heart to pump up blood, of the eye to see, and even, as affirmed by Vogt, of the liver to secrete bile.

But all this would not suffice for a complete materialism, even if satisfactorily proved. For there still remained the belief in a Supreme Mind, unshaken by this materialism, even if it be fully granted that what we call our minds are in all respects products of the brain machinery and nervous telegraphy. There was still the belief, deep in men's minds, which Bacon, the initiator of the inductive and positive philosophy, and himself sometimes classed with the materialists, has given expression to in his essay on "Atheism:" "I had rather believe all the fables in the Legend and the Talmud, and the Alcoran, than that this universal frame is without a mind." Moreover, there were proofs seemingly cogent and unanswerable adduced in support of the belief. In particular, there was the famous argument from design and Final Causes. But now it appears that Darwin has at last enabled the extreme materialist to attack and carry the design argument, the last and hitherto impregnable fortress behind which Natural Theology had intrenched herself; the argument that even Mill admitted, as having the balance of probabilities in its favour; and from which Kant himself, the great conqueror in these regions of speculation, after a close siege, at length, contrary to his usual practice, drew off his investing forces, having finally accepted it, as at least subjectively true. And what was the argument that so universally recommended itself, and that was treated with such respect? Briefly: that the seeming marks of design, and especially the exquisite adaptations in the organic world, prove the existence of a designing mind. The wing of the bird, the fin of the fish, the eye and hand of the man,—these and countless other constructions exhibit such admirable and astonishing adaptations, are so perfectly fitted to their proper ends of flight, of sight, of infinitely various mechanical effort, that they must have been planned and conceived by an infinitely intelligent mind, and constructed by supreme executive skill. The animals did not make themselves with all these wonderful organs, and blind Nature could not make them, therefore there must have been a shaping and intelligent Deity. But how, suggests Darwin, if all these skilful products were only slowly brought to their present perfection, if they were all improved, like human inventions, from an elementary stage partly because their individual possessors made use of them, partly because those, who through chance inherited the best, succeeded best in the battle of life, and handed on to their offspring the acquired advantages? How if the perfect eye were an instrument thus slowly achieved, and one which was improved gradually, as a telescope is improved, though without inventor or improver other than the possessor who by use improves it, assisted by natural selection, which picks out for survival those who possess the best instruments? How, in fact, if all these admired constructions were *results* that remained, instead of preconceptions executed all at once; if they seem *chefs-d'œuvre* of workmanship, solely because Nature, like an artist careful of his reputation, has exhibited only her best works, and has destroyed all her inferior ones?

In fact, Darwin assures us the eye was constructed by endless selection on the part of Nature, who, commencing operations on a mere nerve sensitive to the rays of sunlight, by ever preserving those individuals with the slightest perceptible improvement in the organ after this rudimentary stage, at length perfected an instrument so indispensable for the needs of most animals. The improvements in all organs were made by Nature, herself in reality of most uninventive genius, but who always acted on the simple rule, which cost her the least possible trouble, of selecting those who by chance had already got an advantage in any of these organs, and entrusting to them the honour and responsibility of continuing the species together with the acquired advantage. And this simple method, requiring so little reflection or genius, this rule of thumb so to speak, if invariably acted upon, and especially if it is carried out faithfully for countless ages, seems fully adequate to accomplish the final marvel. Let Nature but favour and keep the best specimens of her species, and ever drop the inferior ones, and at the end of ten thousand or a hundred thousand years, she will have some surprising and most select results to show. The perfect result which now so much astonishes us in the human eye, is but the final sum of an infinite series of small incremental advantages acquired in this way during the countless ages since the first germinal eye mysteriously appeared in the starfish or mollusc. It is true that Nature, having learned her art, now does her work far more easily and expeditiously. She constructs a hand, an eye, a whole body, and multitudes of them, in a very short space of time comparatively, because when she has once gained any advantage, or learned an art in the organic sphere, she holds to it by a blind conservative instinct, and faithfully reproduces it in the next generation, through the fact of inheritance. Though even in these cases of rapid reproduction, embryology teaches that the embryo goes through the same successive stages in the womb that the long line of its phylogenetic ancestors passed through, only that the steps of the process which it cost Nature millions of years to learn in the case of the species, are now, in the case of the individual, abridged into a few weeks or months.

This is the whole story. And here the design argument, as formerly understood, loses its point and force, apparent design being explained by and resolved into natural process and the fact of inheritance. What we mistook for a preconception in an infinite mind, realized by an almighty and skilful hand, is a most excellent result that chance has spared and that natural selection has brought to the front. And suppose an objector were to maintain that this conservative faculty of Nature's; this obstinate holding on to an advantage once gained, and passing it on from parent to offspring; this marvellous faculty of repeating in a few weeks or months all the creative skill which it took millions of years to acquire; this facility of reproducing at a few sittings the choicest masterpieces of her work, elaborating the human eye in a dark region, carving the human hand, and laying up the tender cells and coils of the future brain; —that all this is to the full as extraordinary and transcendent workmanship as was ever the supposed sudden creations of species with all their organs and adaptations. Yes, the materialistic biologist tells us, it is quite as wonderful; but it is a fact, however astonishing, and as a fact it is conceivable, while the other account of supernatural creation is a fiction, and of the worst kind, because it never *could* be made conceivable to us under our existing mental conditions. Moreover, extraordinary as is the evolution before birth of any living being, human or other, there is no appearance of the action of a mind at work unfolding each stage of the process; on the contrary, science, which has lately been deeply engaged on the subject, tells us only of the action of matter, the evolution one after another, and according to regular ascertainable laws, of the wonderful properties stored up implicitly in all-powerful and mysterious matter. A mysterious, universal, immanent power is here manifested, if you will; the materialist affirms that it is a power inherent in and belonging to matter, and most certainly it is not mind in any sense of that term to which we can attach a meaning. Even if we grant a universal power at every point and pulse of the organic, as of the inorganic world, existing everywhere and at all times, still this would not be a universal mind, but a universal power or agency; and if we are to use our words with any definite meaning, we cannot affirm that there is a supreme mind at work, shaping the individual organs by supernatural power before birth, when science assures us that it is all done by natural processes. There is no more trace of mind in the short process of evolution which the science of embryology surveys, than in the long processes of evolution of which Darwin tells us this is but a very brief epitome. The evolution of the individual, with all its exquisite adaptations, is as wonderful truly as the evolution of a planet, as the evolution of the human species; but it is no more brought about, than were those others, by the action of a supernatural mind planning it or of a supernatural hand achieving it; which are clearly mere words that convey no meaning. It is done by regular, natural steps and processes which science is learning to trace and exhibit to us as invariable laws, mysterious and marvellous in the last result, indeed, but only, as all ultimate facts and laws are and must be, from the laws of embryonic development and natural selection to the law of gravitation, although they, in the long run, relate only to matter and its various manifestations.

§ 2. Thus, the new materialism seeks to draw renewed life and nutriment from Darwinism. Can it be said to this materialism, which bases itself upon doctrine of evolution, that, whether there be or be not marks of infinite wisdom and goodness discoverable in the entire cosmic process, yet a God, intelligent and moral, must be postulated as the Author of conscience and the moral law in man; a God who, moreover, still exists as a moral Legislator and Ruler, and who will finally make virtue and happiness coincident hereafter, as we feel they should be, though they never actually are, upon the earth ? This is Kant's argument for the existence and moral government of God, reproduced in Mr. Matthew Arnold's "something not ourselves that makes for righteousness."

But in answer to this we are assured, not merely by the materialists, but by scientific moralists like Darwin and Spencer, that from the circumstances and necessities of the case, men themselves must have invented morality, slowly but surely—a conclusion which is confirmed by

Tylor's and Lubbock's researches into the primitive history of mankind. The germs of all morality, we are told, are contained in two primitive instincts—the instinct of self-preservation and the reproductive instinct; in particular social morality, or morality proper, implied in our obligation to our fellows, is to be traced to the former. Morality is a necessary corollary from the instinct to live, so much so that, being given three, or even two, social, not to say human, beings agreeing to live together in any kind of union, however loose, morality of some degree and amount, however slight, must result. Three men, three ants, could not live and labour together without manifesting the essential elements of morality. Union, besides allaying mutual fear and distrust, secures certain evident advantages: two can obtain by their united labours more than double the amount of food and raiment that each working separately could procure. Here the self-preserving instinct comes into play. But they could not have the advantages of union unless there was mutual trust, a fair division of labour and of its acquisitions; and here we have the essential germs of truth and justice. Further, if in a primitive tribe of men, as in a colony of ants, there was not some zeal in individuals for the common good, the society, as a whole, would not flourish, and the individuals themselves would be the losers. So surely, in fact, as the primitive units in a state of isolation, under the instinct of self-preservation, must act in ways that we could generally predict in pursuit of food, so surely when they come together, though still at first under the guidance of this instinct of self-preservation, or self-advancement, they will observe, in their mutual intercourse, a rudimentary moral behaviour, which will in time become customs and then recognized laws, with a power lodged somewhere to enforce them.

All else follows in the natural course of evolution: the gradual improvement of morality will be accomplished by natural selection favouring those tribes or groups in which the social as well as other virtues, as courage, and sacrifice, were most observed and practised. All the virtues necessary for society will be thus developed if men live together—sociability, sympathy, pity, as well as regard for veracity, justice, and the general weal. True, the vices may also be developed in individuals, because at the bottom man remains a being with an obstinate instinct to seek his own advantage, which urges him to violate his duty to others; but the united interest of the society is always a force antagonistic to these selfish impulses, and exerts itself to repress them. Of course, the looser the cohesion of the primitive societies, the less scope there is for the development of the virtues, which, in a state of savage isolation, may be, as we still see, almost non-existent, or may exist only in so far as the mere primitive unit, the family group, implies some small recognition of them.

Morality is thus no special fact in human nature necessarily requiring a supernatural being to produce it. The moral law was not specially handed down from heaven to guide men's actions. Given only the self-conserving instinct inseparable from all living beings, given further the germs of the principle of sociability so widely spread in the animal kingdom,—and all social animals, man included, must of necessity invent some system of morals. Morality in this respect stands on the same level with art, science, mechanical invention, that they are all equally of man's creation and device. Morality, indeed, presupposes some rudimentary form of society, to whose interests it is strictly related, while the others, although they find their fostering and encouragement in society, do not necessarily imply it, being possible in solitude. Morality, too, was earlier in the world than art, or science, or even religion (itself of natural origin). It was probably not earlier than some rude mechanical arts; but just as certainly as these were the devices of men themselves, so were moral notions and rules. Indeed, the first inventors could with better reason lay claim to inspiration than the first moralists; to invent and to execute being a gift of the few, to perceive the need of moral conduct being common to all. But as we believe that no God was required to teach men to shape their rude stone hatchets, their spear and arrow heads; as the more skilful conceived and shaped these, urged thereto and taught solely by the necessities of their position under the instinct to live; the bee and the bird, under like impelling forces, displaying a like mechanical ingenuity;—so men discovered, though much more easily and generally, the need and utility of the primary virtues. The real difficulty never came from not seeing clearly their necessity; this was obvious enough, even to individuals of the earliest and rudest human hordes, just as it is instinctively obvious to the lower social animals to-day. The difficulty was, and, though in much less degree, still is, to reduce moral sentiments and rules to practice, in opposition to the powerful antagonistic forces of selfishness and sensuality, which are in their essence instinctive, unreasoning, prone to boundless excess, and regardless of the good of others. Indeed, the difficulty in ruder times of curbing the ungovernable egotism of the individual was felt to be so great, that as soon as men had come to conceive the notion of supernatural and powerful personalities resident behind the forces and phenomena of Nature—fetishes, demons, deities—the aid of some of them was specially invoked in order to give a supernatural sanction, the fear of the god's displeasure, in addition to the ordinary natural ones that society supplied. In still later times, we find the law-givers and founders of religions, in their several sacred books, affirming that they had received the moral precepts inculcated by them from heaven. But not the less was morality a matter of man's invention, and practised long before the pretended revelations which afterwards came in to reinforce and confirm it; of human invention like the mechanical arts, but so obviously and instinctively apparent in its necessity, that where even two or three human units were aggregated together, there morality was sure to arise in the midst of them. Social necessity was the mother of morality, as individual necessity of the mechanical arts; but necessity was as much the mother of the one species of invention as of the other.

Very early, too, but not till they had quite parted all company with their non-human relations, our forlorn and helpless ancestors must have experienced some dim religious feelings, begotten of fear, and awe, and ignorance, and blind dumb wonder, which Nature and her formidable forces, sometimes terrible and destructive, sometimes again seemingly beneficent and kindly disposed, would naturally stir within them. The primitive man found himself cast helpless into a universe fraught with manifold dangers, where all was uncertain, and the sentiment of absolute dependence on Nature and her capricious powers, unless he could find some way to placate them, was borne deeply in upon him. But haply, by figuring the powers of Nature as beings like himself, as he would naturally do, they would be conceived as capable of being moved in a human way and rendered more favourably disposed. Hence came religion into the world, born of fear, as Epicurus truly declared; and hence religious practice soon followed, in the shape of ceremony, sacrifice, and supplication to please the powerful demons and deities.

But morality, as already said, was prior to religion. Men had moral notions at least as early as religious feelings, and moral practice long before religion became organized into a system of worship with prescribed rites and ceremonies, so that religion was in no sense the source, but only appeared subsequently as an ally, of morality.

Long after religion had appeared, when a breathing-time in the fierce battle of existence was allowed, when leisure was possible, in an auspicious climate, and amidst happier conditions of life, art was born, and, following quickly upon art, science and philosophy—not from an immediate material necessity as in the case of practical inventions, nor from a social necessity as in the case of morals, but in order to satisfy a new and inner need, a higher craving born in the souls of men for beauty and truth.

And, indeed, when one reflects, it might with a far greater show of reason be contended that a God was required to teach men the rudiments of art and science than of morality; to implant the new perceptions of beauty and the new relish for truth—both such strange and unlikely visitants to the primitive savage soul—than to sow the seeds of morality, or teach men the primary virtues, so certain to be developed amongst them from the evident necessities of the case, without any external instruction. Or, if a divine author were postulated, to produce the first *dispositions* to moral practice, the first dim feelings of pity, of sympathy, of affection, and still more the disposition, so antagonistic to his inmost essence of self-conservation, to carry virtue to the extreme of self-sacrifice, the argument might have some force. But, couched in the Kantian form, that God exists as the original Author of the moral law, the argument, as we have just seen, has as little foundation in reason as it has historical justification under the searching modern criticism of the sacred books of different peoples.

And as for the fact of conscience, continues the evolution moralist,—the feeling of duty and moral obligation now existing in men, upon which so much stress is laid by intuitional moralists and theological advocates, this, so far as it is a real fact (though it is far from being a universal one), admits of a quite natural explanation.

So far as it is a fact, it can be naturally accounted for; though in reality conscience is to be found in all degrees, from its almost non-existence to its very moderate average amount, and up to the high and very exceptional degree that makes the hero and martyr accept death rather than be false to it. The existence of the sentiment of duty is admitted, as also its occasional intensity; but even in the extremest case, no supernatural cause or origin is necessary. Conscience, we know from science and history, has grown from the zero state to its present limited degree and range in the average individuals of civilized communities; we know already the natural causes of its commencement, and the natural history of its genesis and development is not far to seek. The explanation of the present fact of a developed conscience in man is simply this: Man being naturally a social animal, the social conscience has been worked into the species by ages of dearly purchased experience, the results of which were handed on from generation to generation by inheritance. This experience it was that, ever enforcing the lesson—evident enough, one would have supposed, without it—of its absolute necessity, not merely for the general social weal, and to save it from internal dissolution, but still more pressingly to save it from destruction by external antagonist tribes, who, besides being braver, were more firmly knit together by the common social bonds of mutual trust, a sense of justice, and regard for the general good. The societies, in fact, which, besides being braver, were more moral, and had a more generally diffused conscience, were those that were favoured by natural selection, and survived. And the scientifically established fact of the transmission by heredity of acquired moral and mental qualities, explains why modern societies have a greatly increased moral, no less than industrial and intellectual capital, since each generation starts with the accumulated inheritance of the preceding, which, in its turn, it should hand on to the next in at least undiminished amount. We to-day are "·the heirs of all the ages," morally no less than intellectually. It is true, some societies may be in a state of moral retrogression; there may be a period of almost general moral degeneracy, as in the decline of the Roman Empire before Christianity arose; but there comes, as then, an epoch of reformation, a new moral illumination, often brought about by one superior spirit, who, mistaking his own enthusiasm and the higher intensity of his own moral feelings for a divine voice, announces himself as specially commissioned from heaven to proclaim anew the moral law and the will of God. And by the powerful contagion of a great example and a great personality, through the fact of sympathy existing in the mass of men, the great prophet or moral reformer has been able to communicate in a measure his state of soul to others, and so at length to raise society to the height it had lost, or even to a still higher moral level.

Thus is to be explained the existence of conscience, and even, having regard to long periods, a continual increase in the clearness and range of its moral light. Our moral dispositions are thus strictly an inherited bequest. And virtue remains indestructible in the species as a whole, whatever deterioration it may undergo in a particular society or in particular individuals. So long as the structure of the brain and nervous system remains constant, as it does on the whole, conscience, morality, remains safe from open assault or secret sap. If we have inherited a good conscience, like a good constitution, from our parents, we shall keep it. And morality in general, it may be safely said, will not be destroyed by the scientific teaching, because it is hidden and stowed away safely in an inaccessible region, in the inmost molecular constitution of the coils and cells of the brain and nerves, and can only be deteriorated or destroyed with these. Morality is as indestructible as art or science; its tendency, like these, is to further development and diffusion, not to a deterioration. Thus, then, in fine, there is no need to postulate the supernatural either for the commencement, the improvement, or the continual preservation of morality; and the voice of conscience, that now speaks with the accumulated moral experience of thousands of generations, is no more the voice of Deity than the perceptions of beauty or truth, likewise inheritances, are special inspirations from Him.

§ 3. Whence, then, the need, demands the evolution materialist, of postulating a supernatural cause? Not, certainly, for morality; for we show you its natural earthly origin from the necessities of man's life. Not for the creation of the earth and sun and planets; for we can show you how they must have been born from physical and dynamical laws. To produce consciousness, you will probably say. But consciousness, including its higher stages of self-consciousness and reason in man, was slowly evolved in the entire animal kingdom, culminating in the human species, from unconsciousness; just as it was evolved in yourself, who, between birth and maturity, have passed through precisely similar stages. This wonderful miracle of evolution has happened in your own case, as it has in that of all men ever born, who attained to man's estate; why, then, may it not have happened in the entire animal kingdom? Doubtless the supposition implies the descent of man from the brute, as well as of all conscious life from unconsciousness. But we show you, there is no *a priori* impossibility in either of these suppositions, and we refer you to Darwin for further proofs of the first, and to Haeckel for a probable proof of the second. Moreover, science at the present moment shows us conscious and sentient life fading into unconscious and insentient forms in the debatable border-land between the plant and animal world; it shows us unbroken continuity from the plant to the human soul, as it is trying to show and has all but succeeded in showing unbroken continuity between chemistry and consciousness. You think, however, there is a gap between chemistry and consciousness shown in the first appearance of life itself. But why resort to the *Deus ex machina* here more than elsewhere? The first appearance of life, as of all things, is mysterious: we grant it. It is difficult to trace the laws which govern the successive stages of the evolutionary process; still, science is fast discovering them in embryology;

and life, you must allow, now begins with matter, whether you admit or deny the possibility of spontaneous generation. Matter is unquestionably first in the field to-day, in all cases where life afterwards emerges. Matter must be first given, without life or mind, even though life and mind afterwards result. But a Creator, you think, with Darwin, must be postulated at the beginning, in order to produce the first few forms of life, granting that the laws of organized matter can accomplish all the rest. But what if chemical combination, aided and supplemented by natural selection, having infinite ages to make many chance trials and failures, and working under more favourable atmospheric or oceanic conditions, on the cooling surface of the globe, or better still, in the dark ocean beds,—what if, between them, they should have hit at last by accident upon some faint rude attempts at life, some rudimentary structureless forms, possibly like the *monera* as now exhibited; which, having been once successfully launched into life, and well under way, afterwards, by the continuing favour of fortune and natural selection, grew and prospered, and were developed into much greater things? What, in a word, if chemical affinity and natural selection, that is to say, matter and its necessary laws, and neither on the one hand Chaos, nor on the other a personal world-fashioning Creator, were the original father of things?

And as for this rival hypothesis, this supposed supernatural process of creation, reflect for a moment, and see if it be not a mere word expressly invented to cover our ignorance—an empty name, which men pass off on themselves for a real explanation. For, only think, what could this impossible process of creation from blank nonentity be—this sudden miraculous summons and precipitation of a host of suns and planets from the empty void, made from no pre-existent materials? If your mind can really "think the great thought of creation," in this fashion—so different from either the Hegelian or the Darwinian conception of it—then indeed the process of miraculous creation might be possible in the cosmos, since your mind at least has accomplished the marvellous process of creation, has constructed its thought out of no existent or conceivable materials! And the sudden creation of a single living form, of a caterpillar, from nothing, is no less difficult than the creation of a world or a host of worlds (possibly, indeed, it would be the more difficult feat of the two); for the mere physical magnitude makes no difference in the intrinsic difficulty, or, let us say rather, in its utter inconceivability and absurdity, even as a possible notion. But chemical combination to produce life!—this, you say, is equally inconceivable and impossible. Not so. We merely conceive new properties to result from a new arrangement of the chemical constituents of matter —a thing with which the eye of Science is very familiar in her analysis and interrogation of Nature's processes. But, again you say, we cannot conceive how life should have originally resulted from a particular arrangement of molecules. Can you conceive, then, how it now results from such an arrangement, though it does as a fact, as the most eminent embryologists have shown us? Or can you conceive how, at the present moment, as the basis of life there is only protoplasm, in the last analysis produced merely by the physical and chemical properties of oxygen, carbon, hydrogen, nitrogen, with some other elements in small proportions, duly combined together? Can you conceive, in fact, how anything which is wholly different from its elements should yet proceed from them?—how water, for instance, should come from oxygen and hydrogen? and yet it does as a fact, however inconceivable and inexplicable, and how little soever we could have expected such a wonderful transformation beforehand. At bottom, indeed, can you conceive why anything should come from anything, beyond the fact, which the senses constantly show us, or which Science, assisting our senses, discovers for us, that it actually does so happen? In the end, all final facts, all the first appearing and becoming of things, even all associations of particular effects with particular antecedent conditions, are, as our scientific thinkers from Hume to Mill and Spencer allow, equally inexplicable, equally mysterious, equally, if you will, miracles. But it is the business of Science to ascertain the laws and conditions under which these facts and appearances present themselves, to discover the constant relations governing both their successive and simultaneous states. These laws Science can discover; to do so is her special work, interesting to the thinker and the savant, and useful to the world; but she has learned, from the futility of all such speculations, to decline the further questions why matter has such properties, why it is governed by such laws, why it undergoes such Protean transformations. She has long since handed over the question of the *why* of phenomena to metaphysics, reserving to herself the question of the *how*, the question of fact. Nor has metaphysics made much of the other problem of the why, over which she has so long puzzled herself. In the end, we must confess that we cannot tell why final facts are so, why they have been so, or why they should continue so; and certainly the miracle and final mystery of Nature's ultimate facts and processes is not diminished by the postulate, which can never be proved, of a power lodged behind Nature, acting after the human fashion, moving, constructing, meditating, selecting as we men do, and still less by the further supposition of such a power acting in a manner entirely supernatural as well as inconceivable, in the evoking of worlds and organisms from pure nonentity, or the void of space.

§ 4. Here appear the outlines of a new and formidable materialistic system. Here once again the hydra-headed materialism, so often slain in the course of the history of philosophy, rises up alive and aggressive; and this time seemingly armed at all points, and threatening to all the higher interests of man, the belief in God, the reality of virtue, the hope of a hereafter. Surely, we are inclined to think, these recurrent phenomena, this repeated resurrection and apparition of the spectre of materialism, betokens something significant. What may it mean? And can we give any answer to it? For a real answer seems urgently required in our time once again.

You have, indeed, shown, we say to the new materialist, that the universal mind has not worked according to men's former rude conceptions; that it did not suddenly call the spheres into being from out the blank and empty abyss; did not conceive, create from nothing, and then fashion and piece together the parts of animal organisms as a watchmaker puts together the parts of a watch. We allow that the Power which we postulate did not reveal His will to men in the moral law handed down from heaven by special miracle to chosen instruments. Nevertheless, though you have shown how matter and mechanical laws might have been the parent of the physical worlds, you have not yet, we conceive, satisfactorily shown how they could have been the sources of the spiritual world; and you have not shown us what first moved matter itself from its original state of eternal rest, or what impressed law and order on the materials of the universe.

You have not shown how mere homogeneous matter, be it hydrogen gas or other uniform substance, however refined, could run of itself into order and harmony, as disclosed in the mathematical figures and motions of the earth and planets and myriad sidereal worlds; motions so labyrinthine, with never a collision, time so exactly kept that the earth is never a fraction of a second late in her vast annual journey. Nor have you explained how these huge spinning spheres, some of them hundreds of thousands of miles in thickness, are hung in the heavens self-supported. Are they really so? No, the law of gravitation keeps them all in their places. And what is gravity? A universal property of matter, like inertia, you say. And why is not matter rather a property of it—of this mysterious invisible something that admittedly governs it everywhere and at all times? What is this gravity? We cannot tell. It is a word for universally observed effects; but we believe there is a cause for it which is not matter itself. To say that matter moves itself, and that gravity is a necessary law of matter in motion, looks like an explanation, but is really none.

Then, according to your story, after innumerable tentative trials, at last elementary life appeared. Life was a happy hit, a fortunate and unexpected product, entirely uncontemplated by Nature! Let us grant this too. Did it appear first in the plant or the animal? We cannot say positively; probably simultaneously, here affixing itself to a particular spot as a plant, and there finding itself wonderfully endowed with the faculty of locomotion. Still, this new property of self-movement at pleasure is a very remarkable fact, for though the planets move, they are not supposed to be self-moved, but must obey a fixed external law of movement. Whence have the elementary forms of organic life this singular difference? Then the feeling of sentiency, and its gradual increase to consciousness, is a still greater marvel. Automatic movement and life might, it is faintly conceivable, be products of chemical and physical law, and be expressible, as our automatists say, in terms of such. But the light of consciousness and thought, —how can we even faintly suppose this to have any relation to a particular collocation of the chemical elements? Is there not a gulf between chemistry and consciousness, admitted by the most eminent authorities in science; a difference for ever, than which none greater is conceivable, between mind and matter—between the internal and unextended states of knowing and feeling and their external and extended material conditions; an abyss not to be bridged, between the cerebral atoms and thought, their supposed product? But it is acknowledged that the word "product" is to be taken in Hume's sense of something that invariably follows after something else, though we see no reason why it should so follow. Be it so; but in that case your materialism and monism break down and become dualism; for if matter is not the efficient cause of thought, but only an antecedent, wholly unlike its consequent; if matter does not itself always actually think, or if one of its associated forms of energy is not transformed into thought, as the hardier materialists would affirm;— then there are two acknowledged things or entities in the universe, totally different in kind—matter and thought.

However, lest we should be thought to snatch at a merely verbal victory, extorted from particular scientific concessions, of the difference between matter and consciousness, we are ready to grant the materialist that if he can prove, beyond doubt or question, that matter—adding all its properties, if he chooses—was first in the field at the beginning, and that there was nothing else either behind it or immanent in it of a totally different nature, then materialism in its most real and significant sense is proved. We will allow it proved, without pressing him with the concessions of physicists and naturalists like Dubois-Reymond, Helmholtz, and Tyndall, who have admitted the gulf between consciousness and matter; for at least matter—the cerebral atoms—though unlike thought, produces it, is the cause of it in the scientific sense, the antecedent, without which it would not be; while again, ages ago, matter was the parent of it, and of all things that have since been slowly evolved therefrom.

The controversy between the materialist and those who differ from him in thinking his explanation of the universe wholly insufficient, may fairly be narrowed to this point: Was matter, and nothing else, first in the field at the beginning of things, or from all eternity? and is matter, and nothing else wholly different from it, to-day at the bottom of all things—life and thought included? Was matter the first, and is it still the last and deepest thing in the universe? This is the real and only important question; and if, as said, the materialist could really answer it satisfactorily in the affirmative, materialism in its most serious and important sense would be established. And further, we are ready to accept the materialist's own statement of the nature of matter, various and comprehensive as that has now become. We give him the hard, indivisible atoms of physics, though these are rather an hypothesis, or, as Professor Bain terms them, "representative fictions;" we give the protoplasm in the organic sphere, and the molecules in the brain, as equally material; and, if he wishes, we are ready to regard the various forms of energy that play on or about matter as their solid basis of operations, as material likewise. Heat, electrical, chemical, and nervous energy, invisible in themselves, but which demonstrate their existence by visible or palpable effects, we shall grant to be material, because they have been found only in conjunction with phenomenal matter. In fact, all that Science has been able to observe in this Protean matter, together with something which she has not observed, but the existence of which she only suspects, we are ready to grant; and yet we feel compelled to ask—Is there not something more than all this phenomenal matter, and all this phenomenal energy? Is there not something manifested in the universe wholly different from it?—something of which these things are effects; but which is more than these, and different from these, which in future ages will show far more effects than these, just as to-day it shows an infinitely more expanded variety of matter, if so we must call it, than it did in the pleistocene period, and still more, than when it manifested itself as only a diffused fiery vapour.

Was matter the whole at the beginning? Was there not something behind? At least, was there not a principle of development and evolution—an immaterial thing, you must allow—something which required matter to work upon as material, and by means of which it showed all its marvels? This process is not matter, and yet this is the essence of the whole universe in time, as it is still the most essential fact in all existence. This process of development requires time, infinite ages, in which to declare itself. It has declared itself on the earth in the various forms of matter, and it has also reached thought. What might not its translations and expressions be through other infinite worlds? Still only matter, you say, and thought as its product, if there be thought. But are you sure? and would matter under a sixth or seventh sense, revealing a wholly new side of existence, be our matter? Would thought, its supposed product, be our thought, if it received its materials through wholly different sources and avenues, perhaps going far deeper into all possible existence than ours? Has there not, then, been at work throughout the process of evolution, even on our earth, a mighty and mysterious something?—a something which, if we will speak at all of it, we must describe as a purpose, moving beneath and irresistibly pushing its way, unfolding itself, ascending higher and higher? And the deposition of the germs which afterwards flowered so gloriously in religion, art, morality, even science itself,—can this be said to be within the power of matter alone? Have we not here creation after all? At one time and at one moment there did not exist in the universe certain things which have since appeared—life, consciousness, human affection; at one moment they were not, afterwards they were. Is this evolution or creation? Indeed, the name is indifferent; but nevertheless, this fact of evolution or creation, call it which you please, still is—and you allow it—the very life and essence of the world. This is the one process for ever going on, and now more prodigiously than ever. The birth and growth and life of every insect, of every flower, of every man, are instances of it. The universe is still a perpetual process of evolution or creation. And what is the working power? What evolves all the stages of the process? What transforms all the energies? Matter, the universal blind mother, brings forth all from her dark womb! and the energies of matter transform themselves for ever and ever. To state it thus is indeed to proclaim loudly the futility of materialism, and yet this is all that materialists themselves give us for explanation.

Further, in all this process of evolution, in all these transformations of energy, where all is wonderful, there is one thing, one evolution, one transformation, pre-eminently wonderful. There is the evolution of consciousness and thought, the supreme marvel of the universe; there is the unique energy that slowly awoke to consciousness, that alone knows and contemplates all the other energies as well as itself. We might almost conceive that everything else might be brought into connection with matter as the central principle; that all the other facts in the universe might conceivably be hung from the plastic and flexible principle of matter as now viewed; but consciousness, with all its wonderful contents, this and its evolution are inexplicable by materialism, and can only receive explanation by postulating a principle wholly different from all that we know of matter.

Or was consciousness, too, as well as life, only a lucky accident that Nature blindly stumbled upon? Did Matter, blindly groping, while sorting her old materials, while arranging, and rearranging her atoms, at last hit upon this splendid thing by chance—this most surprising thing, had she any intelligence to perceive it and to be surprised. For a spirit arose beneath her blind passes, her fortuitous motions and combinations, destined, if not to give eyes to Matter to read herself, at least to be her master and ruler; a spirit that read into the face of Matter and Nature a divine beauty, and found in her breast a truth unsuspected by herself; a soul, too, that found in itself infinite affections as well as immortal longings for a divine something nowhere discoverable in nature or on the earth; a soul that, in process of further evolution, began to nourish ambitious and dazzling hopes of a future continued life as its inherent right and privilege, that dreamt of equality with the angels, and of an immortality like the gods:—such being the startling phenomenon that was one day born of matter in a mindless universe, the product of a lucky accident!

§ 5. The sinister question that lies at the root of all our new materialism, and which is brought prominently forward by Darwinism, is precisely this old and threatening one—Was the universe born of chance? And are all the grandest things that have since appeared in it—thought, will, affection, beauty, enthusiasm, like random products? This is the real question forced upon us by the latest aspect of the materialistic philosophy, in alliance with the doctrine of evolution; and now we are face to face with it.

Was it accident that first deposited the tingling nerve sensitive to the sun's rays, that afterwards, under favour of natural selection, developed into the miracle of the human eye? Was it accident that endowed the optic nerve with such very remarkable properties; and that awoke the inner and totally distinct seeing power—the reader behind the refracting lens and the optic nerve, who uses both? And finally, was it accident that awoke all the other senses, together with consciousness and all its varied components—emotion, sensations, and thoughts?

Let those who can believe this; I for my part must believe differently. We must believe that, in some way, though possibly only faintly analogous to our design and intention, the great results attained by Nature were intended by her, and that she reached them by a route which was not any of the cross-roads of chance. They were both intended to appear, and they were not reached at haphazard. We are compelled to interpret the course of evolution as being under guidance; to believe that the final results were aimed at, that Nature did not stumble on her best works by sheer accident, the further results of which would have utterly astonished herself had she eyes to see. Let us freely grant that the intention, design, plan, and purpose which we must read into Nature, and which we must suppose in some way to be there, is and must be very different from ours, only remotely analogous to ours, because we cannot postulate the existence of a Person in which it resides; but yet we must use the notion of design, because the only other alternative, chance, is still wider away from the facts. If we must elect between the two agencies, chance and design, the latter must be nearer the truth. Design we know already in our own case to be a true shaping power, while chance effects nothing but evil in the long run. Chance, as an explanation—and if design be denied, chance must be offered as the explanation—is a word expressing nothing, a word which, under pretence of explanation, affirms nothing whatever. It is this; but it is also much more serious; for it is the express denial of God, and is thus genuine atheism.

For even if we could prove the existence of a God that cared not how the world went, and in no way controlled the course of its evolution and history, although perhaps we could not justly be called atheists, yet the voice of the world, since the days of Epicurus, has regarded the belief that the gods are careless as practically atheism. A power that called the world into being, and immediately resigned all control over it, abandoning it to a chance fate, would scarcely be deserving the name of God. In some way, then, we are compelled to suppose that Nature did not grope her way blindly and blunderingly to her most splendid achievements,—to life, to consciousness and its contents, to the poet's vision of beauty, the martyr's enthusiasm for virtue, the thinker's thirst for truth. These high things could not have been accidental. The best things that have resulted on earth—love, joy, peace, virtue, truth, beauty,—these and possibly grander things elsewhere realized, Nature, or rather a power behind Nature, meant, contemplated, and intended. Give what latitude to the word "intention" that your imagination enables you, but it is by some such analogy that we must interpret Nature's operations; and her evident continuing kindness to us in the daily rising of the sun, in her corn and wine, her fruits and flowers, is a confirmation of our faith in her sympathy with and good will to men.

And even if the universe, with its present law and order, could conceivably have come from chance, we are sure it does not thither tend; for we men have now the course of it, at least on our earth, in large measure in our hands. We are now co-labourers with Nature, and it is by our conscious efforts striving to further her aims that the further work of development is to be carried on. It is in and by us men that the higher level, spiritual, artistic, moral, social, to which she is aspiring, is to be reached.

Can it be said to all this, that if Nature had not reached her present most excellent things, the *chefs-d'œuvre* of her workmanship, she would have reached others as great or greater, though of a different sort; that it mattered not which of the cross-roads of chance she took at any critical moment in the evolution of things; that if she had not accidentally struck on life, and afterwards on consciousness, which carried with it all its glorious after-contents, she would have found something else as good or better? May it be said of Nature (as of man himself) that if she had not taken one path at a critical moment in her career, she might have prospered just as well by trying another, or on the other hand, that what she has attained to, and now holds by, might possibly have been far surpassed; that, far from having taken the tide at the flood that leads on to fortune, she missed it rather on the earth, from whence resulted "the shallows and miseries" of the remainder of the voyage, which the pessimist now so loudly laments; that, in fact, far greater things were in the list of possibilities originally held in her hands, but which have been for ever missed on the earth by a wrong turn taken at a decisive moment,—possibilities which, perhaps, nay, certainly, have been realized in happier spheres, through the exhaustion of chance and errors, and by the trial of ever new combinations and arrangements? Or shall we hold, with the optimist, unflinchingly, that our world is as good as it could have been; that none other or better was possible under the circumstances? The question is finally a matter for faith, but faith appealing to reason, and I for my part hold to the latter view. I believe that the highest things attained on the earth are equal to the best anywhere attained, and further, that they were intended to come out in the end, in process of time and evolution. Better or worse of their kind may be realized elsewhere, and even wholly different things, which may be very good; but nothing greater than the finest things our own old earth has shown us—virtue, knowledge, affection, beauty, and the peace and joy which comes from these; while nothing good has anywhere been arrived at by chance.

Professor Huxley contends that the final results on the earth were rigidly necessary from the inherent properties of matter, and could have been predicted by an infinite intelligence, had there been any such contemporaneous with the original "cosmic vapour," just as, being given the somewhat different physical conditions of the planet Jupiter, the same intelligence could have predicted with equal certainty a different result. Being given the physical conditions, there was only, he thinks, a mathematical and dynamical problem to work out, though one of much complexity when considered in its details. Professor Oscar Schmidt, in his work on *Darwinism and Descent*, in appearance differing from Professor Huxley, but only in appearance, discerns in the evolutionary process, as its most essential attribute, the fact of contingency, or as we have simply described it—chance. Professor Huxley's physical and mechanical necessity is quite compatible with this metaphysical contingency; indeed, as he himself tells us, it implies it, for he assures us that Darwinism is exclusive of teleology—of all design and purpose. And when he speaks of a hypothetical intelligence that might have predicted the final results on the earth—life, consciousness, and all the rest that followed from these—he only means to say that if such an intelligence had existed, capable of seeing clearly the chance combinations that might result and that would result, then he had only to make his mechanical or physico-chemical calculation to know what would follow. The properties of unchanging matter would determine the rest, if only the contingent combinations were known or given. But it is quite clear that, even admitting the actions of all bodies and even all animals to be as physically necessary as the motions of the planets round the sun, there is still endless room for the play of contingency, just as there is in the course of a man's life, though, on the necessitarian view, as maintained by Huxley, all his actions are in like manner determined, and even in the end physically determined. If all be physical necessity, there is ample room for contingency, for chance, unless, indeed, there was not only a hypothetical but a real intelligence of some kind, and not only an intelligence but a power that in some way exercised a control over the course of evolution, and in some way aimed at the final good results.

Another eminent naturalist, Professor Asa Gray, contends that the doctrines of Darwin are compatible with design and final causes, as, indeed, with the opposite views. They are compatible with design, I allow; but only on condition that the Darwinian acknowledges a purpose in the process of evolution, while we allow to him that the meaning of the words—"will," "design," "purpose," "intention," are to be widened, and freed from their old anthropomorphic contents. There was a general intention and purpose, which is still shown in the physical universe, in its rigid relations immutably held since the cosmic vapour cooled and condensed into suns and planets, attracting each other by mathematically measurable law; and there was intention and purpose, though not as ours, in the power manifested everywhere in Nature, and moving under the process of evolution to reach the best that has been gained. In the organic world this power, though still having its special aims in each single being, nevertheless, by the very fact that it has sundered itself into so many individuals, has seemingly lost its unity of aim and purpose in the animals and in man. But, nevertheless, it has an aim, and steers for it, though in a way seemingly laborious and circuitous, and in some respects clearly incomprehensible. What is it aiming at now in our species? A better world on the earth, towards which so many powerful tendencies point,—a higher and also a happier one; of this we are sure, for these are the desires and aims of men, which are amongst its chief aims, though they must be realized by men's conscious efforts. In conclusion, we must believe in aim, will, and purpose in the universe, other than the human; but not in the old theological and anthropomorphic sense. To adhere to the old conceptions of will and purpose, which were either strictly framed after human models, or else tied to a particular metaphysical determination of personality, is as wrong as the emptying of the universe, after the manner of our modern physicists and naturalists, of all will and purpose. But the former is a pious error; the latter, with its logical result of a universe drifting nowhither, is one which would destroy all religion, and all morality so far as bound up with religion.

CHAPTER III.

ON THE DEVELOPED CONCEPTION OF GOD.

§ 1. WITH difficulty will any of the past forms of idealism be able to make head against the new materialism in association with evolution. For excepting the theological idealism of Berkeley, idealism, in its later forms—English and Germanic—is compatible with the evolution materialism. And Berkeley's proof of the existence of an Infinite Spirit resembling the human, but vaster, is precisely the part of his system that subsequent philosophy has found least acceptable. But setting aside this part, the remainder of the Berkeleian idealism is quite reconcilable with the extremest forms of materialism, which asks only the phenomenal matter—that Berkeley freely grants—in order to effect all its purposes. Indeed, Professor Huxley distinctly allows that the arguments of "pure idealism" are unanswerable, and can be all the more easily shown to be irrefutable the more completely we accept the materialist's position.*

But besides materialism and idealism, there is yet a third monistic conception of the universe, at least as old

* His words are: "The more completely the materialistic position is admitted, the easier it is to show that the idealistic position is unassailable, if the idealist confines himself within the limits of positive knowledge."—*Life of Hume*, p. 82.

as the days of Spinoza—a system which, though it has been obscured, now by materialism, now by idealism, as one or other acquired temporary ascendency, yet has ever reappeared again, and at the present moment seems likely to prevail more and more, and, by drawing to itself the truthful elements in materialism and idealism, in the end to cut the ground from beneath the feet of both; deriving, moreover, as it has done, ever fresh life and strength from the great scientific discoverers of the past two hundred years, and certainly not least support from those of our own generation.

There is the conception which represents the Ultimate Principle of the universe as something deeper, wider, greater than either matter as we know it or consciousness as we know it; something of which matter and thought are merely special forms, appearances, expressions—the only ones, indeed, that we can know, and that only by means of one of these themselves, but which are, nevertheless, far from being exhaustive of the transcendent nature of that One Eternal Substance and Power at the bottom of these things that we know, as well as of innumerable other possible presentations of itself of which we can know nothing.

This great conception, Spinozistic in its origin, has been unfolding itself for more than two centuries past in human thought; has been working ever deeper into the philosophic, poetic, artistic, theological, and even lately into the scientific consciousness. It was the conception of God in which the soul of Goethe, naturalist and mighty poet, finally rested. It was the conception of Schliermacher, the father of rational theology. Even Kant, thinker and man of science—though from the practical reason he reached a different result—from the speculative side could find no other conception than this of an Absolute Being, the final unconditioned Substance, "the sum of all realities;" while at the present time, Herbert Spencer, the philosopher of evolution, adopts this idea as the one most reconcilable with modern physical and natural science, as well as with the whole process and doctrine of evolution.

§ 2. There is in the universe an Existence over and above all phenomena, whether viewed as unconditioned Existence with Kant, as infinite Substance with Spinoza, as an inscrutable Power with Spencer; a transcendent Something, of which matter and mind are alike merely phenomenal manifestations or modes, which are far from being exhaustive of its whole nature. There is an Ultimate Reality, in which, according to the great conception of Spinoza, as according to Herbert Spencer who has adopted it, mind and matter, subject and object, thought and thing, are finally united; a reality vaster and deeper than all we know or dream of in matter; grander than all we can think of or imagine in mind—which, as we know it, is perhaps only a fugitive, though glorious, flower, thrown out from it here on the earth in the course of its long evolutionary march. There is an Absolute Existence, as according to Hegel (though not essentially Thought, as described by him), unfolding itself slowly in the transmutations of matter through the ages, aspiring constantly higher, from matter to life, from life to sensation, from sensation to consciousness, from consciousness to spirit; a Power one and the same with that which now exhibits itself in the various Protean transformations of the stock of physical energies, which are merely so many phenomenal masks it has assumed, without any or all of them conveying

2 A

a full or true description of its real nature. There is a mighty living and universal Power which, though not itself individual, is for ever bursting forth into endless individual life, in plant, or animal, or man, or angel; a Power which, though not personal, yet lives and moves in the inmost being and essence of all persons; a Power resistless, but beneficent, which, partially suspended in winter, bursts into a glorious resurrection of life and beauty in spring,—in bud and blossom, in insect, bird, and brute; a Power gracious and renovating, which temporarily suspended in our exhausted hearts, yet ever wells up again in inner secret and satisfying springs of hope and joy and peace, life-restoring, light-giving, to our heavy-laden souls. There is a Power, of which matter and energy, life and light, thought and volition, are but forms; a Power, too, whose exhaustless life and energy are but slightly drawn upon by all the various demands made upon it in our little earth, working as it does simultaneously as one and the same power in each of the myriad stellar systems dispersed through infinite space. In the most distant orbs, from which Science, by her searching analysis and improved methods of observation, has recently brought back her spectroscopic, supplementing her telescopic, reports, the same power is displayed in the composition of matter and in the maintenance of law as at home on the earth; and probably in many of those distant spheres it works in the production of life, while probably also, nay, somewhere certainly, and whether working by other and superior art or working, as here, by natural selection chiefly, it has attained to grander and more excellent results than the choicest terrestrial things,—to something greater than truth, beauty, virtue, happiness, or if only to these, then to a higher species of them, to a peace more serene and settled than ours, to a truth more clear and free from error, to a beauty more pervading, to a happiness less fugitive and more unalloyed, to a virtue superior to our smirched earthly product.

But further, this transcendent and stupendous Power, however far it has progressed in its mysterious but glorious march of evolution, will, according to Science, exhibit itself in still more surprising results and perfect productions in future times, at least in our earth; in productions which we can now no more conceive than could our rude prehistoric ancestors conceive within their dark and narrow brains all the marvellous discoveries, inventions, and improvements of our modern life and civilization.

This Ultimate Power in the universe, mysterious and unfathomable for ever, however much we or future generations may know of its manifestations, is thus described by the philosopher of evolution, Herbert Spencer: "There is a power behind humanity, and behind all other things; a power of which humanity is but a small and fugitive product; a power which was, in the course of ever-changing manifestations, before humanity was, and will continue through other manifestations when humanity has ceased to be." *

But the Power is unknowable, he assures us, save only in its manifestations. It would be equally incorrect to describe it as either matter or mind; for it is more than both, and more fundamental than either. In both cases alike, should we attempt to describe it as material

* According to Spencer, this mysterious Power is the original and abiding source of the religious feelings, which can never find a proper object in any "religion of humanity" as conceived by Comte (*Study of Sociology*, pp. 311, 312).

or as mental, we are only applying our imperfect, phenomenal, and provisory predicates and notions, our scarcely approximate symbols and words—anthropomorphic when borrowed from our minds and actions, materialistic when borrowed from matter and Nature's actions—to something wholly beyond the reach of any combination of human symbols, material or mental, however skilfully and subtly put together by even the greatest thinkers, to adequately characterize. Language can give no more than an approximate description of the manifestations of the Power, which itself remains for ever inaccessible and unfathomable. It would, indeed, be the easier of the two, according to Spencer, to offer a solution of the problem of the universe and the transcendent power manifested in it in terms of mind than in terms of matter, but both solutions would be inadequate. "It would be easier to translate so-called matter into so-called spirit, than to translate so-called spirit into so-called matter (which latter is, indeed, wholly impossible); yet no translation can carry us beyond our symbols." The materialist's solution of the world-problem, he thinks futile. The idealist's is also inadequate; for though idealism can express the phenomena of matter in terms of mind, yet matter exists as a mode of force. Its reality, though relative, is as deep as that of our thought. We cannot conceive its non-existence. In one sense, matter is perhaps a more essential predicate of the Ultimate Power than mind; for matter was first in the field on the earth, as geology and the doctrine of evolution assure us. Moreover, this matter extends through all space. Far as gravitation extends, there reigns matter; and its probable ultimate unit, the hydrogen atom, has been reported in Sirius and Aldebaran by the spectroscope; while we cannot affirm with equal confidence the existence of mind or consciousness closely resembling ours in remote parts of the stellar regions.

According to Spencer, we do not know this Ultimate Power, and we shall never know it. Neither we nor any of the human species, however enlarged their intelligence may in future become, shall know it. In fact, it would appear as if no conceivable intelligence could ever solve the final enigma of the world; certainly no human intelligence will ever be adequate to the problem. The Ultimate Power "is no more representable in terms of human consciousness than human consciousness is representable in terms of a plant's function." While men remain subject to the limitations of consciousness, they cannot compass in thought an existence transcending all consciousness; and men must be for ever subject to these limitations.

However, though so much is inaccessible, we may even now know something of this noumenal existence and Ultimate Power. We can know its existence, infinity, eternity, universal agency and efficacy, and its final utter incomprehensibility. The latter predicate may seem a contradiction in terms, but it is not so. It is real and important, though negative knowledge, to know that the Final Power and Being in the universe *must* for ever remain unknown, not only by us, but by the most exalted intelligence that can come after us; for men have long and persistently believed the contrary,—believed that by searching they could find out God, or, on the other hand, that He could communicate with and reveal His real nature to them.

We can know something more, and what more immediately concerns us than the universal and negative predicates just named. We can know the sides of His nature that this Universal Being has turned to us, the small illuminated segment of the vast inscrutable sphere of existence. We may know the manifestations of this transcendent Power both in ourselves and in the external world. This knowledge, science and a sound philosophy rightly interpreting the facts and conclusions of science, provide us with; and such knowledge, a real and true revelation and guide of life, of greatly increased clearness and range, men may haply have to-day as they never could have had in any former period of man's sojourn on earth.

§ 3. This Ultimate Reality in the universe is God. The conception which we have illustrated in some detail coincides, in its main features,* with that of Spencer, though he was by no means the first to propound it or to shape it forth to the world. The conception is essentially due to the great Spinoza, the profoundest philosophical mind of a century prolific in the production of great thinkers, as it was also the conception accepted and further illustrated by Goethe, the greatest modern poet. Moreover, something like this, and differing only from this in the ascription of purpose, is the notion of Schliermacher, the founder of modern rational theology. Kant, indeed, a great and original thinker, came to a different conclusion. For, although he had himself destroyed the old and stock arguments for the existence of God, and though from the furthest frontier of his own understanding commanding the most advanced outlook, he could discern nothing but a shadowy something—a merely "limitative" concept of a thing-in-itself at the end of all experience, a something which was no real thing, though constantly mistaken by the metaphysicians for

---

* In its main features; for, as stated, we recognize one element, the most important of all, namely, *purpose*, which is omitted alike from the Substance of Spinoza and the Ultimate Reality of Spencer.

such;—nevertheless, Kant recovered his belief in God from another and an unexpected quarter. He recovered it, first, in the shape of an *Idea* of the Reason; an idea that the understanding, dealing only with concepts pure or empirical, could not supply, but which the reason, a different faculty, finds herself necessarily and unaccountably possessed of; an idea or goal that invites and beckons the reason to follow it, and which finally shows itself as the most abstract and attenuated conception of absolutely unconditioned being, further described after the manner of Leibnitz—as if to infuse some life and reality into it— as "the sum of all possible realities." But secondly, and in a more concrete form, Kant proved the existence of God from the Practical Reason. God veritably exists, and stands in a most important relation to us as the Author of the moral law; a postulate which the practical reason is compelled to make from the absolutely imperative and unconditional character of the notion of Duty—a notion which we find in ourselves, which admits of no human origin or explanation, but which constantly refers us back to a Divine Author and an abiding Will, at once intelligent and virtuous, as its only conceivable source. Such was Kant's manner of proof; and it may be added that in this notion of duty, followed up, he recovered all the interests that he had himself put in jeopardy,—not only God, but freedom of the will and immortality.

"We ought, therefore we can;" we feel the categorical order of duty, therefore it must be within our power to follow it. In this argument Kant recovers free-will. And a future life is necessary to bring into final harmony virtue and happiness, which reason requires, but which never has place in this world. But subsequent criticism has not ratified Kant's practical proof, or rather postulate, of God's existence. It has been considered as irreconcilable with the remainder of his philosophic system,—an after-thought, prompted by the weakness of age and an unwillingness to part with the personal Deity of his youth and the masses. On the other hand, his destructions of the old proofs of the existence of God has been accepted as complete and decisive. This, however, leaves God, in Kant's system, where He is posited before Kant's refutation began, as an absolute Being behind all experience, the finally unfathomable but real ultimate source of the phenomena of mind as of matter; a notion in all essential particulars the same as the conception of Spinoza reproduced by Goethe and Spencer, which we have already presented.

§ 4. This conception of a grand Reality, whose phenomenal projections in space and in our consciousness alone are knowable, is a great as well as philosophical conception, and probably that with which all thinking men will finally close as the worthiest that finite faculty can frame of Deity. It has the merit of reconciling *most* of what Science has been teaching with all that Philosophy—whose special business it is to decide upon the question—has yet been able to agree upon. Further—and this is important—it satisfies the demands of the imagination, as shown by its general acceptance by imaginations of the grand order, as those of Goethe, Wordsworth, Shelley, Carlyle; it falls in also with the instinctive beliefs of the human race, which, at bottom, and ever in its own blind wisdom, both believed in God and acknowledged His final incomprehensibility.

But will this conception offer any effectual check to the new and all-menacing materialism? Yes; we think so. For the universe is no longer regarded as made up solely of matter, nor yet of matter and energy in conjunction. Matter has not so completely filled up the universe, either as diffused ether or as solid bodies, but that there is room for an all-important principle that it is not material behind. Nor has energy, whether chemical, electrical, mechanical or thermal, exhausted all possible forms of phenomenal energy, and still less their source, which is not a phenomenal thing. Whether we include the energy of the soul amongst the list, or exclude it as of more ethereal sublimation, there is something deeper than either it or them, and the source of both. Matter remains merely one of the two most general modes or expressions of a transcendent power, which may have other modes manifested elsewhere and cognizable by superior faculties or more numerous senses. Nay, even our phenomenal matter, which, in our conception of it, is strictly relative to our five senses, and about which it is supposed we know everything,—how might it not appear to beings in one of the planets, with a sixth or seventh sense added on to ours, and as informing to them as the eye is to us ? Matter is not even a fixed and rigid thing in the eyes of modern science. For we must radically change our notion of it, Professor Tyndall tells us. The distinction between organic and inorganic matter no longer holds, says Professor Haeckel, and in "a certain sense matter is itself alive," he further tells us. It is only known as a theatre of forces, which are the real efficient powers, affirms a third. But how can we endow with creative power that of which the very notion is thus shifting and illusory ? How can we make our metaphysical system to depend on a conception that we cannot fix ? The creative power of matter is taken away, because we do not know what matter is, and the more we try to fathom matter, the clearer becomes the conviction both that we cannot know even it, and that there is something deeper behind it. Matter, as far as we do know it, remains and will remain what Kant reduced it to—mere phenomena, with something behind to support them; and energy remains phenomenal energy, with something beneath it to make it efficient. Nor does the solid universe exist merely as Hume conceived it—a sheet of phenomena with nothing behind it, a series of outside aspects of unreal things temporarily painted and effaced on the canvas of consciousness—the canvas itself scarcely real, a bubble that might at any moment burst, having nothing in the inside of it. There is a Power behind phenomena, which produces them; a substance one and the same at the bottom of the universe and of our thought, which preserves them both in law and order; a power whose existence is our only final guarantee that the physical universe will not resolve itself into chaos before our eyes, and that the universal reason will keep steady on her throne. This Power removed—if we could or dare suppose it—anarchy in the atoms, universal chaos within and without, in the brain and in the cosmos, is conceivable; this Power present and eternally supporting all is our guarantee to the contrary. And, once more, this final support and Power is God.

§ 5. And can Theology accept this conception? Will it suit her exigencies and requirements? To this it must be replied at once that it will *not* suit a theology that insists on standing on a non-scientific cosmogony, or on a discredited chronology, or on particular anthropomorphic sketches of the nature and character of God, or one that exacts, as the only true test of theism, our ascription of certain inscrutable metaphysical attributes to Him. It will not suit any of these, nor hardly, indeed, any form of dogmatic theology; but when supplemented by the attribute of purpose, which Science on her side must grant, it will harmonize very well with a theology which allows that there may be development in theology as in all other knowledge, and development in our conception of Deity as development in our conception of the universe, which is His manifestation.

Theology may dislike the seemingly pantheistic notion, and may refuse it for a time; but in the end she will accept it. And there are evident proofs, notwithstanding a tacit agreement to ignore the fact and an unwillingness to acknowledge it, that even the most dogmatic Churches can, with time, slowly change and accommodate their theological conceptions. Development is possible even within the oldest and most dogmatic Christian Church, notwithstanding the very narrow range allowed for it by the dogma of infallibility. The advance of knowledge and the wider vision of truth can still infuse fresh life into the old religious doctrines; they can still "wake a soul under the ribs of death," to which, of themselves, petrified scholastic propositions and metaphysical dogmas respecting God so surely tend. And there is no manner of doubt that the imperative necessity is being felt and silently accepted by all theologies desirous of preserving a continued life, of reshaping their conceptions of the Creator, His ways and works, more in accordance with the great revelation vouchsafed to men through the scientific discoveries of the past three hundred years.

In particular, this conception of God will not suit the theology that insists on ascribing to Him the attributes, at once metaphysical and specially human, of personality and consciousness; the former being the precise one that it is so difficult to get any clear conception of even in ourselves, and both, especially consciousness, being, as Fichte and other philosophers have irrefutably demonstrated, inapplicable and directly contradictory to the notion of an Absolute Being. For consciousness and personality, whatever else they imply, clearly imply the notion of limits and conditions, neither of which can, without contradiction, be applied to an absolute and unconditioned Being; to a transcendent, tremendous, and universal Power, the chief fact in our knowledge of which is precisely its freedom from all the limits which govern and bind our finite being.

It is much better not to yoke the fortunes of religion with any dogma, proposition, or assertion of historical fact, the truth of which the progress of science and thought may afterwards compel men to discredit; better not to subject religion to the serious hazards involved in her acceptance of particular chronologies, cosmogonies, miraculous stories, that may have to give way before better-verified accounts and stricter tests of evidence; and better not to test the quality of our faith, its truth and purity, by our acceptance or non-acceptance of certain metaphysical determinations of the attributes of the Deity, made in unphilosophic and prescientific ages, and still existing in petrified forms in ancient confessions of faith, but which though still challenging our assent, the highest human thought has shown us are either unmeaning or wholly inapplicable in their reference to the Absolute Being. It is better, we say, not to put theology, and especially religion— which, though not identical with theology, is in the closest relationship with it—in such perilous alliance with what is questionable or untrue; for when the day comes, as it does, when the false must fall off and the unmeaning must be surrendered, there is some real danger that the whole of religion may be discarded with the perishable accidents with which it had been united, or at least some danger of its eternal truth and reality being for a time obscured from the eyes and effaced from the souls of men.

§ 6. It has, however, been affirmed that much more than this limited and negative knowledge, which alone a sober philosophy professes to have of God, is possible; it has been affirmed that men, or certain privileged men, have a special sense or faculty for the immediate and direct cognition of God as a separate Being and Personality; and that this sense presents them with a special class of intuitions, which are specially and particularly related to the Divine Personality as no other intuitions are. It has been asserted, and it is still asserted, not only that God can be known under the metaphysical attributes of personality and consciousness, as cognized and proved by the human intellect, but also that a direct cognition of Him, and a divine communion with Him, is possible by means of the religious sense or faculty, which is intermediary between God and the human soul. There is, say those who thus believe, a part, or side, or faculty of the soul—call it Reason, Imagination, Illumination, Religious Sense, or by whatever name—that reveals God directly, as a mighty and mysterious Power, it is true, but also in certain specially human or other important relations, as the compassionate God-Father, the Author of good and of grace, the Whisperer of Truth, the Inspirer of vision beatific of Himself. This religious sense the old saints and mystics had—Plotinus, St. Augustine, St. Bernard, as also the old prophets and holy men, and their modern representatives, though in less degree, still have it. It still gives them inspiration of the true and aspiration to the good, intuitions issuing from the infinite fountain of goodness and truth, and yearnings again to it. And it is not to be denied as a fact, that throughout the history of theology and philosophy, we find a long line of saints and martyrs and mystics, who were fully convinced that they had immediate cognition of God, the felt knowledge of His presence or absence, and the privilege of occasional communion with Him. St. Augustine, St. Bernard, À Kempis, Pascal, all saintly and devotional minds, so believed; as did also others of a somewhat different stamp—Plotinus, Boëhme, Swedenborg, and many besides. Indeed, with the Alexandrine mystics like Plotinus, the communion at rare and rapturous moments seemed to amount to actual union with God; a union ineffable, unspeakable, but rarely vouchsafed and quickly lost again. Nor have there ever since been wanting representatives of both types of soul, even up to our own days. It is in this same spirit that an eloquent and thoughtful contemporary writer still speaks when he contends against our modern materialists that "the upper zones of human affection above the clouds of self and passion take us into the spheres of a Divine Communion."* Nevertheless, modern psychology, to which, if psychology is a true scientific map of the mind, the question of the existence and analysis of any mental faculty properly should belong, is chary in her admission or recognition of any such religious sense. Can it be said, in reply, that the fault may lie with psychology, or rather with the psychologists; that if these regard only the phenomena of the general or vulgar consciousness, it is no marvel if they should miss what only appears in spirits more

* *Religion as affected by Modern Materialism*, by Rev. J. Martineau.

finely touched, and what in these is only to be read by the possessors themselves, and not by the psychologist, unless similarly endowed; that, in fact, the mistake lies with psychology in ignoring the mental experience of the highest class of minds for the consideration of the average experience of common minds; and if thereafter psychology affirms she can find no trace of a religious sense or faculty, so much the worse for her, the confession only showing the strict limits of her province, and the small value of her scientific pretensions. Psychology, it is said, as it properly deals not with the minds of children, or savages, or imbeciles, but of grown and civilized men, so amongst these it should not omit the highest order of minds, or the exceptional phenomena there presented, especially when they are supposed to have reference to a question so high and delicate and important as that of the possible cognition of Deity. For have not some men in like manner a special artistic sense, which divines the several species of beauty hidden from others, in mere sounds and visible symbols ? Are not the special beauties of eye and ear, of form and colour and sound, incommunicable and unintelligible to those who are destitute of the artistic sense; for whom the sounds, which are a revelation and a speaking voice to the musical artist or poet, are mere vibrations on the tympanum of the ear; for whom "the primrose by the river's brim" is only a yellow primrose, while to the poet it is a suggestion and a significant whisper of so much more than even its own evident grace and beauty ?

So argues the religious spirit in opposition to the scientific. This view of the matter would transfer the question of the existence of a religious sense from the sphere of the general science of psychology to particular applications of it in the study of exceptional minds. But even so regarded, there would still be required a trained and delicate psychological eye to read clearly the phenomena in question; and there would be further required a very considerable faculty of faith in others to credit the assertion that any such private and personal illumination is a guarantee of such an objective fact as the existence of a personal Deity, and not a mistaken interpretation of intuitions emanating from a widely different and natural, though it may still be a divine and noble, source.

And even granting the reality of the analogy between the religious and artistic senses, it still remains a fact that the possessors of the former are constantly becoming rarer, while the sharers in the artistic emotions and perceptions are constantly becoming more numerous with the diffusion of a liberal culture. Could it be said that the religious sense once existed more universally and more intensely because it was more needed, but that now it has fallen into general disuse, and in most cases is a merely impotent organ? That the sense once existed, because in the early dismal days of Christianity, when the saints and martyrs were driven into deserts and caves, under the scourge of persecution, added to their conviction of the vanity of life, the felt presence of God as a support was an imperative need; but that in modern days, the need being less pressing, the religious sense or feeling is feebler, amounting in most to no more than a kind of rudimentary spiritual organ, which only testifies to the former different spiritual wants and environment?

It might be said, and possibly with truth; but what we know, and what concerns us here to note as fact, is that those who lay claim to a special organ of communion with a personal Deity are becoming rarer; that when the modern representatives of Plotinus or St. Bernard attempt, though less confidently than their prototypes, to describe their mode of apprehension of the Divine Personality, and their manner of intercourse with Him, they are for the most part above the logical understanding to which their experience is untranslatable, and that modern psychology, which tries to explain the artistic and moral perceptions, has reserved no place or name for the so-called religious intuitions, or for the religious sense.

§ 7. For the most part, we have said, that the believers in a religious sense are unintelligible, and their soul experiences untranslatable. It is, however, not altogether so. And it is just a possible explanation of the state of soul of all such people, that they are mistaking the real nature and sources of a very genuine and a very important class of emotions. For Nature, the visible, bountiful, beautiful, mysterious Cosmos itself, may powerfully stir and agitate the soul, while yet the effect may be wrongly referred by its recipient to an invisible personality resident behind or apart from it. Nature, or the power behind Nature, one with and in sympathy with the power at the bottom of our souls, may effect the communion with God already referred to. More particularly, there are certain great emotions which the contemplation of Nature calls up within us, which, taken singly or in blended composition, may be the very identical intuitions supposed to be specially related to a personal conscious Deity. There is before us mighty and infinite Nature herself, the benignant and beautiful mother, known but unknown, all-producing, all-absorbing; full of mystery and awe and terror, as well as of grace and bounty and beauty; the all-sustainer, the all-destroyer; who produces us for a moment and then swallows us up; who has passed already through unimaginable and eternal years, but who is still more fresh and beautiful than in her earliest youth. Her infinity and grandeur, her myriad worlds, her infinitely prodigal life, the bounty scattered by her hands, the ever-changing beauty of her face, the impenetrable mystery at her heart,—these, as well as the reverse side of her face, her seeming cruelty and callous indifference, the misery as well as the mystery of life, are all calculated to arouse those mingled emotions of awe and reverence, of fear and hope, of love and gratitude, as well as the sense of absolute and complete final dependence on her,—emotions which are the original source, as they are the abiding essence of all religious feeling; emotions really aroused by Nature, but which men have habitually referred to personified powers or to a single personality behind her. The emotions begotten by the contemplation of Nature are well calculated to beget the sense of a perpetual, mighty, and universal Presence and Power. But the presence and the power which exists is that of great Nature herself, who is, as Schelling conceived her, divine and identical with the divine in us; and the noble emotions so vivifying to our souls which flow directly from the contemplation of her, eternal and exhaustless, increasing and not diminishing with the advance of the ages,—these it was, and these it still is, that the religious soul has mistaken for special intuitions of God. It was communion with Nature direct that was mistaken for communion with God (and Nature *is* at least the only symbol of the invisible power behind it); it was communion with her such as the poet and the artist, who derive their strength and inspiration from her, still delight in; only that the poet knows that the pleasure in the pathless woods, as well as the rapture on the lonely shore, is to be referred to the grace of Nature, as does the artist, who, in love with her fair features, which he tries to transfer to his canvas, refers to her the quiet pervading pleasure in her presence, which is the moving principle of his art and the chief secret of his skill. It was in all these cases communion with Nature; but it was also, if the theologian likes it better, a mysterious attempt, in the case of some of the greatest spirits, at intercourse with the Infinite, with which the soul of man, of the great poet, artist, thinker, mystic, or sage, at all times, and now, as in the days of Plato, of Plotinus, of St. Bernard, feels itself in some real but indefinable and inexpressible relation. It was an attempt, at intermittent and supreme moments, to transcend human conditions, to pass the furthest frontier of thought and emotion; an endeavour, however vain, to fathom the mystery, to catch the furthest light, to reach a final support, which the mind of man has ever, from its double sense of impotence and infinity, been vainly assaying.

We are, indeed, in relations of the deepest sympathy with visible Nature, as well as in profoundest final dependence upon her—relations deeper than those of the child to its mother; why, then, should not this mighty and mysterious yet ever visible and beautiful presence stir us deeply and at times most strangely? She is alike so lovely in her golden sunsets and silver clouds, in her splendid summer dress and soberer autumn colours; so beautiful in her glassy seas and flashing waves, by meadow, grove, or stream, in flower, and bird, and man, and brute; and then she is sublime and awful on the lonely summits of her mighty mountains, august and terrible in her lightnings and ocean tempests. But again, she is goodness itself, and shows her kind intention in her cooling fountains and fruits, in her corn, her olives, and her grapes, ripening in her valleys and mountain slopes. The flowers scattered on the wayside, while, showing the consummate artist she has become, are innocent whispers of her friendliness to man. And all the while, whether she shows herself as bountiful, or beautiful, or angry, or terrible, she moves calmly for ever under her own appointed and unchanging laws; all the while, too, we feel that she is profoundly and utterly mysterious, and that none can penetrate beneath the exterior of her impassive breast to read the final secret that she nourishes in her awful and inscrutable heart.

Thus, then, the attributes and qualities with which man endowed God, are truly attributes of Nature, and all the emotions referred to the one are directly begotten by the contemplation and consideration of the other. Communion with God was communion with Nature, including or supplemented by communion not only with the heights but also with the depths and solitudes of man's own soul. The intuitions of the religious sense are naturally produced in the meditative poet by the contemplation of Nature, at least as naturally as any other class of emotions; and to the true poet of Nature, who is always, like Wordsworth, the high priest of her worship, the cosmos, supposed by certain theologians to be merely the garment of an indwelling Deity, becomes at last identified as both sign and thing signified with Him, its appearances and symbols become His veritable speech and thought, its laws the expression of His will, and the entire visible universe, with its immanent energy and final unresolvable mystery, becomes God, His living reality and totality.

§ 8. Does Science object to such a conception of God? On the contrary, so far as her unaided efforts can go in the framing of such a notion, this is the one to which her discoveries are vaguely pointing; this is the result to which the scientific conception of the cosmos tends, that is to say, the conception, so far as it is competent to Science without the aid of Philosophy or Art to frame it. And is this atheism? Then the noblest spirits, including the greatest modern poets and eminent theologians, are atheists; then Wordsworth Nature's poet, and Goethe universal poet, then Schliermacher the theologian, and Schelling the philosopher, must all be held as atheists—a result sufficient to refute the charge.

Science shows to us an eternal and infinite cosmos, its sum of contained matter from eternity to eternity the same; its stock of energy, passing through thermal, mechanical, electrical, vital forms, without the least fraction being ever lost or gained. She has shown us, too, the slow steps, and in some cases at least, the simple means by which Nature travelled from the inorganic to the organic, from matter to spirit, from the rude tentative to the finished production. She has completed for us the disastrous and yet glorious history of life, and above all, of man,—glorious at least so far as relates to our favoured species; for life has been prodigiously multiplied, happiness ever widened, and art, morality, religion, knowledge, have been born and wonderfully developed amongst men. To-day Science shows us the universal reign of law, but teaches also that the very inflexibility of Nature's behaviour constitutes her chief claim upon our gratitude, since it is this invariability of law which makes science, invention, life itself, with all its conquered advantages, possible and permanent things. She has shown us that where Nature is apparently cruel she is really kind, and that while she punishes ignorance of her laws or rebellion against them with merciless severity, to those who know her laws and fall in with them she will grant all things liberally to enjoy.

And Art has added to the scientific conception in discovering for us a new divineness spread over all the face of Nature,—a divine beauty, invisible to the people of the infant world, invisible even for the most part to former civilizations, because the inward perceptions which create the external beauty were not yet born in men; and Religion, which still lives in man's soul as ever, reinforced by Science and Art, sees Nature powerful, benignant, working by fixed law, beautiful but also at times awful and terrible to all, and in the end profoundly mysterious as well as regular in her ways. Religion discerns a purpose through the course of evolution which Science shows—a purpose sometimes dark and shrouded, but again revealed, and which is for her accordingly the chief article of unshaken faith. Religion discerns in Nature, and the Power which she divines behind Nature, both the present support and the final disposer of all; that on which we are in the end dependent for all things—for life, for thought, for happiness, now and hereafter, if such hereafter we are to have.

Thus it is from Religion, reinforced by Science and Art, that we get the complete conception of Nature, and of God the purpose within it and the mystery at the bottom of it. But if, as Schliermacher contends, we separate the notion of God from that of the universe, we have only a name for that portion of the total conception which is inexplicable, and which contains the mysterious and unknowable quantity; if we do not separate the notions, then is God identical with Nature or the Cosmos, plus the final mystery, where, however, only the first part of the conception, the cosmos itself, has any real and positive signification for our minds.

CHAPTER IV.

OBJECTIONS TO THE EVOLUTION ETHICS.

§ 1. THERE are some who apprehend from the whole new teaching, and especially from the Darwinian theory of the descent of man and of the origin of morals, something if possible more serious than the dethronement of a personal Ruler,—the destruction, namely, of conscience, His last voice and representative on earth, of the moral law that the German transcendental philosophy, which destroyed so much else, had anew pronounced sacred.

There are those who are now becoming anxious for the fate of virtue itself, whose inmost essence and dearest life seem threatened by the doctrines of science. There is a deepening fear in desponding moments, at the hearts of men who are just and true and good, that the great ideal lights and guiding beacons of Truth and Justice and Benevolence are soon to be extinguished in the moral heavens; that, together with Religion, Morality also is about to receive her quietus; that along with faith and hope in a hereafter of compensation for so much amiss here, that which is greater than either faith or hope, namely, charity, the disinterested love and labour for others, for our kind, will slowly die in the hearts of men from the chilling, by the sciences economic and sociological, of the internal heat that supported it, and through the teaching of our evolution moralists of the former low source and the present vulgar utilitarian sanction of the disinterested virtues. Even the sentiment of duty, it is feared, the sentiment that found a lodging-place in all but the most abandoned breasts, and that sometimes visited even these ; the sentiment that some actions must be done and others left undone, without once counting cost or thinking of consequence ;—even this, the source of all that is morally good or worthy in man, and which chiefly exalts him above the brute, seems in danger of being sapped by the psychological account of its origin in the individual, and by the evolutionist's account of its origin in the species.

Such are the fears, not to say the beliefs, of some ; and it must be confessed that there are not wanting some grounds for the apprehensions. For what is virtue, according to the latest light thrown back on its origin, and according to the evolution interpretation of the facts ? A thing of human contrivance, an invention which men were forced to make, as well from mutual fear as from selfish calculations, a discovery, a device, which if it had not been made neither their society nor themselves would have existed. Morality was at first, and still is in its essential features, a set of police regulations, devised originally by the more politic heads of the tribe to keep the unruly and anti-social spirits in order. It was devised in the general interest of the tribe, to produce harmony within, and strength against the external enemy. Morality, in short, was a discovery of man, like any other, a discovery easy to make, if necessity had not forced him to make it, since he had already inherited the moral germ from his humbler quadrumanous ancestors. He had but to improve and develop these, and in doing so he had everywhere examples to copy from, in the ants, the bees, and other social animals existing around and practising the virtues of industry, disinterested labour, courage, and others necessary for the good of the community. Morality, in fact, was an invention, to which men, as well as other social animals, were driven by the necessity for it and encouraged to improve, by the utility of it. It was an invention, and, like all such, susceptible of improvement from age to age, as suited better to the altered social needs of men. Moreover, it was susceptible of variation, as suited to the somewhat different social conditions of different people. It was not precisely immutable, as the former moralists represented it. The habits of veracity which suited one community with a particular moral nature and physical environment, would not equally suit another community; and hence, to tell the truth, might be honoured in one society and but lightly esteemed in another. But nevertheless, some virtues were necessary for all; and amongst these a minimum at least of what we reckon the cardinal virtues— veracity, justice, charity—were indispensable for the continuance of any, even the most incoherent, kind of social union.

On this account, certainly, Virtue, if she was not the earthly and baseborn child of fear and selfishness, as Hobbes had characterized her, had these at least as important constituent elements and shaping factors when she first appeared in the primitive human world. The story of her heaven-descended origin was a pleasant poetic fiction of later ages, invented by self-deluded but well-intentioned enthusiasts, the founders of religions, and encouraged by crafty and politic rulers and priests in their own interests, by moralists and poets in behalf of the general interests of society. It was a fiction almost believed in by its first inventors, and justified by the disbeliever on account of its necessity for restraining the selfishness, and breaking in the boundless passions of the individuals composing the more primitive social organizations.

And now, if such were the true earthly origin of Virtue, the supposed offspring and "darling child" of Jove ; and if her essence at bottom to-day in no way belies her selfish and utilitarian origin, as the teaching of Spencer and Darwin implies, then the question is raised, how can Conscience justify her present pretensions to be the absolute ruler of conduct.? For that she now has, and legitimately has, such pretensions, is maintained no less in the amended utilitarianism of Spencer than in the high transcendental morality of Kant, or the modified English intuitional morality. It is maintained, but it is not explained. Again, if to assign the origin be to mark the limits and sphere of morality, as the evolution ethics seems to imply, how is it that Virtue has so far transcended alike her selfish and social origin ? Still more, why should she aspire to do so ? Why should she not confine herself to the earth, from which she sprang ? why should she aspire ever to grander ideal heights, to a purer justice, to a more perfect and diffused truth, to a greater good embracing ever greater numbers ? If selfishness lie essentially at the root of life and conduct, we should naturally expect it ought still to show itself in the grown flower of the most developed conduct. But does it do so ? Is there not self-forgetting and self-sacrificing conduct, in spite of the evolutionist's picture of the eternal and necessary struggle for existence ? There is truly, but the fact has not been explained by the theory, nor can it easily be explained.

For even if social and disinterested sentiments have been, in the course of countless generations, gradually superinduced on the original selfish root; even if the self-regarding sentiments were slowly transmuted by a moral and physiological chemistry, itself not explained, into the unselfish sentiments;—still these last principles can find, on this evolution theory, no adequate justification for their action, should they come in collision with the self-regarding principles in us. Why should we follow disinterested principles against our clear self-interest, the first of obligations, on the evolution theory of life as a ceaseless competitive fight? It is not open to the evolutionists, as it was to the benevolence moralists, to say we follow them because we derive greater pleasure and satisfaction from them. And when a collision arises, such as must constantly happen, between the self-asserting and the self-forgetting impulses, between our supposed interest and conscience, why may we not deny the authority of Conscience, that can only show such questionable credentials of her claims to rule as a mere inherited tendency amounts to? For this fact of inherited tendency is all that Darwin and Spencer give us on which to found the right of conscience to be the ruler of our actions. True, indeed, Spencer allows that conscience *should* rule; but the difficulty is, with the utilitarian origin and the utilitarian final end, and with the conception of life as in some sort always a competitive struggle, to establish any valid and incontestable claim to rule. It is ruler *de facto*, he allows; how it is ruler *de jure* is not explained; and should we feel inclined to shake off its yoke, to deny that a divine right can come from the fact of inherited tendency, there seems no real reason why the rule of conscience might not be disputed in theory as well as disallowed in fact. The pretension, in short, might be denied as a usurped authority.

More especially, it is argued that the moral casuist will be disposed to rate the authority of conscience lightly when he is further informed that conscience itself, this inward monitor and light, together with our inherited tendency to certain virtues if not too costly in their practice, were the slow products of a process whose essential feature was the desperate individual struggle for life. And how conscience, the absolute commanding voice, the warning and seemingly unearthly light, could be born on such a battle-field; how morality, that was to be the mitigator and moderator of the wild and selfish struggle, could at all arise in the brief pauses of the strife, how it could be evoked out of the very strife which itself was partly to heal, or how emerge from the moral chaos, to compose which was its chief business, has not been at all satisfactorily explained to us. For to say that savage societies and tribes, as a first condition of vigorous external war, must first have secured some harmony and peace within, must have secured some mutual understanding amongst the internal units, amounting to a low sort of morality, is not a sufficient explanation of the height and disinterested sacrifice to which moral conduct may reach, even amongst savage tribes, notwithstanding all their immorality. Some other and higher origin still seems requisite to make the moral feelings do their work. Even to give the dog his fidelity and affection, the ant its courage and devotion to the interest of the colony, asks for higher origin than the instinct of self-preservation or the fear of punishment, as these virtues in the lower animals require even now some higher prompting to their practice.

But if, indeed, from such an origin and by such a route

virtue really reached the earth, men may well repeat the desperate sarcasm of Brutus—

> There, vile jade Virtue, thou'rt proved but a word!

If virtue is but the result of a convention, as Hobbes affirmed, and as evolution confirms; if it is in its essence only a set of police regulations, conceived and drawn out in the interest of the social order;—then, indeed, it has no substance or reality. Virtue is then only a name, and not what some of her deluded followers, faithful even unto death, believed her to be—something deep as the central foundations of the universe, beautiful beyond all else, and real as life itself; that towards which, above all, Nature pushes and tends as her highest aim and goal; that on which she has most determinedly and passionately set her heart; and that too which, albeit her efforts seem slow and vacillating, and her progress fitful or interrupted, she will surely at last attain.

If, objects the moral idealist, morality is essentially, as by implication it is in the evolution ethics, a selfish compact or transaction whereby we engage ourselves to restrain certain of our selfish impulses, for the sake of a larger ultimate net return to self in a different shape, and not necessarily to a higher self,—then virtue is destroyed in idea, as it assuredly will be in practice, whenever this ethics is adopted and acted upon. For assuredly the selfish man will seek, and justifiably, to evade or perform imperfectly his part of the moral contract, whenever he can with safety, and especially wherever his supposed interests come into collision with those of others. In short, with such an origin, virtue is effectually destroyed; and, indeed, vice not less; for there remains no essential or real distinction between them. The difference is for us one of name, of convenience, even of provisional names and of changing convenience. The human world that we imagined the only moral world becomes the most completely non-moral world, since man is the only animal that, having a conscience, is able to analyze it away, and thus escape from its authority.

And does it not follow, from this account of morality, that the thief or burglar is justified in taking, if he is able by force or fraud, from a society composed only of selfish atoms and reposing only on the fact of possession and might, that which he deems necessary for self-preservation—the first and strongest and most pressing obligation, on the showing of the evolutionist? Further, it is evident that neither truth nor justice will be striven for very ardently in a society which adopts such a benumbing moral faith, as Herbert Spencer himself is inclined to admit, if not to approve of.[*] Why, indeed, should they, if the pursuit of such visionary ideals involves costly personal effort, perhaps sacrifice, and the destruction of self—the centre and end of all our actions? In a word, with the evolution origin for morals, no moral obligation remains. There remains only the obligation of interest; for the individual—the primary obligation to exist, and to attend to the interest of self to the utmost extent within the limits of law and conventional opinion; and for society—the primary obligation to defend its own existence and interests, including its own imperfections, however opposed they may be to truth, justice, and the greater good both of itself and of future society.

And the feeling of duty, what is it, on this showing, but a noble delusion, of which, whenever it presses heavy on

[*] *Study of Sociology*, p. 402.

us or prescribes arduous or dangerous service, we, as prudent and sensible persons, may conveniently rid ourselves? And a nice sense of honour, what is it more than a sense of duty, when duly weighed in the scales of the evolution ethics? It is a word, a thing of air, "a trim reckoning," possessed by him "who died o' Wednesday," as Falstaff described the other honour related to glory. And Falstaff's practical conclusion as regards this species of honour—" I'll none of it "—would be likely enough to become the general one, as regards both duty and honour, under a general acceptance of the new ethics, especially if there was no promised payment in their service of an immediate and tangible kind.

But, on the evolution theory of the origin of moral sentiments, how shall we explain the fact that men up to the present pursue truth regardless of results, contend for justice, are ready to incur danger in defence of the down-trodden, to efface themselves for others, or to die for duty? And why should our species, deluded, if science has truly gauged its character as essentially self-asserting and selfish, ever and anon, and not less in our own than in former ages, make such passionate and prodigious efforts to enthrone truth and right in some more perfect form in the earth, or in their own society—efforts repeated again and again, and in which individuals have dashed themselves to pieces in pursuit of a glorious but impossible goal? Nay, why should the apostles of the scientific faith furnish us themselves with such bright examples of the contrary of their moral teaching? Why should some of them furnish us with the best examples in our days of the devotion of the martyrs of the past to truth, if they do not believe the interest of truth to transcend every other? A

Socrates, and a Giordano Bruno,—we can understand how they could devote their lives and give their blood rather than betray the sacred cause of truth, because they believed that the interest of truth transcended the supposed adverse interest of all human societies and institutions; but our evolutionists, who, like Darwin, Spencer, and Huxley, follow truth regardless of consequences, and yet accept the utilitarian ethics, which founds truth on its social utility, what shall we say of them? What, but that there exists an unreconciled contradiction between their ethical creed and their own practice; and that their deeds give the best refutation to their words?

§ 2. There are even graver counts in the indictment against the morality of science; that it tends to dissolve society as well as poison virtue. It is argued that to regard morality as merely a thing of human invention, evolved and perfected by the pressure of the social necessities conjointly with the action of natural selection; to consider it as a set of relations really conventional, and necessary only in the sense of being, in great measure, indispensable for the well-being of the average units composing the social whole;—to assign to virtue only such a low origin, and to make right and wrong depend only on the uncertain and variable sanctions of external reward and punishment, is, in effect, to destroy virtue and to cut the inmost nerve of virtuous endeavour. The effect of this ethical teaching is to poison virtue by slow degrees and with small doses, even in the virtuous man, who should accept it. As for the generality, the mass of the species, as described by evolution, they will be nothing loth to be free from their old moral bonds and fetters; nor will they be long in putting in practice the pleasing lesson of their future moral emancipation. The moral yoke of science will indeed be easy, its burden light and almost pleasant. But neither the first nor the final social result which might be predicted with some degree of scientific confidence, from the many examples of history, which show an invariable sequence between moral degeneracy and failing civilization, will be quite so pleasant for the next few generations or for future society. A deluge of immorality, and moral materialism as bad as immorality, will set in as the first result of the general ethical doctrine of science, so well in keeping with her discoveries and inventions, resulting mainly in the mere multiplication of material joys and comforts. A deluge of moral materialism—something far more serious than metaphysical materialism, which is at least compatible with a high ideal life in its advocates—will set in, which will indefinitely postpone the happy millennium, promised by Herbert Spencer as the result of continued natural selection; and in the resulting moral nihilism our tainted civilization, with its mere material prosperity here high piled up and alongside boundless want and misery, our boasted modern society, with its external pomp and glitter and perfume and its internal hollowness and corruption, will go down to sure and deserved destruction.

A society and a civilization with moral conviction sapped, for which the eternal beacons of truth and justice no longer shine as guiding or warning lights, which has extinguished the illusions of faith and hope, and for which even charity can scarce exist, if the evolution teaching prevails; a society, in short, which will have lost its soul and replaced it by its senses, must go surely down to destruction and chaos, after the manner of all past societies from which the inner light and life had departed.

It will go down as the Roman civilization, morally sapped by the Epicurean, the true prototype of the Evolution philosophy, went down before the vigorous external barbarian, who had not tasted of the tree of knowledge of good and evil as raised by Epicurus:—only that in the case of modern society the Goths will probably be internal—the toiling many in its midst, who labour for the rest, but who, with all their misery and vices, have yet more of the virile virtues of humanity than the superior and ruling classes.

To specify more precisely the stages of moral decay:— if the feeling of the sacredness surrounding the notion of duty; if the absolutely imperative authority and character of the mandates of conscience, as insisted on in the Kantian ethics, be once called in question; and, still more, if the notion of duty should be dissolved by scientific analysis, or the evolution explanation of how it naturally came by slow development through natural selection,—not only will the evil-disposed throw over at once all remaining restraint of conscience, if only they can with safety; not only will the selfish throw down with alacrity the moral burden which science has so much eased from their shoulders, but, what is worse, the arms of the virtuous will begin to grow weary and their hearts to wax faint in the long and losing struggle with the constantly augmenting forces of evil. It is true they will continue to fight, but they will not be able to make way, and their efforts will only serve to delay the general moral decay and final social dissolution, not unaccompanied by social catastrophes.

Nor will it suffice to say in deprecation of such apprehensions that, with respect to many actions, men must continue to feel a moral obligation to do or to refrain; that the moral imperatives, *thou shalt* and *thou shalt not*, must continue to be felt by men, whatever account analysis or evolution may give of the genesis of the feelings. For men will reduce the area of this field of felt obligation, and will not allow the feelings to press with inconvenient severity upon them. They will contract the domain of morality as they have already contracted that of religion. They will reduce the sphere of its prohibitory precepts to the smallest minimum consistent with escape from legal punishment or from the unfavourable opinion of those who can hurt them. The internal punishments, the pains and penalties annexed to wrong doing, they will resolutely overlook, till these will gradually become remitted, and at length die a natural death, from the gradual hardening of the heart, the alienating of the moral perceptions, and the slow corruption of conscience, the moral judge, by a continual bribing process. And when men have thus wholly or partially slain the inner moral self, the reduction of the area of moral conduct (if, indeed, any true morality can be said to remain) will be very great indeed, considering how many evil actions men may perpetrate that no external punishment can reach —neither law, nor the unfavourable opinion of the good, which might not be regarded, nor yet that of their fellows, which would be regarded, but who themselves will be, in general, men of the same relaxed moral principle.

In the same manner, as they have reduced the prohibitive, men will reduce the sphere of the hortatory and positive moral precepts to such actions only as promise rewards of an outward tangible and visible character, to results that admit of a ready material investment and with a prospect, if necessary, of immediate realization. The inner satisfaction from duty done or conscience followed, they will lightly rate, and, indeed, properly, as they will but slightly feel them. Nor will it be only positive moral conduct that they will thus reduce; all other kinds of conduct, all pursuit of ideal aims, all heroic action, all action to any end which does not promise prompt material payment—the only result they will have any capacity in their souls to enjoy—they will be disposed to dispense with.

And all the more will men be so disposed to act and to live, when they are informed, as they now are by a school of scientific moralists different from the evolutionists, that all our actions without exception are determined by the interaction of natural forces resident within the body, which, in the last analysis of the materialist, are physical and chemical forces, blindly at work, however orderly may be at times the results of their action,—forces over which, as such, we can have no sort of control; when we are told that man is the subject essentially of mechanical, which are exclusive of moral, laws, the universal authority of the first leaving no space for the operation of the second; when we are assured that our character is given to us and not made by us, and that, in a word, there is no ego or moral subject by and through which we possess a moral freedom and initiative, or can be made responsible beings, but instead of it a collection of natural forces in a temporary connection with the material organization, whose interactions really determine all resulting actions, as well as volitions, emotions, and thoughts. In a word, and to sum up the indictment, when men discover that the only actions in a real sense obligatory on them, are those where the external force of law or opinion can be brought to coerce them, as they will not be slow to gather from the evolution ethics; and when they further learn from our new atomist and materialist philosophers, that even with respect to these few the action that finally takes place will be determined by natural and physical forces in any case, thus absolving them from all consequences of the decision;—should they put this double doctrine together which the men of science are everywhere inculcating, there will not be much space left for that morality or conduct which an influential writer has maintained should cover at least three-fourths of life,* and which, on any reckoning other than the scientific, should extend to a very large proportion of it.

* Matthew Arnold, *Literature and Dogma*, p. 15.

CHAPTER V.

CONFLICT AND PARTIAL CONCILIATION BETWEEN THE NEW AND OLD ETHICS.

§ 1. SUCH are the various apprehensions of religious and moral men, such the general spirit and the chief forms of the objections urged to the new morality by the spiritualist, the moral idealist, and the intuitionalist. Attempts have been made to answer the objections here urged, though I cannot think that the full weight and point of some of them have been fully felt or adequately met by any of the expounders or defenders of evolution in general or the evolution morality in particular.

Some of the objections urged by the idealist may be without sufficient grounds, some of the apprehensions are doubtless baseless or exaggerated, but nevertheless is there real and just cause of alarm for the future of morals; and my aim and desire in the remainder of this work is to make some attempt at discriminating between objections resting on real and rational grounds, and those founded chiefly on chimerical fears; as also, in some degree, where such seems possible, to effect a conciliation, or at the least a better understanding of the points at issue between science and morality, or rather between the evolution ethics on the one side, and moral idealism and spiritualism on the other.

I believe, indeed, what will appear more fully in the sequel, that much of the apparent contradiction (though not all) rests on a confusion between real and ideal morality; between the scientific generalizations of conduct founded on man's actual behaviour, and the higher morality founded on the hypothetically perfect man; between the morality which aims to lay down more or less definite rules for man as scientifically known and placed in certain general relations to his fellows and social environment, and the morality of the Kantian, the idealist, or the intuitionalist, which severally require the moral subject to follow the unconditional imperative of duty, the dictates of conscience, or the lead of the great ideals to which he is impelled by moral forces within. There is confusion in idea, as well as incompatibility to a certain extent in fact, between what science teaches us from our nature and the exigencies of our social environment we *must* do, and that which the moral law, the authority of conscience, and the force of ideas tell us we *ought* to do; though, until men's moral nature is both more perfect and more in harmony with its surroundings, they never can accomplish other than approximately that to which their highest moral conceptions point.

To the end of conciliation between the evolution and ideal morality, there is only one safe position to be taken up and held by the evolutionist, no less than by the idealist or intuitionalist. Let the scientific moralist maintain that whatever may have been the primitive origin of our present moral sentiments, whatever the history of the magic transformation of the self-regarding into social and even self-sacrificing impulses admitted as existing facts, that the true meaning and reality of these last is to be sought for in the conscious feelings and impulses themselves as now felt and manifested in us; and this wholly irrespective of their scientific origin and slow development through the course of man's natural history. The meaning is to be sought for and found only in the feelings themselves, wholly irrespective of any knowledge of their derivation, whether in ourselves in our short life, or in the species in its lengthened one. Let the evolutionist grant, as he can quite afford to do, that the true meaning and intention of our moral principles of action is to be found in their developed form as shown within ourselves to-day, and is not to be found in the rude primitive germs, the first fugitive moral gleams in our remote human or animal ancestors; that, in fact, if we had neither psychological nor evolution teaching as to their origin, we should still know the meaning of our moral impulses. More especially: to go back to their origin in our species ages ago for light, is as useless and misleading as it would be for the man to revert for an explanation of those sentiments and principles of action which govern his conduct as man, to their first appearance in the boy. He would not obtain light by such a course of retrospection; on the contrary, he would be leaving light, only to find it fade more and more into final and utter darkness. We should not thus find the true meaning, or nature, or aim of pity, or love, or ambition, or sacrifice, nor even of the sociable feelings; for none of these exist in the boy or in the undeveloped man in other than rudimentary, that is, not in their real and proper form. They have not the emotional and moral content which is necessary to constitute them truly moral principles, as in the fully developed man. They only contain faint intimations of the future principles. Indeed, strictly speaking, our earliest sentiments and principles no more resemble these when fully matured, than the grub the butterfly, or the embryo in its several stages, the later-developed animal. And not less is the difference between the moral sentiments as shown in the infancy and in the maturity of the race.

Above all, it is useless to turn to the origin, if we would know what course of action our present moral intuitions point to. To consult the dark oracle of the primitive man, even could we reach the strange interior of his moral consciousness, would avail us to this end just as little as the careful psychological scrutiny of the moral instincts of his nearest existing representatives, would now avail us. In all such investigations, however carefully conducted, we are leaving the light which is in ourselves and round about us in the world of man, and going into dark regions in search of it. That light is nowhere to be found, save in the feelings themselves as manifested and interpreted by ourselves, corrected by the interpretation of the highest specimens of our species who have had the same feelings in highest form— in the feelings of pity as we now experience it, in the love of justice, of truth, of charity, of our kind, or whatever other social or disinterested sentiment is strong within us. The meaning of these principles is given in the principles, and that meaning is action, to which they unmistakably point; —but action regulated by reason and advised by science, which give a commanding view of the possible remote as well as the immediate consequences of such actions.

If, then, the evolution moralist would really obviate the objections of the spiritualist or idealist, let him thus acknowledge that the true meaning of our moral ideas and impulses is to be read in their present full-grown and developed form, as shown in the most superior spirits, and not in their germinal form, whether as shown in children, savages, or the doubtful traces of the primitive man. Let him acknowledge further, as Herbert Spencer in effect does, that though in their origin they had the good of the tribe in view, yet veracity, justice, and benevolence are now to be pursued for their own sakes, under the guidance of reason; the good of society being too large an aim in its totality, too shifting and uncertain in any special form, to constitute a steady object of pursuit. Let the evolutionist admit freely, as he well may, that if we are filled with a passion for truth or justice, the significance of these moral facts for us is that they require an issue in action correspondent to them, and their meaning in the moral economy of the universe is that, in an unjust world which hates the truth, there must always be spirits thus strongly touched with a passion for truth and justice; and that if these and such as these, above all, do not stand up for these ideals, and at times, if need be, stand prepared to quarrel in their behalf, injustice, and falsehood, and fraud, and violence (like rank and poisonous growths) would reign supreme on earth, until at last society, composed wholly of such immoral and warring elements, reverted to its proper chaos, and effected its own destruction.

But he who feels strongly the sacredness of the sentiments need not stop to inquire how the feeling of sanctity has grown around the original ruder and simpler form of the feeling. Let him accept the fact of its sacredness, as given in the feeling, in all faith. He need not care to analyze it into its constituent moral elements with the psychologist, nor to trace the history of its growth with the evolutionist. There is little use in either the analysis or the history for him who is strongly filled with the sentiment, and who wishes to act. And, in fact, such a one does not care to verify the legitimacy of his moral impulse, for fear it should prove an illusion. He embraces it and he acts upon it in full faith that it was meant to urge to and to point to its proper actions. He may or he may not know that the true final aim of justice is the well-being of mankind as Darwin and Spencer say, or the greatest happiness of the greatest number as Mill and Bentham teach; he may or he may not know that the natural external origin of justice was the exigencies of society, and the internal origin the first appearance of a strange sentiment which is now strong in him; in any case, what he feels is that the sense of justice and right exists in him, and demands appropriate action.

Doubtless the just man, the righteous, loved of Heaven, should act under the guidance of reason as well as under the impulse of his sense of justice; and therefore, though bound to do justly in all the relations of life, he is not bound, unless he occupies a very exceptional position of influence, to aim at a comprehensive realization of justice in his society or in the world. For even the statesman, the legislator, the moral or practical reformer, who might hope to make the claims of justice more fully felt or more widely extended, must first carefully consider the facts and conditions of his society, before he can hope to effect any change either in its sentiments or institutions which might give justice a broader and deeper foundation. With respect to this, the most important of the social virtues, all that can be considered as incumbent on the generality of us, as distinguished from statesmen and reformers, is that in so far as the conditions and exigencies of our social surroundings admit, so far as our circumstances, our talents, our opportunities allow, and consistently with the discharge of other necessary and possibly conflicting duties, we should, by seconding the aims of those who have the claims of justice at heart, endeavour to hasten the reign of justice and the bringing in of righteousness on the earth. These are doubtless large limitations and abatements of the absolute aims of the idealist; but science to-day, as in the days of Aristotle, and with stronger reasons, insists on our having regard to the categories of time, place, and persons, to the considerations of possibility and suitability in our moral endeavours.

Men can always do something, by word and equitable deed, for the cause of justice; at a favourable moment possibly more; but it is only on great spirits specially elected, and on the rare occasion of a great opportunity presented, that the high duty may devolve of striking their strongest for the cause of justice without regard to cost or consequence. At important moments in the life of nations, in certain great crises in human affairs, in great reformations or revolutions, the great man, who is also the just, whether statesman, reformer, soldier, writer, is called upon to speak and act in bolder and more decisive manner. But all are not called to this high service, nor yet the greatest spirits, save at the fitting hour. To the thinker belongs the elaboration of the growing idea of the just; on all men it is incumbent to act justly in the common relations and intercourse of life; but to strive after a more comprehensive establishment of the ideal of justice in our still unjust world, is only asked of the great men, the masters of affairs and of action, and from them only when the fulness of time has come, when, indeed, they may call upon the rest to strongly second their efforts. Within these limits the claims of the moral idealist in behalf of justice must be reduced.

In like manner with regard to our duty to truth. If we are haply the chosen depositaries of important and universal truths which it concerns mankind to know, we should seek to diffuse it at all hazards; even if we only know something more than the limited circle which we can hope to influence amongst which our life is cast, we should try to share our superior truth and knowledge; yet should we do so in this case with especial care and caution, lest we do more harm than good to the ultimate cause of truth, if not harm to our friends in disturbing their mental peace, while a regard for their happiness constitutes at least as weighty an obligation as that we are under to the spread of unwelcome truth.

We should aim at the good of our kind, beginning with our friends, and we are also to aim at the spread of truth; and hence may easily result a collision of duties difficult to reconcile. There is, indeed, but one mode of partial reconciliation possible, namely, by adopting a qualification like to that laid down as applicable in the case of justice. We must maintain that while the truth naked and unveiled, will ultimately be for the good of the world and mankind; and while, therefore, a Socrates, a Luther, a Spinoza, must and should proclaim it, though it bring not peace but a sword to men, and not peace but perturbation within the proclaimer's breast;—yet that the like is not asked from the mass of men, save as seconders and supporters of the superior men. Nor are even superior men bound at all times, and to all men, to speak the faith that is in them. There should be fit occasion and fit audience. All men are under obligation, with the known exceptions, to veracity, without which no society could exist; but all men are not called upon to be either the apostles or martyrs of truth, nor yet, except possibly once in the course of centuries, to take up arms in her behalf and fight.

§ 2. Neither science nor evolution can have anything to say against these views of the nature and meaning of our present moral principles. On the contrary, science must concede that it is in accordance with our present developed moral nature that men should act; that under these, guided by reason, they do, in fact, act. And the evolutionist may very well agree with the idealist on the matter of fact alleged by the latter—that the species is scarcely less now than at any former period in its history, governed and swayed by moral ideas. He may reply to the idealist that the moral sentiments are not likely to be sapped by a knowledge of the germs and roots from which their highest flowers have sprung in the later history of mankind.

The evolution moralist, as well as any, may assert the fact, which is merely in accordance with the general principles of evolution itself, that the moral consciousness of mankind has become both more widened and deepened in modern times; that men, in all civilized communities at least, are now more generally regardful of the claims of truth and justice; that they have a clearer perception of the extended relations to which the developed notion of justice applies; that they show a greater respect for veracity in their speech, and a clearer appreciation of the claims of discovered and established general truths on their regards. Further, they may contend, too, that men now more actively pursue the good of others, and, though the fact is certainly not insisted on by Herbert Spencer, that their souls are as inflammable as ever to the influence of great disinterested ideas. For, in fact, the emotions which are the inner force and fire to the higher virtues, exist now, at least in potential form which might easily be stirred into active existence, in more developed amount and intenser degree in the individual, as they have also extended their sway over a larger mass of mankind. The sentiments social and political, which have no reference to self or personal interests, but to race, country, class, or kind, are far more widely diffused, and have shown themselves in more pronounced and potent form in modern times, and certainly not least strong during the past quarter of a century. History, since the epoch of the French Revolution up to our own day, gives abundant proof of the power of mere ideas over men, apart from every question of their origin or even legitimacy. Men have struggled for ideas as passionately in the nineteenth century as in the sixteenth or in the age of the Crusades, save only that the ideas have changed their form and the colour of their attractions, being now humanitarian rather than religious. Men have struggled for them simply because they find them existing within themselves, and because they feel their imperious sway over them. They have not cared to analyze them with the psychologist, feeling that they were meant for action and not for analysis. And men will still continue, in spite of disappointment in attaining the reality, in spite even of their disappointment in the reality itself when attained, to struggle again and again, with unwearied faith and patience, for the ideal glorified in imagination. And what an amount of effort, of blood, has been freely spent during a whole century for ideas—for liberty, for unity, for brotherhood, for humanity, nay, for revolution and anarchy itself, which have for some become strangely consecrated as the conditions precedent of curing the actual and obstinate evils of society!

And what enthusiasm, too, have not men of science, of speculation, of learning, shown in our age for truth for its own sake, apart from its apprehended good or evil results to themselves! What love of it; what sacrifice for it; what faith in its final efficacy! Let, then, our scientific moralist freely concede to the idealist that man cannot live without ideals, which he trustfully accepts, and, indeed, sometimes blindly and desperately follows, without caring to know their origin, without doubt as to their ultimate beneficial social tendency, although he has not primarily such social good in view, but simply the glorious ideas themselves which he would serve. And even if these sometimes appear to delude and deceive, man will still act again in accordance with them. Their votary refuses to disbelieve them, refuses to see blemishes in the divinity that he loves. Though all others should even see only ugly and repulsive features, the true believer sees only beauty, and passionately follows his ideal—be it Freedom with radiant mien, Justice with front severe, Truth with her fair features, nay, even the dark phantoms of Nihilism and Anarchy with the dagger and torch in hand,—all alike exercise a strange and sublime, sometimes a terrible, fascination for the believer. The evolution moralist cannot, indeed, deny the force and reality of such disinterested sentiments during the past thirty years, from whatever source they derived their mighty energy. And that moral and social energy still exists in modern societies. No part of it is spent or disappears without producing its proper effect. None of it, at least, is lost. If in appearance finally lost or dissipated, it is only momentarily and only in appearance. It is again gathered and recruited, and again applied to the progress and development of humanity, which in the end is always moved by these great sentiments at its heart. And whatever be the origin of these or other sentiments, whether in himself or in the species, whether they first appeared yesterday or ages ago, is immaterial to the social man of to-day, so far as relates to action. They exist now in his breast, and man as naturally acts from their impulse as physical forces act to produce their proper effects. But should they do so? is the disquieting doubt and question raised by the evolution moralist and sociologist, Herbert Spencer. Are they wise in so passionately following their political and social impulses, so foolishly and thoughtlessly their philanthrophic and benevolent ones? It matters not; since wise or imprudent they *will* so act, even in spite of his moderating gospel. For such a being social man is to-day, in this the latest stage of his natural history. At present, ideas, which may prove illusions, urge him to act for their fuller realization. That such social and spiritual forces are necessary, is shown by the fact of their existence; and in spite alike of the despairing pessimism of Hartmann, which treats them as illusions, or the qualified optimism of Spencer, which expects nothing from them, but all from time and natural selection, man will still be governed, naturally and necessarily, by ideals, and the species will still be urged forward by aspirations within its breast.

Neither, then, shall ideal aims be destroyed by scientific analysis or research, nor yet virtue, as some are apprehensive. For if we look at the subject from another and a more strictly scientific point of view, virtue is safe. It is safe because its foundation and source lies in a region inaccessible to hurt, impregnable alike to external assault or to internal sap. Morality, virtue, is safe in its essence, however its accidents be affected, because its essence resides in the inmost structure and essence of the nerves and cells of the developed brain of the species, which has been developed with even a more special reference to the moral than to the intellectual or material needs of men. Morality can only be deteriorated by a change for the worse in the composition of the cells and fibres of the brain, and these cannot be suddenly or easily changed in the race, whatever accidents they may be subject to in the individual. The doctrine of heredity and continued development is on the side of morality, and this doctrine is one of the most assuring conclusions which recent science has given to men. Further yet, the social exigencies more imperiously demand obedience to moral rules in modern complex than in former simpler societies; and, therefore, there need be no fear of a relaxation of the social imperative as regards either legal or moral rules essential to social existence and development, but only of those which stand opposed, and which should, therefore, be rather regarded as immoral than moral commands. Until, then, the physical basis of the brain and nerves is deteriorated in modern nations, men will not be less moral; and unless the universal laws of life, and the eternal requirements of every society are mutable, the primary virtues—the core of virtue—will remain immutable, while the growing body of virtue will be mutable only in the sense of being more developed. This is, or should be, the answer of evolution to those who fear for the interests of morality.

Morality will not be touched in essence, but it is quite compatible with this and not unlikely that its essential features may be in future more clearly recognized, as also that there may be a new valuation of the old virtues. It is quite possible that, on taking a new inventory of our moral capital and moral practices, it should be pronounced by a competent ethical valuator that there was a change in the relative worth of some moral habits and virtues; that some had suffered deterioration; that others had improved in worth; nay, even that some new ones might be now required by our changed and changing modern society. It is more than possible that, by our new moral teachers, certain old and now useless practices will cease to be regarded as virtues, while others, hardly now esteemed as such, or at least placed low down in the scale of virtuous excellence, will receive more honourable recognition. It is not likely that asceticism, or fasting, or supplication will be as highly esteemed as heretofore. The merit of uninquiring faith, or of assent without due grounds, will be rated much less, though that the many should repose faith in the more carefully verified conclusions of their superiors in wisdom and knowledge will be always requisite. The wickedness of doubt, as such, will itself be greatly doubted; as doubt will be held a meritorious mental state, or the reverse, according to the mind in which it appears, and according to the subject to which it refers. Even sacrifice, although it must always occupy the highest rank in the virtues, since it will be always called for more or less in the discharge of our appointed function or duty, will be less highly rated outside that sphere, unless for great and worthy ends, to which only the few are called. On the other hand, the old virtues which respect self will be as much required as ever; possibly more : courage will be as much needed, though not so much of the merely physical sort; temperance will be more required in the front of greater temptations, and with our nerves more excitable; while prudence, implying judgment, will be more necessary in the midst of the more complex conditions of life; above all, the old stoical spirit of combined fortitude and resignation will require cultivation to support the shocks of fortune and the defeat of cherished hopes, which must continue to be frequent, though brain and nerves are now less firm to bear them. On the social side, the claims of the great social virtues—veracity, justice, charity—will be more than ever imperatively recognized and enforced, both by conscience and opinion. Sympathy, not merely with the sorrows, but with the general mental states of others, will be more and more felt as a pressing want of human nature, both as a mitigation of sorrow and as a multiplication of satisfactions; while sympathy, in the form of pity for the misery and want around, including an active disposition to relieve it, will long continue, in spite alike of the depressing economic and sociological doctrine, to rank amongst the holiest feelings and the best springs of virtuous conduct in human nature.

Virtue, then, will not be destroyed. Morality, as well as religion, will remain. It will remain as an eternal necessity of our social nature and of our condition in the world. Its field may, indeed, as already implied, be contracted in some directions, but it will receive a more than equivalent augmentation in others, so that a larger total area of life will pass under the sway of morality. A greater number of our actions will become moralized, to use the new and significant term; that is to say, we shall come to feel, with regard to them, that the doing or not doing them is not a matter of indifference, but of some degree of moral obligation. But the obligation to these new virtues will be of a lighter kind than to the older ones shown to be necessary through a longer and a universal experience; so that, though morality may increase extensively, it may still become a less costly intensive effort to the doer. It will be so because there will be less real sacrifice asked or needed in future, since action in behalf of others, owing to men's widened sympathies, will become more easy and even pleasurable, and since also, if the sacrifice is of a more serious character, others will the less ask or expect it of us, even should we be disposed to make it. In this, which is no invidious sense, the moral yoke of science might be described as easy. But its code can never be very light so long as duty is recognized, and life remains in its essence what it is.

§ 3. So far the evolution moralist might successfully defend his doctrine against objections urged. But in order to do so a large faith in the future is necessary. Meantime is it not a fact that there exists at the present moment an irreconcilable contradiction between the new teaching of science, biological and sociological, and the currently accepted teaching of the moral sciences; between the morality which conscience points out and prescribes to us, and the actual behaviour which science shows us the deepest laws of life and the necessities of existence impose upon us; between the moral law which imperatively declares *we ought*, and the scientific law which clearly shows us *we must?* Is there not, too, a contradiction between the moral facts within; between the fundamental instinct of self-preservation, and the equally certain fact of self-sacrifice; between the impulses of pity and sympathy pleading for the mitigation of others' woe, and the fact of self-assertion in the ceaseless competitive struggle of life urging us to regard only our own weal?

It must be granted that there does exist the contradiction, which is palpably and prominently brought before us by the new evolution morality; and the contradiction has not been satisfactorily reconciled by any of our evolution teachers, either by Darwin, Spencer,* or any other. But the real fact is, that this moral antinomy has always existed; the new moral philosophy has only served to bring into clearer manifestation the contradictions latent in the conditions of life, as well as other more obvious ones.

There always was and there always will be a collision of interests amongst men, as well, indeed, as a certain conflict in our own moral nature even when there is no question of a collision with the interests of others. The ideal and the real in morals can never be brought into more than partial or momentary, not to full and final, harmony. Their spheres can never be brought into complete coincidence, not even should our species continue to exist and to improve until the final day prophesied by physical philosophers, when our old and worn-out earth shall fall back

* This chapter was written before the appearance of Mr. Spencer's *Data of Ethics*. An attempt is there made at a conciliation of opposing theories; but the attempt is not very successful. It could not be, in fact, for Mr. Spencer treats Ethics exclusively from the standpoint of evolution and the generalizations of the sciences, without regard to the evolution of the science itself, through a series of thinkers from the days of Aristotle.

upon the parent sun to recruit her exhausted fires. There are, however, some hopeful considerations. There is a tendency to greater harmony in the conflicting conditions of life, and in the contrary moral impulses within us. Although, as evolution teaches, the most central fact of life should forbid the perfect and final harmony between the interests of the individual atoms composing the social aggregations, or between the various united groups and interests as against each other, yet is there the most undoubted tendency to a diminution of mutual interference of real interests. This much, at least, evolution and sociological science have shown us.* The moral and industrial and social progress of society has greatly consisted in the gradual creation or discovery of common interests, common pleasures and sources of enjoyment, and also, it must be particularly noted, in the distinct evolution and transmission by heredity of affections and sentiments lodged specially in the breast of each to consider the claims of others in the cases of competition, and sometimes to induce us to surrender our own pleasure and satisfaction for the sake of others. Reason and reflection teaches us that often there is no real antagonism between our good and that of others where we supposed there was such; and that often a seeming conflict may be resolved into a real community of interest, while even in the case of a real opposition there are developed principles existing within us—the sense of justice, the fact of benevolence, the judgment of conscience whose business it is to consider fairly the competing claims of others, and sometimes even to take the part of others against ourselves; at least, as in the case of the impulses to benevolence and mercy, to consider it better "to give

* See Spencer's *Data of Ethics*, ch. xii.

than to receive," to forgive than to revenge. In such moral factors as these lies our hope of future moral progress, as in the recognition of them lies the possibility of a partial reconciliation of the real and ideal morals, of the scientifically ascertained facts and conditions under which men must live and act, and the unconditional commands of the moral law as conceived by Kant, or the supreme authority of conscience as proved by Butler. But there can be only a partial approach to harmonization between the opposite moral schools, as there can be only a nearer approach to coincidence between the real and ideal spheres of conduct.

For there are contradictions in our own nature as well as in the external conditions of things. There are the self-conserving instincts at the bottom of our being, which must ever produce a certain interference with the happiness at least of some others. And besides pity and sympathy, there are facts of our nature antagonistic to pity.* There is the fact of anger, the fact of antipathy, together with a certain hardening of the heart naturally produced as a sort of moral covering or protection by the many shocks incident to our life of probation. There is also, together with competition, the disastrous life of chance, in part the result of overflowing population, in part of our individual *régime*; and these facts of competition and chance, pressing more heavily on man in modern times than in the days of feudalism, bring home to the individual in the thick of the competitive and pitiless struggle, the fact and the reminder that life is still, in spite of our moral progress, in a real and most serious sense, a struggle of each for himself, and a struggle not merely against his competing fellows,

* See Book I. ch. iii.

but also against the threatening chapter of contingencies from within and without. Having reached the stage of social progress called individualism, where each one is entrusted with and must take care of himself, such a state of things must exist; and we must accept the good and evil of it together,—the good being that we have large individual liberty of action, as the natural complement of the state; the evil that, under this system of universal competition and individualism, where each one thinks first and above all else of "getting on"—to use the significant phrase, which marks the essence of the system—there is a wider front exposed by the individual to the assaults of the formidable impersonality called Chance, and a consequent greater danger of lapse into the dreaded and dismal social abyss which hides the forlorn and hopeless host of the failures.

It is true that the present is only a transitional stage in the great march of social evolution. True also that there are hopeful signs, too many and various to be misunderstood, pointing to the fact that the era of unmitigated competition and individualism is being left behind. Where competition has shown itself injurious, men are giving it up. The community of interest in so many departments of life is too evident, and the necessities of mutual support and aid and protection too pressing, not to produce a certain mutual understanding and merging of destructive internal competition amongst the units that compose a class, or who are associated in an interest. That very sense of mutual dependence, and of a community of interest, to which all society owes its origin, is now seen to be applicable to many subordinate classes and groups and sections of a modern complex society, applicable everywhere, in fact, where an interest common to numbers, however few, may appear. In such cases men seek, and they will seek yet more, to minimize hazard and chance to the individuals, by making all associated partners in a common fortune. But though men will continue to do so more and more, as society progresses, its necessity as well as its advantages being so obvious; yet they will not withal be able to dispense wholly with competition, either amongst associations, or the united interest, or nations, or even amongst individuals whose interest, though common in certain respects, may yet be incompatible in others with that of their fellows in their own class or association.

While man remains man, even in the extremest conceivable type of a socialistic community, competition in some form must continue amongst individuals; as while he remains an animal, however far he may have transcended his lower animal origin, there must cling to him some of his old selfish and sensual nature. He may become a more social, a more intellectual, a more spiritual being, his development moving forward on all these higher lines, but yet the progress is slow, and the ideal goal will never be fully gained. We can hardly even imagine a time when the facts of anger, and envy, and jealousy, and acquisitiveness will be extinguished. " Virtue cannot," as Hamlet tells us, "so inoculate our old stock," but we will relish something of that which diverges therefrom. Neither the social, nor the sympathetic, nor the sacrificing virtues can ever be so far developed as to wholly fill up the area of life and exclude all interests antagonistic to others; and though it is conceivable that a competition having the good of others for its object may become not uncommon, yet such would still subsist side by side with the old egoistic competition for a share of the divisible satisfactions which two cannot possess or enjoy at the same time. This egoistic competition, though with slowly diminishing intensity, this conflict of interests, though within a slowly lessening field, evolution and the social sciences assure us must continue; and this part of the new teaching is so far ethically significant that it lies on the transcendental and ideal morality, either to refute it or to accept it and accommodate its own teaching to it.

THE END.